THE INHERITANCE

THE
INHERITANCE

America's Military after
Two Decades of War

MARA E. KARLIN

BROOKINGS INSTITUTION PRESS
Washington, D.C.

The Brookings Institution is a private nonprofit organization devoted
to research, education, and publication on important issues of domestic and foreign policy. Its principal purpose is to bring the highest quality independent research and analysis to bear on current and emerging
policy problems. Interpretations or conclusions in Brookings publications should be understood to be solely those of the authors.

Library of Congress Control Number: 2021946136

ISBN 9780815738459 (pbk)
ISBN 9780815738466 (ebook)

9 8 7 6 5 4 3 2 1

Typeset in Calluna

Composition by Elliott Beard

To Mom and Dad with immense gratitude

Contents

Acknowledgments

I kept hoping someone else would write this book. It is a terrifyingly immense topic—and a terrifyingly critical one at that—and I was concerned about doing it justice, about ensuring that this exploration of the legacies of the post-9/11 wars was thoughtful, rigorous, and respectful. Nevertheless, the book needed to be written and I hope that this effort represents a reasonable attempt to tackle this thorny, unwieldy, and visceral topic.

There are many, many people who played an integral role in helping me research and write this book. Above all, I want to express my deepest gratitude to those who sat for interviews; without their insights, this book would be a shell of itself. I simply cannot thank my dear colleague and friend Paula Thornhill enough for her endless wisdom, extraordinary support, and frank feedback. A number of tremendous colleagues read drafts and offered their constructive inputs throughout this process, including Scott Cooper, Jim Mitre, Nina Wagner, Kaleb Redden, Susanna Blume, Ethan Saxon, Alice Friend, Loren DeJonge Schulman, Alex Pascal, Nora Bensahel, and Dave Barno. Five different graduate student research assistants spent long days and nights shaping this manuscript over the last few years. Kathryn Olson and Jon Austin helped in the early stages, Chenny Zhang was critical to the structure and organization, and Phoebe Benich and Sam Wilkins played massive roles in researching and editing what were often rather hideously formulated ideas and drafts. Their consistent support and enthusiasm were remarkable and

I'm honored to have worked with each of these young professionals. I am also indebted to Jeb Benkowski, whose immense talent and indefatigable approach improve everything he touches.

I feel very lucky to be part of the U.S. national security and foreign policy community. My former colleagues from the Pentagon during my nearly ten years of service there shaped my thinking in countless ways, as have my current colleagues from Johns Hopkins University's School of Advanced International Studies (SAIS), particularly those in the Strategic Studies Department, which I have been honored to direct, including Thayer McKell, Stephanie Papa, John McLaughlin, Thomas Rid, Adam Szubin, Eric Edelman, Tom Mahnken, Eliot Cohen, the aforementioned Paula Thornhill, Nora Bensahel, and Dave Barno, as well as the enthusiastic SAIS librarians. The thoughtful Strategic Studies students at SAIS influenced me in inextricable ways; I hope they understand that their professor learned as much from them as they hopefully learned from her. My colleagues at the Brookings Institution have been immensely supportive as I pursued this project and helped ensure clarity and rigor, particularly John Allen, Mike O'Hanlon, Jen Berlin, and Leah Dreyfuss. And the 2018 and 2019 participants of the National Security Professionals and Practitioners Program run by the Philip Merrill Center for Strategic Studies continue to inform my perspective on these issues as well.

Working with the Brookings Institution Press was, in a word, delightful. Bill Finan did a masterful job pushing and pulling on this book. I'm grateful to Kristen Harrison and Cecilia González at the press, as well as the anonymous reviewers whose feedback made this book better.

I appreciate the assistance of the Department of Defense's Defense Office of Prepublication and Security Review, particularly Paul Jacobsmeyer for his diligent work and responsiveness, as well as the efforts of Brian Arakelian.

Finally, I am thankful to my family and friends for their consistent support as I wrestled with this tome. In particular, Frances Z. Brown, Dipali Mukhophadhyay, Deborah Saxon, Nora Rigby, Anna Fruttero, Luca Flabbi, Julia Zuckerman, Liz Rosenberg, Miriam Szubin, Kelly Magsamen, Alice Brennan, Julia Doan, Buzz Phillips, Tamara Cofman Wittes, Jim Slife, Kori Schake, Caitlin Talmadge, and Eric Reid.

And to my family, I have yet to find the words to express my deep gratitude. My wonderful and devoted parents, Charlene and Hooshang Karlin, who over the years simultaneously taught me that anything is possible and everything will be okay (even when I doubted); my fantastic siblings, Tami and Raymond Rokni, David Karlin, and Jennifer Karlin; my amazing nephews, Arya and Alex Rokni; and my dear in-laws, Bonnie and Jack Jacobson, who have supported me every step of the way. Above all, my remarkable husband Reuben and children Daniel Amir and Emma Yasmine deserve all the thanks in the world.

PREFACE

"Shadows from the past were still there."

We were trying to focus on the future. For more than a decade, the U.S. military—really, the entire national security community—had been overwhelmingly focused on terrorism. But inside the Pentagon in 2013, it was increasingly difficult to dismiss China's efforts to destabilize an Asian-Pacific regional order that had upheld a good deal of stability and security for the better part of seventy years. The year before, the secretary of defense had released the Defense Strategic Guidance formally announcing a rebalance to the Asia-Pacific, and now it was time to draft the congressionally-mandated defense strategy.

The resulting 2014 Quadrennial Defense Review largely reinforced the same points as the 2012 Defense Strategic Guidance, as would the 2018 National Defense Strategy a few years later. All three underscored that the U.S. military had to prioritize great power challengers like China (Russia would be added to the list after its 2014 invasion of Crimea) and to deprioritize terrorism and insurgency in places like Afghanistan and the Middle East. But in 2013, like today, the security environment made that hard. The seemingly endless pull of terrorism, manifested by the Islamic State of Iraq and the Levant (ISIL) in particular, was hard to resist.

But what made it much harder then, and continues to make it hard to this day, was our inability to reckon with what had happened since the September 11, 2001, attacks.

I write this book as someone who has devoted her career to national security, who cares deeply about today's U.S. military, and who fears what tomorrow's wars may bring. Throughout the post-9/11 wars, across two administrations, I repeatedly engaged in national security debates inside the Pentagon that left me concerned about the state of the military and the lack of productive dialogue by those in and around it—including civilians. Often, senior leaders slated to discuss one topic seemed plagued by a mountain of neuralgia just below the conversation's surface that occasionally poked out with vitriol and frustration, threatening to debilitate our efforts entirely.

Seemingly technocratic discussions about the future size of the U.S. Army devolved into blame sessions over the Iraq War. Dialogues about the permutations of the next war descended into bitter grumbling about the mistakes made after 9/11. These issues percolated perniciously below the surface. I recognize, of course, that I am part of the complex I am analyzing, This gives me a certain, somewhat unusual, perspective as both a scholar and a former policymaker. It also gives me both an intellectual and professional responsibility to scrutinize this period as rigorously as possible.

In writing this book, I sought to examine what the military has inherited from being at war since 9/11. I came up with long lists of positive and negative legacies. Our ability to find, fix, and finish practically any target anywhere in the world. A homeland that has not faced a catastrophic terrorist attack in nearly two decades. A public that celebrates its troops—but also does not know, can rarely understand, and does not seem terribly interested in what is being done in their name. A force whose veterans commit suicide at historic levels amid a fledgling support system. It is, perhaps, natural that the book focuses more on the negative legacies, as those are the ones least likely to be interrogated.

What most puzzled me, however, was the infrequency with which a conversation about the last two decades of war occurs. How did the most capable military in U.S. history—indeed, in the history of the world—

fight to, at best, a draw in its longest contemporary conflict? And why has this not been the subject of greater reflection and debate?

Some, of course, have offered answers. They attribute blame to the places in which the military has waged war, the enemies it has fought, and the characters of the conflicts themselves. I do not dispute that these are valid elements. Those outward-looking attributions, however, miss or dismiss the important role that the functions and dysfunctions of U.S. civil-military relations have played in the course of U.S. national security policy in the twenty-first century. In addition to the inability of the American public to engage in conversation about their last two decades of war, the three-way relationship between military professionals, civilian managers of violence, and the American people is increasingly fraught with tensions that many do not want to acknowledge, much less analyze.

But, acknowledge it we must. Reconciling with the hard legacies of the past two decades will strengthen the will of future military members to engage in war when civilian leaders deem it necessary. Moreover, the future national security leadership team—civilians and military alike—will be more united in understanding the respective strengths and roles that each brings to the fight.

For now, we rarely talk about these dynamics: not as a society, not as a national security establishment, and not even as a military. But acting like they do not exist does not mean they will go away. This book argues that, as a result, the next president will inherit both a military and a military-society nexus deeply in need of not just dollars but also deep dialogue, discourse, and debate.

This may not sound new. Indeed, it has become commonplace to compare the post-9/11 wars to the Vietnam War. To be sure, there are a lot of similarities—not least, I suspect, that reconciling the Vietnam War's legacies has taken generations. The Vietnam War, however, is endogenous to the legacies of the post-9/11 wars because the same institutions that waged war in Vietnam led the campaigns into Afghanistan and Iraq decades later, often on the basis of the putative lessons learned from failure in Vietnam itself. These wars rhyme, but, ultimately, contain their own rhythm. While researching his 2001 book *War in a Time of*

Peace: Bush, Clinton, and the Generals, author David Halberstam reflected his surprise over the Vietnam War's presence in wars decades later. Despite the different "politics . . . players . . . constituencies . . . shadows from the past were still there, ghosts . . . still loitered in the hallways and meeting rooms."[1] Twenty years later, those old words have taken on new meaning. Halberstam's ghosts have been joined by the specters of an even longer war, as the reader will soon discover.

In that sense, this book is an attempt to inspire a dialogue that has been long in the making, is frankly much overdue, and, bluntly, must take place if we are to learn from the past to do better going forward. Precisely because I value the U.S. military and want it to be as strong as possible, I believe the nation needs to grapple with these issues. I hope this book manages to help it do so in a thoughtful, respectful, and, above all, productive manner.

1

Why Should We Care

Legacy, Myth, and Memory

"All wars are fought twice, the first time on the
battlefield, the second time in memory."[1]

It is both too soon and too late to write this book. It is too soon because
the post-9/11 wars have not ended and appear unlikely to do so by the
time the book is published. And it is too late because much of the U.S.
military has already decided it has learned its lessons from them—and is
moving on to prepare for new and different types of conflict far different
and far away from the painful classrooms of Iraq and Afghanistan. But
the institutions doing so have fought for the longest stretch of time in
their histories. Nearly two decades of conflict have irrevocably shaped
the U.S. military, as has incessant fighting in conflicts, many of which
could generously be called inconclusive, against non-state actors span-
ning the globe. The epitaph of the post-9/11 wars, when it is finally written, will likely combine three words: perplexity (over why they lasted

so long); ambiguity (over their focus or lack thereof); and anxiety (over what, on balance, they achieved, prevented, and exacerbated).

What has the U.S. military inherited from nearly two decades at war? This book is about how the U.S. military—its leaders, its troops, its thinkers, its doers, its veterans—is dealing with the legacy of the wars since 9/11. The legacy, or legacies, of these conflicts have serious implications for how the United States will wage war in the future, but there is a stunning lack of introspection about these conflicts. At best, there are ad hoc, episodic, and unstructured debates about Iraq or Afghanistan, or operational-level studies of certain battles. In the military, myths about why, how, and who it has fought have emerged and matured, often consigning those who still worry about the wars' legacies to a strange clergy of historians and axe grinders. The national security apparatus as a whole now seeks to move on to the next perceived threats: China and Russia. The American public, for its part, remains disinterested in the post-9/11 wars—they rarely come closer than casualty lists in the newspaper summarizing horrific events in far-off places, or scattered applause on airplane flights and at baseball games for those who have served. And many Americans are questioning whether it even makes sense to invest in the military given problems at home and doubts about whether U.S. military involvement abroad really can be a force for good. Simply put, there is neither serious nor organized stock-taking by public intellectuals on this inheritance.

But the United States cannot simply hit reset and ignore the legacies from its nearly twenty years at war. Ultimately, its lack of a postmortem dialogue will continue to feed a dynamic in which different constituencies learn different lessons, come to different conclusions, and, therefore, foment a vacuum of introspection and dialogue that neuters the history of what has transpired. When debates do occur, they often are characterized by fierce, visceral disagreements over the facts—potentially leading to hollow analysis. This is "gnawing at our military's zeitgeist," as one soldier explained ruefully when I asked him about the legacy of these conflicts.

For that reason, this book focuses primarily on exploring this inheritance and then offers practical antidotes to begin correcting it. It examines three civil-military crises fomented by the post-9/11 wars. Then, looking through five lenses, it explores how nearly two decades of conflict are influencing how the military goes to war, how the military wages war, who leads the military, who serves in it, how the military thinks about war, and, above all, the enduring impact of these wars on those who waged them.

The post-9/11 era is not necessarily over. Indeed, we may see only its conclusion in retrospect. Those who wrestle with its legacy are frustrated, exhausted, and rarely have a serious opportunity to reflect on it. Yet, if the U.S. military seeks victory in the future, it must acknowledge and reconcile this inheritance. It must recognize the positive and negative baggage it takes on its pivot toward the next wars. This book seeks to help them do so.

ARGUMENT AND APPROACH

While the term "inflection point" is often both overused and inaccurate, it is entirely appropriate in the case of the September 11, 2001, attack. For the U.S. military, it felt like everything changed overnight. Throughout the 1990s, the military had lurched from one conflict to another, in places as varied as Somalia, Haiti, and the Balkans, on a wide array of missions. But after the September 11 attacks, a perception grew that the military's purpose was now crystal clear: fighting terrorists and those who sponsor them. Over the next two decades, that crystal clarity shattered under the impact of nearly two decades of unrelenting war, changing the military in the process.

It is easy today to take for granted the many aspects of our system of government that are so long and deeply held as to be unquestioned yet fundamental to the nature of our republic. The role of the military is one of those. It is worth recalling, however, that decisions about the use of military power—including who makes decisions about the use of force, and the military's relation to society as whole—were a key concern at America's founding. Questions about the United States's self-conception of its role in the world and, thus, its military's activities abroad, often have been a subject of key concern for leaders and the public alike. How-

ever, for much of the post-9/11 wars—indeed, for much of U.S. history—
foundational questions like our national security priorities, the proper
use of force, and how civilians should control the military have received
less introspection than they merit.

Two interrelated dynamics require us to think harder about these
issues now. The first is a broader societal dynamic: the public is less connected to the military now than at any point in modern history. Few
citizens now serve in the military, so those who do not serve neither understand it nor acutely feel its sacrifices. Decisions to pay for ongoing
military operations through deficit spending means no Americans feel
any immediate financial costs for the military's activities.[2] The result
is a military that garners tremendous respect from a public that knows
little about it. This societal dynamic exacerbates and is exacerbated by
a second trend: the U.S. military has been at war for the longest continuous period in its history, but the outcomes of these post-9/11 wars
are inconclusive. The average citizen's attention has largely moved on.
In combination, these twin dynamics mean that never have such long
wars demanded so much of so few. The military feels the wars' painful
effects, but—critically—also seems to feel as if these effects are poorly
understood by others. This book seeks to tackle that inheritance.

Three insights about the U.S. military emerge in this book. First, how
the U.S. military processes the results of twenty years of inconclusive war
can best be understood as encapsulating three interrelated crises. Each
crisis aligns with one of the institutions that Prussian military theorist
Carl von Clausewitz identifies as comprising the political-structural
"social trinity" that influences warfare: the military, the people, and the
government.[3] The first, a *crisis of confidence*, focuses on the military's relationship with itself. This crisis includes both strategic- and personal-
level understandings of why one fights and what victory looks like. The
second, a *crisis of caring*, focuses on the military's relationship with the
American public. This crisis is illustrated by the superficial public interest that has overwhelmingly characterized the post-9/11 wars. And the
third is a *crisis of meaningful civilian control*, which concerns the military's relationship with civilian national security leaders in the government. This crisis highlights some in the military's tendency to blame

civilians rather than simultaneously engaging in more serious introspection; the resurgence of the Powell Doctrine (and its exceedingly narrow criteria for using military force); the popularity of the phrase "best military advice"; and efforts to minimize civilian oversight in crucial arenas. Taken together, these three crises represent the strategic-level inheritance for the U.S. military from the post-9/11 wars it is carrying toward future conflicts.

Many in the military are bitter and frustrated over the course of the post-9/11 wars, and feel they no longer know what victory looks like. To be sure, many of those grievances are serious and valid, and have driven an outpouring of perturbation from members of the military about their service.[4] Those grievances largely have not, however, generated sufficiently serious and hard thinking about what victory means and how to achieve it. Brief interludes of introspection have been technocratic and tactically focused, or brimming with vacuous platitudes that discount the dynamic and inherently political-military nature of conflict. Blame abounds, particularly for civilian leaders, and the gap between these two communities is growing into a gorge. Many members of the military feel alienated from U.S. civilians, question why more Americans do not appreciate or understand their sacrifices, and are resentful of this public indifference. The implications of these dynamics are profoundly worrisome for the all-volunteer force and those it protects.

Second, despite resulting in the most experienced military in U.S. history, the post-9/11 wars have left the United States woefully unprepared for critical future threats. Military forces can be defined by three attributes—time, space, and the spectrum of conflict—and the longest period of war in modern U.S. history has, understandably, resulted in a force specialized along each of these dimensions. It has focused on winning the wars of today at the expense of fighting the wars of tomorrow. It has focused on wars in places like Iraq, Afghanistan, Pakistan, and Syria rather than in places like East Asia or Eastern Europe. Finally, it has focused on enemies like terrorists and insurgents rather than adversaries like China or Russia, and has thought comparatively little about conventional or even nuclear conflict.

This all is logical, of course, but still carries costs. The military—

largely following the civilian guidance it received throughout the first decade of the post-9/11 wars—has become so specialized in handling unconventional and irregular warfare that it is not sufficiently ready for a future of interstate competition or conflict. Such future fights could result in tens of thousands of casualties and could involve attacks against the U.S. homeland, for which we are largely unprepared. The post-9/11 wars have been akin to heartburn; a future high-end conventional or nuclear conflict with Russia or China would be much closer to a heart attack.[5]

If the military does not tackle this inheritance, the consequences could be ruinous. After nearly two decades of war in which the U.S. military seemed trapped in a violent cycle of inconclusiveness, first-order questions are reemerging. These include monumental and thorny topics such as: What should the U.S. military fight for? Who should it be willing to kill and be killed for? And, how can it most effectively and efficiently do so?

It is critical to note up front that this book is not intended to be a critique of any single U.S. administration. The post-9/11 wars now span four presidencies across both political parties. Moreover, some of the societal dynamics at play here have long historical roots. Ultimately, however, this is a book about how the last twenty years have affected the military and society, and what we need to do now. As such, it does not explore all aspects of the international repercussions of these wars. Many other books take up, for example, how the international system and the United States's relationships with other nations (including partners and allies) have been impacted, the future threats the United States may face, and the degree to which the military is prepared for them.[6] These are important topics. But the first step to healing is understanding what has happened to us and how we *can* heal. That is the focus of this book.

LEGACIES MATTER

For any military, the legacies of its previous conflicts inform the institution, the individuals, and the broader society. How a war is fought—and how its society views the conflict—are inextricably linked. Defeat can turn into victory in the public square, as Egypt's government managed when it built a monument in Cairo insinuating success in its 1973 war with Israel despite the reality of catastrophic loss.[7] Blame for losses can be shifted away from the political leadership and the military and toward certain portions of society, as the Nazi leadership did with German Jews in the run-up to World War II. And lost causes can be embraced long after the guns have fallen silent. Some inheritances are "passive" and represent emergent patterns that become acquired norms. Others are "active," such as policy constraints or decisions on how to wage war that are deliberately imposed by leadership. In the case of the U.S. military, some of the most influential conflicts include the Civil War, the World Wars, the Vietnam War, and the Persian Gulf War.

The Civil War illustrates the ultimate futility of burying legacies. More than 150 years after it ended, the impact of this war still is being debated across the country. No work encapsulates its immediate legacy better than Winslow Homer's painting "The Veteran in a New Field," finished in 1865, not long after Confederate General Robert E. Lee's surrender at Appomattox Court House, depicting a former Union soldier who has returned to reap his overgrown and flourishing fields, and he does so with a scythe—the symbol of death.[8] The country had undergone a painful few years, having suffered an estimated 1.5 million casualties, and wrestled over how to reconstruct a "house divided against itself," as Abraham Lincoln had warned.[9] It sought to put the past behind it.

That this resulted in an uneven and unfair approach to issues like equality is clearly evident in the fact of U.S. military segregation through at least 1948.[10] Over the next century, and particularly in the early 1900s, Lee and his lieutenants were deified across the southern United States. Their statues became popular spots in cities like New Orleans, Louisiana, and Richmond, Virginia, as the movement to immortalize those men with monuments was an effort to use the war's legacy to deny Af-

rican Americans their constitutional rights. More subtle consequences
for the military include both its continued overreliance on servicemembers from the South, largely due to base locations, and—given that ten of
the military's bases are named after military officers from the Confed-
eracy, as well as a barracks at the U.S. Military Academy at West Point—a
potentially worrisome deifying dynamic, as well.[11] In recent years, the
Civil War has again come alive, resulting in the removal of some Confederate statues, but the ultimate legacies of a war that tore the country
apart have yet to be fully reconciled. These issues took on new energy
throughout 2020 as the Marine Corps banned Confederate flags and the
Army reconsidered the names of its bases, perturbing a president who
vowed to reject any changes.

The aftermath of World War I illustrates the significance of geography, and especially physical distance, in shaping the United States's use
of force. In the wake of the Versailles Treaty, empires collapsed and some
states were born. But America was shielded from much of that revolutionary upheaval by the Atlantic Ocean.[12] The overwhelming majority
of American troops killed in combat were brought back home for buri-
al.[13] Although the American Legion wanted all Americans to observe two
minutes of silence on the armistice's anniversary, the idea never really
took hold.[14] When the war to end all wars ended, Americans moved on
remarkably fast, content to hope that such carnage would not, or could
not, be repeated in their lifetimes. The size and quality of the interwar
U.S. military reflected this belief.

The legacies of World War II illustrate how memory of a spectacular
victory can change a military. As with all these conflicts, "much depends
on which aspects of the war—and which period of time—one examines,
and which reminiscences one trusts."[15] To be sure, there should be no
doubt that without the U.S. military's involvement in World War II the
world would have looked dramatically different over the last seven decades. It is no exaggeration to say, as President Bill Clinton declared on
the fiftieth anniversary of D-Day, "These men [who fought] saved the
world."[16] More broadly, the war's legacies have been multifaceted and
include a transformed Japan and Germany, the rebirth of a rules-based
liberal international order, and the firm elevation of the United States as

a global superpower. For the military, World War II became the epitome of success, establishing the total defeat of the enemy as the sine qua non of true victory in the minds of its leaders. It is not a coincidence that the Army's newest uniform is strikingly similar to its World War II uniform. As the most senior enlisted soldier in the U.S. Army explained, in designing the new uniform he and others asked, "When is the most prominent time when the Army's service to our nation was universally recognized?"[17] Although World War II is an obvious answer, it is telling that the Army had to reach back more than seventy years to find it.

The Korean War illustrates the opposite: amnesia about a conflict that never ended. Formally speaking, Korea was neither a war nor is it over: it was a "police action" that ceased through a negotiated truce. Due to concerns about whether a future Korean leader would allow Americans to visit the graves of their loved ones, no cemeteries of deceased Americans remain on the peninsula.[18] Often described in the United States as "the Forgotten War" given its virtual absence from the American mindset, the evidence of that conflict can, nevertheless, be found in the flourishing South Korean political and economic space, the broken North Korean state, and the 28,500 U.S. troops stationed in South Korea to this day.

The Vietnam War is especially relevant for this study on legacies of the post-9/11 wars because it illustrates the challenge posed when different constituencies learn different lessons and adopt them following a conflict. Various groups of Americans have had different arguments as to why the United States lost in Vietnam. These include a lack of understanding of the war's character among senior civilian decisionmakers; poor decisionmaking by military leaders; crass motives; the media; public protestors; the draft; unwillingness to see a tough fight through; and, of course, the adversary's particular qualities.[19] One good example of the panoply of reasons for Vietnam's failure is exemplified by retired General Barry McCaffrey, a highly decorated infantry veteran of the war. He alternately blames defeat on "arrogant, blowtorch personalities like McNamara and his 'whiz kids' . . . micromanagement of the war by bureaucrats . . . (lack of) unwavering resolve to support South Vietnam . . . (and lack of) the support of the American public."[20]

Defeat in Vietnam crushed the American soul. As one scholar argues, it "brought a loss of American innocence" that profoundly shaped the future military.[21] The war "polarized the American people and poisoned the political atmosphere as had no issue since slavery."[22] Many in the U.S. military were riddled with resentment for their sacrifices, which the public seemed unwilling to recognize, let alone honor. As an example of myth-making about war, the titular action-hero lead of the *Rambo* movie franchise is a useful proxy for the U.S. Army: he mourns, "I want my country to love me as much as I love it."[23] Some troops, of course, were angrier; as one veteran bitterly explained, "I won *my* war. It's *you* who fucking lost."[24] As the Vietnam War was ending, American society—racked by guilt, disillusionment, and frustration—decided it would largely contract warfighting to a small subset of the population. The all-volunteer force was born.[25]

Frustration over perceptions of civilian micromanagement and meddling in so-called military affairs further colored the Vietnam War's legacy. One sees this dynamic in pockets across the military. The National Museum of the Marine Corps, for example, extols the Marine role in WWII but sees Vietnam as a "'political war' rather than a military 'war.'"[26] Lieutenant General H. R. McMaster is another case in point. His book *Dereliction of Duty,* written when he was an Army major, criticized civilian leaders for setting what he deemed impossible-to-achieve goals and military leaders for quietly enabling them to do so. His book has been exceedingly popular across the military.[27] Ironically, the Army passed then Colonel H. R. McMaster over for promotion twice, and he only finally became a general after senior civilian officials intervened.[28]

Yet, there is reason to question just how much the legacies of the Vietnam War reflect rigorous military introspection. While the military's composition and capabilities shifted in its aftermath, as one scholar argued: "The military has been less successful in adjusting intellectually and emotionally to the trauma of Vietnam. There has been a marked reluctance on its part to accept a share of responsibility for the nation's failure. The tendency, rather, has been to blame a weak-kneed civilian leadership or a lack of public will."[29] Such arguments were, frankly, more popular in the Army than those made by scholar and then active-duty

Army officer Andrew Krepinevich's in *The Army and Vietnam*, his doctoral dissertation and subsequent book, which squarely placed blame on the Army.[30]

Given its complicated legacy, perhaps there should be little surprise that the specter of the Vietnam War lingers. From President Reagan arguing that for "too long, we have lived with the Vietnam Syndrome," to President George H. W. Bush declaring after the 1991 Persian Gulf War that "we've kicked the Vietnam syndrome once and for all," neither America's political elite nor its military leadership could escape Vietnam's discomfiting presence.[31] Indeed, nearly two decades after the drawdown of U.S. ground forces in Vietnam, journalist James Mann found in his research that there was heavy pressure "to overcome the legacy of Vietnam with a clean victory" before, during, and in the immediate aftermath of the Persian Gulf War.[32] More recently, Vietnam has been used as a powerful historical analogy for today's conflicts, compared to the U.S. wars in Iraq, Syria, and Afghanistan. Senator John McCain, a Navy pilot and prisoner of war during the Vietnam War, said the Obama administration's approach in Iraq and Syria reminded him of "another war we lost . . . and that was the war in Vietnam."[33] Senator John Kerry, another Vietnam veteran, warned that the United States had "misunderstood, misread, misplanned and mismanaged our honorable intentions in Iraq with an arrogant self-delusion reminiscent of Vietnam."[34] And, some critics argue that President Obama's team was obsessed with avoiding another Vietnam, perhaps to the detriment of their policy choices.[35]

The Persian Gulf War, in contrast, illustrates the dangers posed by romanticized conflicts for the military and society. The U.S. military was built to fight the Soviet Union in a massive conventional war. It prevailed in a brief war with extremely limited objectives—pushing the Iraqi military out of Kuwait—by employing overwhelming force against an opponent best described, with the advantage of retrospect, as a third-rate power. This victory came after an overwhelming air campaign and a brief ground conflict colored by spectacular technological prowess and the deployment of more than half of the Navy, Marine Corps, and Army's available assets against a surprisingly inept opponent.

Military leaders were informed by the legacies of Vietnam in how they planned and fought the Persian Gulf War, particularly in their focus on combining limited objectives with overwhelming force.[36] More broadly, for the U.S. military, the inherited legacy is that the Persian Gulf War was won because it was conducted without the apparent defects of the Vietnam War: there was no civilian micromanagement; there were clear, limited, and fixed objectives; and the U.S. military devoted all its resources to a single fight. Overwhelming victory against Iraq represented a vindication for the military of everything it had done to rebuild after the Vietnam War. It "learned" that it had done everything right and expunged the ghosts of Vietnam. This, as we later see, set it up for spectacular missteps in the post-9/11 wars.

One could argue, of course, that the military should have considered the many other reasons the United States prevailed in the Persian Gulf War, including the political and military decrepitude of its Iraqi adversary following Baghdad's grueling eight-year war with Iran, as well as the heavy U.S. investment in training and equipping its military over the previous two decades. President Reagan's massive defense build-up, which emphasized new bombers, missiles, advances in stealth, and sophisticated command and control systems, was particularly important in providing the coalition with overwhelming conventional superiority. And, of course, the war ended with Iraqi president Saddam Hussein still in power, U.S. air patrols policing much of Iraqi skies through Operations Northern and Southern Watch, and U.S. troops based in Saudi Arabia. In other words, even after victory, the U.S. military never fully withdrew the military presence it had built up for the Persian Gulf War—a cause célèbre for al Qaeda. These concluding legacies serve as reminders that wars are not bookended but, rather, bleed into one another.

Nevertheless, the muddling of the legacies of the Vietnam and Persian Gulf Wars spurred the rise of what has become known at various times as the Weinberger Doctrine, the Weinberger-Powell Doctrine, and the Powell Doctrine. It first emerged in late 1984, with the painful memory of Vietnam still fresh, after the Marine barracks bombing killed 241 military personnel in Beirut and the United States invaded Grenada. As Secretary of Defense Caspar Weinberger explained his theory of the use of force, the United States should send its military to fight abroad only when vital national security interests are at stake and the intention is victory; when it has well-defined and executable objectives; when it devotes sufficient resources and the military has the ability to employ them as desired; when public support is assured, and "as a last resort and to be used only when other means have failed."[37] In drafting this historic speech, Weinberger was supported by his senior military aide at the time, Major General Colin Powell.[38] Powell would go on to serve as chairman of the joint chiefs of staff during the Persian Gulf War and, in the wake of that conflict, he refined Weinberger's criteria. However, he attributed the eponymous doctrine's conception to national security discussions held before the Persian Gulf War began, rooted in a particular set of lessons from the Vietnam War. As Powell explained:

> The lessons I absorbed from Panama confirmed all my convictions over the preceding twenty years, since the days of doubt over Vietnam. Have a clear political objective and stick to it. Use all the force necessary, and do not apologize for going in big if that is what it takes. Decisive force ends wars quickly and in the long run saves lives. Whatever threats we faced in the future, I intended to make these rules the bedrock of my military counsel.[39]

Once President Bush listened to his recommendation and "doubled the force facing the Iraqis," the concept became part of the national security lexicon.[40]

The Powell Doctrine encapsulates military frustration over two perceived problems: civilian micromanagement and meddling in so-called military affairs, and vague political objectives. While it is inherently flawed given its political naivete (particularly in a system where national security power is distributed so the system will rarely give firm and clear political objectives); its minimal consideration of the adversary's perspective; and its grounding in the linear nature of conflicts and national security interests, the Powell Doctrine, nevertheless, profoundly shaped the young military leaders of 1991—who became the generals of 2001 through 2003.[41]

Scholars Nora Bensahel and David Barno recall the ominous warning by retired General Barry McCaffrey, who said, "I fear the majors of Desert Storm," because he understood that "now a whole new genera- tion of soldiers believed that the overwhelming success of the Gulf War proved once and for all that the Army had learned the right lessons from Vietnam."[42] The doctrine resonated, in other words, and continues to resonate, among a certain subset of the U.S. military and its leadership, not least due to its seemingly straightforward checklist to solving the complex nonlinear issues of war.

And, of course, none of these dynamics are idiosyncratic to the U.S. military. Neuralgia-inspired denial is reminiscent of the French war in Algeria. Despite deploying 500,000 troops, 35,000 of whom died in Alge- ria, the war has "disappeared from collective memory" in France.[43] Con- versely, the French have glorified their population's "resistance" against the Nazi occupation in World War II despite overwhelming evidence that it was far from unanimous and unified.[44] More recently, and closer to the U.S. experience, the Soviet leadership hid the coffins of its troops killed in Afghanistan and often failed to specify where a soldier had per- ished. However, by 2004, Russian president Vladimir Putin said they had "won their battle."[45]

Legacies of war shape individuals, militaries, and countries. They simply cannot be ignored. Failing to deliberately reconcile the impact of these legacies will merely allow them to shapeshift—positively or del- eteriously.

MYTHS AND MEMORY

Exploring the military's inheritance since 9/11 requires difficult discus- sions regarding myths and memories, the stories institutions or indi- viduals tell themselves and others, since they shape our understanding of legacies. Vigilance is necessary in these discussions, because "much depends on which aspects of the war—and which period of time—one examines, and which reminiscences one trusts."[46] Narratives come and go like waves on a beach, and as the literature on memory studies high- lights, memory is complicated, fragmented, and disorienting.[47] Simply put, one cannot ignore the profound impact of myths. As scholar Eliot

Cohen affirms, "Political and military institutions can no more escape the molding hand of history than an individual can escape the influences of memory."[48]

Myths invariably develop around the legacies of conflict. Given how wrenching it is to conduct serious introspection of painful events, myths may, themselves, end up forming the dominant legacies of a war, especially for those intimately involved in waging war or making decisions. Such individuals have developed stories about what happened and why, which may or may not be defensible or even factually correct. And those tales will invariably inform their future actions. President Truman approached the conflict in Korea based on his understanding of the causes and course of World War II; General Maxwell Taylor, General William Westmoreland, Secretary of State Dean Rusk, and Under Secretary of State George Ball did the same for the Vietnam War.[49] "Where they sat depended on where they had *stood* before," scholars Ernest May and Richard Neustadt remind readers.[50] As one author on military affairs reflected, "Mom had grown up an admiral's daughter and said that senior officers functioned so that no truth could betray the myths, of either the past or the mind."[51]

Studies of bias by scholar Daniel Kahneman are particularly noteworthy in this regard, since he smartly highlights the dangers inherent in errors of confabulation and attribution; fallacies of sunk cost; and biases of optimism, availability, confirmation, saliency, and anchoring in making judgments.[52] Now, two decades of cycling in and out of theaters like Iraq and Afghanistan has resulted in many troops going back to the same country—and sometimes the same province—repeatedly. That dynamic colors many military perspectives, invariably informing the lessons they have learned and, just as importantly, the myths they have formed.

Buying into myths does not necessarily have to be disingenuous or nefarious. It often is neither. But it can be dangerous, nevertheless. As President John Kennedy explained, "The great enemy of the truth is very often not the lie—deliberate, contrived, and dishonest—but the myth—persistent, persuasive, and unrealistic."[53]

The post-9/11 wars shaped the military leaders who led them from

the Pentagon, the combatant commands, or in the field. They have
shaped those who will lead the American military in its future wars, as
well. This is important because military myths vary by rank, by specialty
or community, and by service. The Air Force and Navy have told themselves very different stories than the Army and the Marines have over
the years. Within specialties, the lessons learned by those who flew unmanned vehicles differs from those who flew fighter aircraft in combat.
When Winston Churchill reminds us that "at times of crisis, myths have
their historical importance," he did not also acknowledge their often diffuse nature.[54] There is no one story or myth about the U.S. military that
encapsulates the single story of this inheritance. Readers seeking that
unified summary will find themselves terribly unsatisfied. Moreover, in
the vein of George Packer's warning, "Journalists and historians have to
distort war: in order to find the plot—causation, sequence, meaning—
they make war more intelligible than it really is."[55] Caveat lector.

REVIEWS TO DATE

The U.S. military has not conducted its own serious, rigorous, and holis-
tic assessment of its inheritance from the past nearly two decades of war.
The Army authorized a two-volume study focused solely on Iraq from
the years 2003 to 2011, which was reluctantly published after a public
outcry. However, it contains little strategic analysis and has had virtually
no effect on the overall narrative inside the institution.[56] Then Chairman of the Joint Chiefs Martin Dempsey did commission a thoughtful
study on the costs, benefits, and lessons learned from Iraq and Afghanistan, which was conducted entirely by National Defense University
rather than members of the military—although many of its authors are
veterans.[57] And in 2011, Dempsey tasked the Joint and Coalition Operational Analysis division with gathering lessons learned. The final product focused on the first decade of the post-9/11 wars and has received
little attention to date, perhaps due to the anodyne nature of its findings,
such as the difficulty of accurately assessing the security environment,
shifting from waging conventional conflict to counterinsurgency, and
collaborating with partners in and outside of the U.S. government.[58]

There have been various narrower efforts to analyze the U.S. approach to the post-9/11 wars, including on the wars in Iraq and Afghanistan.[59] In this category belong a number of assessments on specific periods in specific wars, most notably the 2006–2007 Bush administration national security discussions that culminated in the decision to surge troops in Iraq and the Obama administration's 2009 decision to review options in Afghanistan that culminated in a surge of troops.[60] As retired General Stanley McChrystal, who commanded the war in Afghanistan, said of them: "I saw good people all trying to reach a positive outcome, but approaching the problem from different cultures and perspectives, often speaking with different vocabularies."[61]

A second category includes the broad defense strategy reviews conducted every four years or so, including internal Defense Department-led Quadrennial Defense Reviews as well as the products of independent panels or commissions appointed by Congress. However, only the most recent of these examined the legacy of the last two decades of conflict, and then only briefly.[62] In doing so, the report states that the "security and well-being of the United States are at greater risk than at any time in decades . . . America's military superiority . . . has eroded to a dangerous degree."[63] A final category of narrower projects includes the tremendous literature on the post-9/11 wars written by those who experienced them from various vantage points, including those who served in the military.[64]

Two key U.S. allies that engaged in the post-9/11 wars, the United Kingdom and Australia, have conducted their own reviews, albeit with varying results. Most famously, the British government empowered an independent panel to study the UK's involvement in the Iraq War and to identify lessons learned. Led by Sir John Chilcot and subsequently nicknamed the Chilcot Report, the scathing report was published after seven years of inquiry—far from those wars' conclusions.[65] Australia's review was more informal. Conducted over three years by a Defence Department analyst, it was released only after a freedom of information act request, as the Defence Department leaders had quashed its publication. The report brims with frustration with and resentment for politicians and military leaders unwilling to provide "strategic direction," and military personnel adrift, perhaps best summed up by one Australian military commander who rued: "We did some shit for a while and things didn't get any worse."[66]

METHODOLOGY

This book asks the question: What has the U.S. military inherited from nearly two decades at war? Chapters 2 to 4 outline three crises that are shaping the military's sense of itself, its relationship to society, and its relationship with its civilian overseers—a crisis of confidence, a crisis of caring, and a crisis of meaningful civilian oversight, respectively—which provide a useful framework for the subsequent chapters. Chapter 5 explores how the military goes to war, including planning for war, paying for war, and perceiving war. Chapter 6 examines how the military wages war, particularly exploring how it makes choices regarding time, space, and the spectrum of conflict; the different impacts of being at war on each of the military services; and the changing role of combatant commands. Chapter 7 looks at those who have served throughout the post-9/11 wars, while chapter 8 focuses on those who have led the military during this period. Chapter 9 outlines some of the approaches to fighting and winning that have characterized these wars and been developed to understand them (as well as the future). Finally, chapter 10 offers insights for the reader on how to productively deal with these legacies.

This book's overwhelming focus is on the armed forces, the civilian managers of violence, and the relationship between them. While it predominantly focuses on what the post-9/11 wars have meant for the military, it is impossible to ignore the role of civilians because of the nature of U.S. democracy. To be clear, many of those civilians have made many mistakes, which a substantial literature has addressed.[67] However, one should be cautious of sleepwalking into narratives that simply blame civilians for the strategic sins of the past two decades. Instead, this book seeks to explore the shared responsibility of those in uniform and those in Western business attire while accounting for the lessons implicitly learned by both.

Exploring issues that are "not dead yet" is a thorny endeavor.[68] Studying contemporary affairs poses its own difficulties and rarely lends itself to formal theory development or highly stylized argument. Some research methods, like process tracing, were useful in examining the range of primary sources that complemented this book's leveraging of the rich secondary literature on particular issues.

Much of the analysis in this book, however, is based on the findings from nearly 100 interviews that I personally conducted from 2018 to 2020. I conducted most of the interviews with current or recently retired generals or flag officers, the highest-ranking members of the U.S. military, and a few current or former senior civilian executives who served in the U.S. Defense Department. All interviews were conducted in a semi-structured manner, used the same list of questions, and benefited from the snowball sampling method. Interviewees were generally asked a broad question about the legacies of the post-9/11 wars for the U.S. military, a more specific question about how the inconclusiveness of these wars may have shaped these legacies, a few questions about the impact of the wars on the joint force and on internal Department of Defense dynamics, a question about their perception of shifts in civil-military relations, and a pair of questions about how they thought about conflict earlier in their career and how they think about the trajectory of conflict in the future.

The interviewees represent a wide diversity of experience, including serving across the joint force, the combatant commands, the military services, the joint staff, and the office of the secretary of defense. They include many of the military leaders who found themselves in positions of influence as they served at the highest levels of a military waging its longest conflict. Some still serve, while others retired or resigned their positions over the last decade or so. Each held multiple positions throughout the post-9/11 period. The senior civilian executives represented both career officials and political appointees across both political parties.

On the whole, however, interviewees were overwhelmingly senior military leaders, like current and recently retired general and flag officers. That makes sense for two reasons. First, senior military leaders shape the military's internal narrative of and approach to the legacies of the post-9/11 wars. Whether through promotions, professional military education, strategy, budget, or doctrine, they transmit their views into the organization. Second, they shape the external narrative of the legacies of the post-9/11 wars by informing the national security debate and by engaging the American public on how it absorbs the wars. To be sure, more junior members of the military have an important perspective to offer. Notably, many of the most compelling quotes come from mid-level and junior officers across the military. However, when examining influence on the broader military organization, the current and former senior leaders have a more substantial impact.

To benefit from the interviewees' frank and honest insights while also respecting their desires for discretion, I have anonymized their words and refer to them generically throughout this book. Quotations in the book without footnotes are interview quotes. I took this approach to preserve confidentiality and trust, which was of the utmost importance to interviewees who shared their frank and provocative insights. I took the triangulation process seriously, weighing the internal consistency of interviews and including as much context as possible to inform readers' abilities to critically interpret the findings. Although much of the research in this field is based on anonymized surveys, expert interviews are the best way to answer this book's question.

As a national security professional and scholar who worked in the Pentagon for five secretaries of defense over two administrations, and who made policy on a wide range of issues, I was granted tremendous access by my former colleagues in and out of uniform. They were generous with their time, their insights, and their connections, such that there remain very few notable senior military officials from the last two decades whose experiences have not been considered in this book—either through interviews or through their public comments.

The observations they share are compelling. Patterns emerged in these interviews to a degree I had not expected, including key terms and ideas that were either repeatedly invoked or repeatedly ignored.[69] Other sources, like the satirical website *Duffel Blog* started by Marine veteran Paul Szoldra, helped unearth the hidden discourse of those servicemembers who were not otherwise represented. *Duffel Blog* is a modern version of *The Wipers Times*, the witty paper that troops on the Western Front in World War I produced to offer a sardonic reflection on the conflict.

All these sources represent different lenses based on their background, role, and temporal involvement in the post-9/11 wars, and were important to access. Nevertheless, the complicated nature of the issues under discussion precludes a neat and tidy narrative. As the reader will find, this book is, therefore, not a theory of things but, rather, a story of things. That recognition forced great humility on me as I tried to tell this story. I profoundly recognize that, like Arthur M. Schlesinger Jr. has said, this book has been written from a "zone of imperfect visibility."[70] Contemporaneously defining the post-9/11 wars and explaining the legacies that come out of them through firsthand accounts comes with risks, but given how consequential the misuse of military history can be, it is a risk worth taking.

One such risk worth addressing now is the book's use of the term "post-9/11 wars." It is clunky and awkward. This is, perhaps, appropriately so, given that the fighting itself has clunkily and awkwardly spanned the globe. There are other names for it, of course, like the Global War on Terror, the Long War, the Forever War, or World War IV. However, these are unsatisfying and each is riddled with its own problems. "This war has no easily visualized ending or telos that lends itself to articulation in a phrase or name," John McLaughlin and I previously wrote.[71]

Moreover, the length of this time period invariably means that different moments in these wars have different characters and rhetorical resonances. The wars in Iraq and Afghanistan are a major part of the post-9/11 wars, but, according to one study, the post-9/11 wars have involved the U.S. military fighting in nearly 40 percent of countries.[72] Indeed, the inability to pinpoint exactly where the U.S. has been waging war over the past two decades represents one of the many ways in which these conflicts have been fuzzy. Using the term "post-9/11 wars," thus, purposively trades rhetorical punch for definitional clarity.

My personal involvement in many of the issues covered in this book while I served as a senior Defense Department policymaker presents its own challenges, as well. Although my background and profile facilitated extraordinary access, that came with costs. I recognize my own positionality in this research and have attempted to control for it to the extent possible while also acknowledging where and how it introduces bias.[73] I hope the approach I offer in this book benefits a field in need of more diverse research methodologies, especially those that can help bridge the scholar-practitioner and civil-military divides.

2

The Military's Sense of Itself

The Crisis of Confidence

"Everywhere I go, I hear 'We don't win anymore.'"

There is a crisis within our military, in its relationship with itself—a *crisis of confidence*. To be clear, the crisis of confidence does not mean, or at least does not only mean, that the military has low self-esteem. Rather, this crisis focuses on the loss permeating those who have fought in the post-9/11 wars of the corporate identity that helps make the military professional.[1] Many servicemembers are confused about what the military does, how it should do it, and why.

This crisis emanates from a paradox that has characterized the post-9/11 wars. The U.S. military is consistently described as the best military on the planet. Months before the September 11, 2001, attacks, President Bush exhorted that "America today has the finest [military] the world has ever seen."[2] In his farewell address to the U.S. military, President Barack Obama described it as "the greatest force for freedom and security that the world has ever known."[3] And more recently, President Donald Trump declared that the U.S. military has "the greatest men . . . the greatest women . . . and the greatest equipment."[4]

Despite being constantly told they are the most capable force on the planet, however, the U.S. military has been unable to clearly win in nearly two decades of fighting against comparatively low-capability foes. To be sure, having prevented another large terrorist attack on the home-land for two decades is, indeed, a stunning accomplishment; however, it does not appear to have been internalized by the military as a true wartime victory. One senior military leader explained, "Everywhere I go, I hear 'we don't win anymore.'" Another general officer underscored that the military's inability to "come to grips with the fact that we didn't win hamstrings us now because we've been told by others and we've been telling ourselves that we're the greatest ever." Similarly, another officer lamented that "we have become an Army that doesn't do anything well."

To be clear, it is not the military's job to define a theory of victory. That is the role of political leaders. However, it is the military's role to translate overall political goals into a military theory of victory. A "mili-tary theory of victory" is defined as "a set of propositions about how and why the behavior of one belligerent in war or conflict short of war will or might affect the behavior of another belligerent in a desired manner."[5] Grounded in a warfighting operating concept, the military theory of vic-tory should be tied to the strategy and resources available, and informed by the adversary's strategy and military theory of victory, as well. The military has responsibility for articulating that a given political objective is unlikely to be achievable, or is likely to be achieved only with a certain amount of resources and in a specific period of time.

This rumbling hunger for success in the face of two decades of war without winning has pushed many to hunt for alternative sustenance. Some, for example, do not want to consider this paradox at all. They want to focus on how hard the military has worked to achieve results—an inputs-based approach. For example, when asked about his experience in the post-9/11 wars after the *Washington Post* published the "Afghani-stan Papers," a compendium of interviews and memos from senior U.S. officials who shaped U.S. policy toward Afghanistan, Air Force Chief Master Sergeant Ramon Colon-Lopez described how hard everyone in the military tried to wage war: the "men and women that have been going back to [sic] since 2002 to perform this mission have been pouring their heart and soul into its success."[6] While his comment is completely appropriate for his role and for that forum, the implication is that giving one's all should be sufficient to forgive a lack of interrogating what they achieved. It sadly represents a conflation between input and outcome. As one senior officer fears, however, this could result in a military unwilling and unable to learn from the post-9/11 wars, "a little bit like a student who doesn't understand why they aren't performing well." As this officer explained, "half-hearted" rejoinders like "political will . . . no endgame . . . impossible to win" are taken as excusing the absence of deeper introspection. Continuing the student metaphor, this officer decried that the military is "accepting our C and moving on."

Those who do want to resolve this paradox could do so in a few different ways. One approach would be to argue that the premise is wrong, because we do not know the counterfactual; that is, how much worse the world might be today if the U.S. military had not done as well as it has. In interviews, this view was best encapsulated by a senior general officer who sighed and said, "Victory may look like keeping it [terrorism] in a box." Another senior general officer explained, "We don't know what has been prevented . . . it could be that this is a huge victory." In this vein, President Obama outlined his view of the military leadership always desiring "more" because the system encouraged such an approach. From his perspective, the military "prided itself on accomplishing a mission once started, without regard to cost, duration, or whether the mission was the right one to begin with." He recognized that "more had not produced victory" but in the case of Iraq, for instance, it had avoided catastrophe.[7]

Another approach for reconciling the paradox of why the military has been unable to prevail in the post-9/11 wars is simply to argue that the U.S. military was given an impossible mission. In this view, the post-9/11 wars never were winnable and it was foolhardy to expect the U.S. military to prevail. One general officer who subscribed to this view judged his numerous wartime deployments as "the best we could do" given the circumstances. A different senior officer recounted that, for a long time, he subscribed to Colonel Harry Summers's famous line about tactical wins and strategic loss in the Vietnam War.[8] As he put it, "I bought into the myth that we never lost a tactical fight." But he demurred and said he finally changed his mind when he realized that "I lost daily. Every time my truck blew up, I lost. I lost way more than I won."

Scholars Nora Bensahel and David Barno examine this premise by using the Vietnam War as a proxy for the nearly two-decades-long war in Afghanistan. They considered how differently one might have perceived that earlier conflict if it had lasted longer but been characterized by a much more limited U.S. role, including fewer U.S. troops deployed, substantially fewer U.S. casualties, and more reliance on the South Vietnamese military. The counterfactual they outlined presents a vision of victory—one in which North Vietnam is held back and the South Vietnamese government remains in power—albeit a rather dispiriting and unsatisfying one.[9]

The military's role as just one tool in the broader national security toolbox reinforced this sense among many military leaders that they had been given an impossible mission. As one general officer outlined in his explanation of the military's role in providing victory in the post-9/11 wars, "We don't define the solution, we're not the only stakeholder, [and] we're not the only lever being applied to the problem." Many military leaders question how effective military power actually can be in this type of conflict. This was evidenced by one senior general officer who declared that "there has been a long history of American theory about the use of the military arm of national power that has been wrong," citing a convoluted list of personnel cuts, hubris, and the negative impact of deploying ground forces abroad. A different general officer worried that "some very thoughtful people rightfully have doubts about the quality or the durability of the application of military power in that [post-9/11 wars] kind of environment." As he explained, "There's this lingering sense that the foundational conditions that prompted 9/11 or allowed it to develop remain very much in place, if not more prevalent."

In a similar vein, former Marine Elliot Ackerman explained to a former Iraqi militant who fought against the American military that we had "lost before we even started fighting. For us, success meant winning.

For you, the insurgents, success meant not losing."[10] And, in one particularly chilling example of how complex, complicated, and convoluted this type of conflict can be, a senior officer described conducting a raid of a home in Afghanistan and finding a saber engraved in English from 1836. Looking at it, he wondered: "Did his great, great, great-grandfather take it off a dead British paratrooper? That was a moment where it was just: what are we doing? We don't have a fucking clue what's going on around here. We have no idea the games that are getting played." His tale highlighted real questions about what defines victory and how realistic it is to achieve it.

A third approach argues that the wars are winnable—the military could prevail—but it has not yet done so for two interrelated reasons. The first is poor leadership among military leaders, civilian leaders, or both. The second, tied to leadership, is that the U.S. military was given the wrong resources and/or pursued the wrong strategy for victory. One former senior civilian policymaker criticized the chasm between strategy and resourcing in the post-9/11 wars. Underscoring that, "at best, we've achieved some operational successes, but they haven't stuck strategically," he was flummoxed throughout the last two decades by military leaders repeatedly declaring "we're on the verge of winning" despite the fact that they "couldn't win with 150,000 troops, but now [claimed to be] on the cusp with 7,000 troops and some airpower." From his perspective, the military leadership's willingness to declare near-victory was entirely detached from the situation on the ground. Similarly, a senior officer criticized what he termed "strategic ineptness . . . an unbelievable inability for senior uniformed decisionmakers to bridge the gap between policy and warfighting."

This approach sometimes includes substantial (and often valid) blame for civilian leaders. One general officer outlined his frustration with civil-military divisions and debates, explaining that "our strategy and policy leadership is not unified enough to sustain an enduring effort that creates the conditions . . . to achieve the strategic outcome that military operations and activities are designed to support." Another senior officer questioned if the military was ever given "the time to accomplish" its objectives in the post-9/11 wars, offering that he feels "guilty that the military could not provide a conclusive victory." Yet another said, "A real viewpoint amongst the military [is] if we were calling the shots, then somehow the outcome would have been different." A final officer said that he and his peers worry that many military leaders believe "somehow the military's hands were tied and if only the armed forces had been able to employ its full might, it could have achieved a decisive victory" in the post-9/11 wars. It should be noted that he hastened to add, "It is hard for me to imagine a more dangerous line of thinking when it comes to the employment of the military option." His fears align, worryingly so, with pernicious patterns of recrimination that followed the military's search for meaning after the Vietnam War.

Many waging the post-9/11 wars simply couldn't figure out what they had been doing and why they had been doing it. In their view, the purpose and end state of the fighting was confused. "We're filling body bags and hospital bags and we don't really know why; there's no end state in sight," lamented one retired general officer. Similarly, a senior officer described the U.S. military's purpose during the post-9/11 wars as "like pouring water in the desert; I can't tell you that anything we did mattered."

These points reflect dynamics that General Stanley McChrystal describes in his memoir. He writes of the frustration that erupted during one of his troop gatherings in Afghanistan while he was leading the war there. Imploring him, "some [of his subordinates] were openly bitter over their loss and the seeming impossibility of their mission. *'Why are we here, Sir? What's the point?'*"[11] Similarly, here's how an officer described his wartime deployments: "Man, you watch really, really good men work really, really hard to do what they think is best and it goes nowhere. Man, what were we doing? For each of these [deployments], I walked away with that same question." The most penetrating comment in this vein came from one officer who reminded me that "there's no such thing as a favorable wind for a sailor who doesn't know where he wants to go." His feelings of aimlessness were palpable. And the punchiest description of this confusion comes from former junior Army officer turned journalist Matt Gallagher, who declared his disillusionment with appropriately powerful language: "Our grandfathers had pushed back the onslaught of fascism. Just what the fuck were we doing?"[12]

The baggage from this uncertainty was repeatedly described as "a sense of futility," in the words of a retired general officer. Echoing concerns about "the futility of it all," another officer recounted his unit returning to Fort Hood from Iraq and then seeing a PowerPoint slide that outlined their impending return seven months later, plus another scheduled deployment back to Iraq a year after that. He recalled how difficult it was to lead troops in that environment, mockingly describing telling his troops that "I know you just got back and we need to do some memorial services, but this time we're really going to win . . . but if not this one, definitely the next one." He then laughed at how "soul crushing" it all was.

He was not alone in bringing up the apparent futility of the war in the context of the brutal deployment schedules it demanded. An officer at his same rank wryly emphasized how "damaging" it was. "We joke in private," he told me, "here we go again, [so] why bother to withdraw [since] we're just going to go right back." A third officer at this rank recounted how many of his colleagues have left the Army. As he put it, "I had a lot of buddies who said 'I love the Army, but I just can't fight for nothing.'" The most colorful description in this vein came from an officer who said the war was "like being at a party, the keg is tapped, the electricity doesn't work, but you're still trying to make things happen." And, finally, one former senior civilian official feared the "corrosive effect" of this dynamic, in which one is "being asked to risk the ultimate sacrifice, but it's not clear we have a strategy or have thought through it."

All these dynamics have fed into the crisis of confidence that has permeated the military's views of victory. Granted, the impermanence of victory is likely as old as war itself. Nearly 2,500 years ago, Thucydides recorded in *The Peloponnesian War* how ephemeral victory proved for the most powerful state at the time, Athens, as a result of both its own decisionmaking and the choices of its opponents. Nearly two hundred years ago, theorist Carl von Clausewitz developed the concept of a "culminating point of victory" and warned that, once it was achieved, one must consolidate gains rather than continue fighting.[13] While he outlined a few different pathways to securing victory, the dynamics Clausewitz highlights underscore his admonition that "in war, the result is never final."[14]

U.S. military personnel, thus, take with them both the baggage of being told they are the best and the burden of their lived experiences over the last two decades, in which strategic victory, for any number of reasons, has proven unattainable. These understandings contradict one another. Unsurprisingly, those in the military, therefore, thrash around for some sort of victory they can grasp, and this paradox makes it much easier to find one.

SEARCHING FOR AN ERSATZ VICTORY

At the strategic level, lack of conclusive victory, whatever its reasons, pushed military leaders to search for an ersatz victory to mitigate the crisis of confidence that erupted. Less generous analysts may see this as deliberate deception and obfuscation.[15] Others will recognize that exhaustion paired with inconclusiveness translates into some degree of trauma, and potentially neuralgia, as the need to assuage cognitive dissonance results in self-justifying reinterpretations of history. In this case, swirling emotions and the imperative to know "why" the post-9/11 wars were fought created a crisis of confidence that requires some degree of post hoc reasoning to salve.

Confusion over purpose and an ambient sense of futility are, perhaps, inherent in counterinsurgency and counterterrorism conflicts. In studies of asymmetric conflict, one scholar found a few relevant themes that can be found in the post-9/11 wars as well. Even though combatants on the more powerful side in these conflicts are in many ways safer from individual injury than their insurgent opponents, nevertheless, "the stronger sides in asymmetric warfare are more risk averse."[16] They particularly focus their risk-taking on protecting those who serve alongside them. That willingness manifests in perceiving "force protection as the highest expression of courage."[17] While some degree of moral injury, or questions of "what is right," inevitably occur in conflict, the character of that conflict shapes its extent, and insurgencies appear particularly harmful.[18] Indeed, urban counterinsurgency environments, which characterized portions of the post-9/11 wars, present a particularly high number of dynamics that can exacerbate moral injury.[19]

For example, one psychologist found a surprisingly high degree of post-traumatic stress in the soldiers and Marines who were deployed to Somalia in the early 1990s. Even though that was a peacekeeping mission, the conflict itself was similar to an insurgency. The findings from that deployment, notably that "American troops in Somalia were disoriented and troubled by 'ambiguous, inconsistent or unacceptable rules of engagement (ROE); lack of clarity about the goals of the mission itself; a civilian population of combatants; and inherently contradictory experiences of the mission as both humanitarian and dangerous'" are very much in line with experiences in the post-9/11 wars.[20]

Many in the military simply developed definitions of victory more achievable than those held by the U.S. political leadership. These included goals focusing on achieving operational or tactical successes, internal bureaucratic achievements, or the protection of comrades in arms. One scholar found that even before the post-9/11 wars, the U.S. military was increasingly focusing on the "operational level of war." This trend has likely been exacerbated over the last two decades as the search for an ersatz victory resulted in the pursuit of operational metrics whose impact on the strategic-level outcome are questionable. The military "wants to fight, that's why it exists, but doing so has a corrosive effect," underscored one senior general officer. However, as a former general officer explained, "Those that have fought [in] it look at it in a smaller scope: I was asked to do this and I did a good job." Victory, therefore, often became defined as "don't die . . . don't get your guys killed and leave it better than you found it," as one senior officer explained.

Alternatively, some found purpose and, thus, victory through others: "14 people that worked for me died [so] my future leadership is for them," declared one officer. In *Restrepo*, a popular movie about the war in Afghanistan, the platoon focuses on defending an isolated outpost named for one of their peers who was killed; indeed, it feels as though their entire purpose in this dangerous part of Afghanistan is to memorialize their fallen comrade rather than to maintain a presence for political-military reasons. One former senior civilian official described hearing about numerous officers who now define their reason for fighting as "loyalty to the team" and victory as protecting their battle buddies, because they either "do not know what the strategy is or are cynical or think it's a bunch of BS."

While that dynamic is not unusual at the unit level, its existence at more mid-grade and senior officer levels is surprising and concerning. Attempts to find value in their efforts are admirable, and the struggle to redefine is understandable. However, they also are, ultimately, dangerous when they detach warfighting from strategy. As one general officer suggested, "Not every tactical engagement or operation contributes to a solution, but that doesn't invalidate the nature of the sacrifice; you have to [believe that] because it's too painful to face the alternative." The longing in his voice was penetrating and unmistakable, almost as though he was trying to convince himself. More bluntly, a journalist who has covered military issues for decades declared, "We saw the U.S. military tactically magnificent, but without a strategic clue. Tactics without strategy is [like] a Ferrari without a steering wheel: it's powerful and fast, and winds up in a ditch." General McConville, chief of staff of the Army, regularly makes it clear that "winning matters."[21] His exhortations that, in conflict, "we don't go to participate, we don't go to try hard" demonstrate a profound discomfort with this inability to define and to capture victory.[22]

This dynamic is an old one. As the foundational study of post-traumatic stress in the Vietnam War found, absent victory, those who survive have real challenges reconciling the purpose of their losses. "The corpses' meaning hovers in the void until the lethal contest has been decided," explains Jonathan Shay, author of *Achilles in Vietnam: Combat Trauma and the Undoing of Character*.[23] Shay's work is a pointed reminder that inconclusive conflicts can cause moral damage long after their last shots have been fired.

Troops' hyper-closeness to the conflicts has played into the crisis of confidence, as well. For many, returning to districts or villages where they previously had been deployed was a disheartening experience. An officer recalled how the vibrant Afghan district he had previously patrolled was a "ghost town" two years later, which "makes you think about what you did and what effect it had." Another discussed returning to the same part of Iraq "because we didn't win the first time," and was disheartened that "the same units we trained are the same units that threw their weapons down and ran." A general officer recounted how the Afghan district that "was in a really good place" when he left the first time had been "completely overrun" on his next deployment. He explained the impact of this experience on his troops. According to this officer, first they asked questions like, "Why did [our colleague] die? Why did we fight? Was it worth it? Was there any value in the sacrifice?" Later, some grew cynical, some left the military, and some "put it in a bin," or compartmentalized it. Psychologists who have spoken to members of the military at more diverse levels than I have for this book have had similar questions raised in their conversations, as well.[24]

Uncertainty over the purpose of the post-9/11 wars, coupled with the desire for ersatz victories, has incentivized efforts to "stay the course." Some officers want to continue fighting because, according to this line of thinking, good people died in previous fights, and seeing the mission through honors their sacrifice. While the first part of that logic is tragically true, the second does not naturally follow from it and, indeed, is a dangerous conclusion. One former general officer discussed a colleague who had served nine wartime deployments. He warned that this colleague's "opinion of it [the wars] can't be trusted because he is too in love with the family farm to recognize when the family farm is no longer a good idea." His "family farm" metaphor suggests that many of those who served in the military are, understandably, too close to the post-9/11 wars and have real difficulty disentangling their operational dedication from strategic-level assessment. He further articulated concerns about "this malaise . . . this overarching guilt" that so many in the military have from their experiences in the post-9/11 wars. From his perspective, the U.S. military tried hard to win and it, ultimately, feels dismayed and perturbed by its failure to do so. Similarly, one former officer discussed what he termed the "schizophrenia" of the U.S. military's approach to fighting the post-9/11 wars. As he put it, "On the one hand, this is absurd—what are we still doing here—and then on the other hand, we can't leave . . . this is insane, but we can't stop." Echoing his views, two former senior civilian officials reiterated how hard it seemed for military leaders to "emotionally" let go of these wars because their "personal and intellectual history . . . has clouded their vision on when is the right time to say ok, it's time for us . . . to put this aside." Of course, given how the post-9/11 wars have bled into one another, it is extremely difficult to pinpoint a moment in time when the United States could have disengaged from its various conflicts, although there were periods in which it was able to dramatically reduce its involvements, such as from Afghanistan in 2004.

The inability to move on from the post-9/11 wars is a troubling issue, and satire provides an important modality through which it is acknowledged and discussed. *Duffel Blog*'s comedy, for example, closely aligns with the sentiments expressed in my interviews, often by more senior-level officials. One piece, titled "War in Afghanistan Turns 16, Earns Driver's License," included a scene in which the war's parents discuss how hard it is to move on. Its mother, fretting that "I just don't think we'll ever be able to let our young war go," is comforted by its father, who responds that "knowing him, he'll still be with us until he's 25 and begging for cash from us until he's at least 40."[25] Another article excitedly declared that "this man was born on 9/11 and gets to fight in the same war it inspired," noting that his father and brother served there, and he expects his sons to do so, as well.[26] A similar piece highlights a teenager born after 9/11 who, in four decades, will command the U.S. war in Afghanistan.[27] That the post-9/11 wars are never-ending is a belief that transcends rank and level.

Another example of satirizing the very real pressure to stay the course in the post-9/11 wars is found in the movie *War Machine*, a fictionalized account of one period of the war in Afghanistan. As the narrator explains, "What do you do when the war you're fighting just can't possibly be won in any meaningful sense? Well, obviously, you sack the guy not winning it, and you bring in some other guy." When the new commander of U.S. military operations takes over, he is exuberant, brimming with infectious enthusiasm. Wry moments abound, like during his first meeting with the Afghan president, when he announces a new strategy. A fictional President Karzai pauses and then quietly remarks that it "sounds a lot like the *old* direction."[28] The movie captures the frustrations of inconclusiveness and the failed attempts to remedy it.

These frustrations also have generated desperation for a real victory, particularly among mid-grade officers. "After 12 years of nonstop deployments, I'd like to be a part of a war we won," an officer told me. "I'd like to get a win in," concurred another. And a third officer, underscoring the losses of military colleagues in combat, also reinforced this message: "It makes you feel like you want a win." Steve Leonard, a retired senior officer and the brains behind "Doctrine Man," a very popular social media presence in the defense community, has noted this desire for victory, as well. While having coffee with a Vietnam War veteran, he is struck when the veteran asked him, "What's it like to win a war?" and realizes that "after two decades of war, I'm not sure I know, either."[29] Indeed, the famous coffee cup quip regularly seen across combat zones and in the Pentagon—"We were winning when I left"—epitomizes the views of many in the military, particularly the rotational mindset that plagued them, according to one journalist who covers these issues.

This crisis of confidence appears to affect different ranks in different ways. In my interviews, mid-grade officers, both active and former, underscored the "staggering physical and emotional toll" and the "guilt" they feel over the lack of victory. One former officer outlined the "resentment towards our senior officers that they didn't know anything," and explained that he would hear quips among his peers criticizing senior military leaders, like "I've been on patrols longer than Desert Storm."

More senior officers may, on the whole, be more comfortable with the lack of victory and better able to compartmentalize it. One former senior civilian official underscored that general officers "tend to recognize . . . and are less troubled by the fact that things are inconclusive . . . they understand, for a variety of reasons," why the post-9/11 wars have taken the shape they have, whereas more junior military personnel "are more frustrated that they've seen their peers killed or injured, they don't feel like the stakes are worth it, [and] they feel we should just get out of it." The deeper understanding displayed by today's senior military leaders is notable. Obviously, however, they do not represent the military's future leaders.

Many of these dynamics are best summarized by a general officer who straddles both the Persian Gulf and post-9/11 wars generations and, in echoing all these points, ruefully acknowledges that "people carry a lot of scars." At West Point, Professor Elizabeth Samet had heard that watching the Persian Gulf War "boosted [cadet] morale and convinced cadets of their invincibility." She found those reactions discordant "with a new sadness and a sober, quiet skepticism" that draped over her students starting around 2005 as the post-9/11 wars took a serious downturn.[30] Comparing the impact of the post-9/11 wars with the Vietnam War, she wondered if those who served as junior officers in both these conflicts will share a crisis of confidence, whether we will have "a generation of senior officers whose sensibilities were formed in an ambiguous conflict that did not go according to plan, soldiers whose youthful idealism and certainty have been tempered by reality and disappointment at the beginning of their military careers."[31]

Notably, the crisis of confidence seemed most undeniable in interviewees' repeated reflection on the therapeutic nature of speaking for this book. Describing it as cathartic, many explained they were grateful for the opportunity to discuss issues that had been simmering below the surface for them. Whether it was the "corrosive" impact of the post-9/11 wars on the military or lamentations about the "hubris" of attempting such expansionist conflicts, they now took the opportunity to think through visceral but often-undiscussed issues. Moreover, for those who still wonder if the post-9/11 wars can, indeed, be "put . . . in a bin," as one general officer described earlier, the most compelling answer comes from one former Marine who analyzed the impact of fighting in the post-9/11 wars. "Even as we want it all to stop, we know on one level that it won't. After any peace deal, now, later, in another decade, we'll still be fighting the war in one place. Our heads."[32]

Going forward, the crisis of confidence can be remedied in a few different ways. One approach is admittedly problematic: to prepare for and fight a different type of warfare, much as the military did forty years ago in the wake of Vietnam. Another approach is more practical: to encourage honest dialogue on the thorny and encumbering dynamics surrounding the character of post-9/11 warfare and victory. But simply ignoring the existence of a problem calls into question the military's willingness to acknowledge hard truths, its prioritization of self-awareness, and its willingness—or even ability—to have such conversations.

The military must wrestle with a discomfiting situation. It is an institution organized to perpetrate violence to achieve victory—yet the inability to define victory, let alone attain it, is fundamentally corrosive. There exist serious drawbacks when an institution can neither clarify nor achieve its purpose. Existential uncertainty and ersatz proxies for strategic victory have bled into the military's mindset.

We should not be surprised that the military has had difficulty acknowledging these issues. One can hope, but should not expect, the military might heal itself. Instead, it is incumbent on civilians to do so. Civilians sent the military to war over two decades, whether indirectly, in the case of the American public, or actively, in the case of civilian government leaders. The military has been pushed into an untenable situation. It has tried hard, but failed, to fill a vacuum of clarity—and it is now in a crisis of confidence.

3

The Military's Relationship to Society

The Crisis of Caring

"The military feels like America's suckers."

The second crisis, the *crisis of caring*, concerns the military's relationship to the public it serves. For nearly two decades, the military has won small victories but even smaller interest across American society. Simply put, the American public gives little thought to who fights, why they do so, the price they have paid and are paying, and whether it is all worth it.

Viewed through the lens of Carl von Clausewitz's social trinity, the United States has effectively been in a situation for nearly two decades in which one of its legs, the people, is disconnected from the other two. Warfare absent public results in a dysfunctional dance between the military and the government, which has influenced the *crisis of meaningful civilian control* discussed in the following chapter. And there is no evidence that this dynamic is shifting. The post-9/11 wars continue; the wounds they have created among those who serve and their families—physical, emotional, and financial wounds—show no sign of abating;

and the public seems little more interested in or knowledgeable about its military than it did in the past decade, or even a generation ago.

Indeed, the disconnect between those who serve and those whom they serve is growing, and this has exacerbated the crisis of caring. Although many have identified this disturbing trend, it has been best captured by retired General James Mattis and Kori Schake, a scholar and former policymaker. They found, as Schake explains, "That connection [between military and civilians] is very broad but very shallow."[1] Their research suggests that only one-fifth of Americans, at most, have a lot of familiarity with the military.[2] Rates of self-identified public support for the military, in contrast, is very high. This means that many citizens support the military on the basis of little knowledge or experience—and suggests that this support is, thus, flimsy. Having a thin connection to those who fight means it makes it easier for the U.S. public to go to war, as many have no personal or civic stake in the fight. If familiarity breeds contempt, moreover, then ignorance breeds awe. A public with little understanding of what the military does has elevated military experience over other kinds of public service, both in terms of trust and resourcing, resulting in outsourcing nonmilitary roles to the military and discounting the roles played by civilians in safeguarding national security.[3] Moreover, while the military does command a lot of public support, there is worrisome evidence that partisan views of the force are increasing. For example, following the June 1, 2020, Lafayette Square events in which Chairman of the Joint Chiefs of Staff General Mark Milley, the most senior military leader, walked in combat fatigues with President Trump for a photo op after peaceful protestors faced tear gas and rubber bullets, a YouGov poll found that trust in the military was significantly higher for Republicans than Democrats. Sixty percent of Republicans expressed a "great deal" of trust, compared to just 25 percent of Democrats.[4] How the military is employed also shapes public support for it. For example, one poll found a significant drop in public support when respondents were given information about its role in a highly politicized issue: U.S.-Mexico border operations. Scholars Peter Feaver and James Golby found that "wrapping the military uniform around a controversial policy comes at a price in overall public attitudes about the military."[5]

The long-term impact of the crisis of caring on the military is uncertain but, undoubtedly, problematic. Many military leaders I spoke with remained frustrated and bitter over the public's disinterest in the wars. This was best described by one former officer who characterized the public's relationship with the military as "20 years of cheerleading mostly driven by guilt and detachment." He fears that the public's willingness to put the military on a pedestal, coupled with what he has termed the military's "self-congratulatory nature," has resulted in a situation in which "we're convinced the military is the be all-end all of all things American." Although the danger this poses to the military is pernicious, as it cannot and should not be expected to solve all of the problems of the United States, the danger to American democracy is even more severe.

A pattern emerges in examining this dynamic, one in which blind support for the military can turn into jingoism that, ultimately, does not serve either the United States or its military well. This crisis of caring may be best summarized by two individuals who are immersed in defense affairs but adjacent to the military. Their trenchant observations demonstrate how knowledgeable outsiders often are able to discern painful truths. The first, a former senior civilian official, made the following argument:

> The military has been whipsawed and resents it. Those who joined for patriotic reasons, post-9/11 or a few years after, they think we tried hard with the surge, then Obama pulled the troops out, then the Afghanistan surge . . . there is no stability, they are still rotating. The idea that you can live the middle class dream and still wear a uniform is a farce. They begin to feel the basic compact isn't true. They are going to worse places. They hear Trump say we should stop being played for suckers and agree. The military feels like America's suckers. These two pieces are related: 1) love us and admire us; and, 2) we're a sucker.

In a similar vein, a journalist offers the following perspective based on his substantial experience covering the military over the last two decades of war: These people feel let down by the military [leadership] and by the government . . . All of them—the combat infantryman who had buddies shot, who shot kids when they had to—what was that all about? You come home and nobody gives a shit . . . Blood, sweat, and tears—given for what? Especially now as they look at the outcomes. Why exactly did I do that?"

Both passages encapsulate the crisis of caring: the sense of frustration and futility coupled with utter sadness and disquietude over the military's relationship with society. Both show the military as a victim, however, representing a dangerous mentality. For many in the military, over the last two decades of war, others—whether the American public or the State Department—did not care enough to show up at the fight. They resent having been left on their own.

A PATTERN EMERGES

The military's relationship to the public can be analyzed from a number of different vantage points, but I focus specifically on the military's views of whom they serve. That perspective elucidates how they view their role and their institution's role in the broader ecosystem. It appears that low expectations may be solidifying into a worrisome reality.

Unsurprisingly, the issue of military-society relations came up repeatedly throughout the interviews for this book. What was most striking, however, is how it came up. The pattern was uncanny and cut across tens of interviews with current and retired general and flag officers in the context of the legacies of the post-9/11 wars. Repeatedly, interviewees would invoke the Vietnam War. They would explain that the post-9/11 wars are not like Vietnam in two crucial ways: (1) this time, the military did not lose (an issue addressed in the previous chapter); and (2) the public did not "make the mistake of conflating the war with the warrior," as one general officer succinctly explained. By this, he meant that whether or not the war's purpose was publicly popular, those who waged the war merited and received civilian support. Various interviewees noted how grateful they are that this was the case. It was "180 degrees out" from the Vietnam War, when there was "a general lack of appreciation by the American people," as described by one general officer whose Vietnam veteran family members had been spit on and asked how many massacres they committed when they returned home—a relatively common experience.[6] The critical role played by society was validated in the foundational study of post-traumatic stress among veterans of the Vietnam War mentioned in the last chapter of *Achilles in Vietnam*, in which the author argues that "support on the home front for the soldier, *regardless of ethical and political disagreements over the war itself,* is essential."[7] The Vietnam War's legacy, of course, very much shaped messaging on supporting the troops in the post-9/11 wars. It is, perhaps, not so curious, then, that the Vietnam War came up almost as much as the war in Afghanistan in interviews of senior military leaders—but it is notable that Vietnam was almost never raised by civilian interviewees.[8]

Later in the conversation, interviewees usually would grow much less positive when asked directly about the state of civil-military relations today. The observations they shared are, in many ways, borne out by the data. But their reactions usually ranged from slight frustration to extreme bitterness and occasional anger, and throughout our conversations, most with individuals whom I admire tremendously, I couldn't help but be taken aback. Many participants articulated feelings of resentment toward those who do not serve and expressed their dismay and perturbation over the public's disinterest. "We've got a warrior class and everybody else," the same general officer who feared a loss of public support bitterly spat. One cannot help but wonder about the extent to which he understands the non-warrior class.

Unlike during the Vietnam War, most of American society "was barely touched by these wars," sighed another retired general officer; one former soldier worried that the public's lack of interest makes it harder on those who fought in these wars. It makes "this idea of moral injury pronounced because there will never be protests in the street" like in the Vietnam War, he feared. The public simply is not interested enough in expending the energy to demonstrate its support for or opposition to these conflicts, and in his perspective, simple public acknowledgment of the wars could help those who fought to reconcile their views of their utility. Another remarked that the military has inherited "a society that is numb to perpetual overseas conflicts," while a third shared his realization that there is now "just assumed popular support for the military at public venues: it's just platitudes, uninformed, not genuine [and] keeps them from asking hard questions about the nature of the military." This general officer pinpointed some of the consequences of such public disinterest, particularly an unwillingness to push the government to reassess the course of the post-9/11 wars.

"America is not at war; the military, the CIA, and parts of the State Department are at war . . . everybody else is making money," declared one senior general officer who went on to describe the "jarring" experience of attending a swanky business lunch and then walking over to Walter Reed Hospital, where he immediately saw a young mother with a baby pushing a double amputee in a wheelchair. It reminded him of just how isolated those who serve are from the rest of society. One officer described the resultant overwhelming but often superficial societal support for the military as "nauseating . . . it feels like they have to say it."

Unsurprisingly, the phrase "thank you for your service" also came up often and requires interrogation. This is a divisive yet popular expression. Some servicemembers like it as an acknowledgement of sorts, as former servicemember Philip Carter explained when he wrote, "It is neither too intimate, nor too invasive, nor too distant, and it correctly captures the sentiment of a grateful nation for those who serve in harm's way."[9] However, many others find it problematic. One scholar conducted two studies using different methodologies to analyze how veterans and active-duty military personnel responded to the phrase "thank you for your service," and found that military personnel were discomfited by the phrase, deeming it "rote," and reporting that it "frequently elicited feelings of awkwardness, objectification, imposter syndrome, and even resentment."[10]

When this topic came up in interviews, it was overwhelmingly negative. One retired general officer had the most penetrating quip: "'Thank you for your service' isn't the issue, more 'thank you for allowing me not to have to think about the military or worry about my family member being forced to join.'" We should "unpack this idea of respectful indifference," lamented another former officer. In a less polite criticism of the phrase "thank you for your service," he chastised how "everybody says they love the military and they respect it, but they really don't give a shit about it . . . not enough to be bought in, informed, or critical."

One general officer described his frustration with private-sector employees who would apologetically remark that he must have joined the military because of a lack of other opportunities. It "cheapens the value of the platitude, 'thank you for your service.' That's nice, but what about you? What about your service to our nation?" Interestingly, two active-duty Army colonels took this phrase to a new level amid the COVID-19 pandemic by writing a piece in praise of health care workers titled "Thank Them for Their Service."[11] One can hope that their attempt to widen the communities toward which this phrase is directed may make it a source of less resentment for veterans of the post-9/11 wars.

Such resentment is dangerous, in part because it could boil over into military personnel discounting the views of those who have not served, including on national security matters. Retired Marine General John Kelly, who openly mocked civilian politicians as "empty barrels," represents one example of a former senior military leader who appears to suggest that a lack of operational experience in a war zone significantly undermines one's ability to make national security policy.[12] Respected civilian defense thinkers over the years, like Senator William Fulbright, Secretary of Defense William Perry, and scholars Thomas Schelling, Roberta Wohlstetter, and Andrew Marshall, would profoundly disagree, although be rather unsurprised, to hear that some believe military service is a prerequisite for having informed views on national security affairs. Indeed, civilians may be able to better see and understand the broader strategic and political environments that shape decisions about the use of force, and are structurally freer to offer critical assessments than are military personnel. The armed forces impose great social pressures internally to conform to group unity of effort, to defer to higher-ranking officers' decisions, and, above all, to follow the chain of command. These are reasonable, if not essential, organizational traits within the military, but they can inhibit innovative or adaptive policymaking.

At a time of particularly acute American political dysfunction, it is neither fair nor helpful for the military to be perceived as the proxy for political knowledge, engagement, and, ultimately, active citizenship.

Indeed, many military interviewees articulated this view, some more passionately than others. Some made disturbing comparisons to warrior societies like Rome and Sparta. Others raised terms like "mercenaries" and "warrior class" in outlining dysfunctional military-society relations. "Spartans fighting and fat cat Athenians sitting back and loving life," is how one senior general officer described it. A soldier asked, "At what point are we dangerously close to becoming a mercenary force that doesn't reflect the country we defend?" One retired general officer questioned if values differ between the military and society, asking whether they are "diverging to a point where you have this warrior class, not well understood, which many people would say have archaic values—that people have sworn to protect and defend?"

"We've got a warrior class and everybody else," flatly declared one general officer. In an almost melancholic tone, another general officer expressed the following fears, succinctly encapsulating a number of comments on this topic raised by other interviewees:

> When we become a society that has a warrior caste and a civilian caste, we become the Roman Empire. Like in the Roman Empire, the emperors increasingly try to buy off the army's loyalty . . . when we become a society that has a warrior caste and a civilian caste, we dissociate our citizenry from the cost of citizenship . . . The citizens remain safe in Rome while the legions go off to pursue the state's interests abroad. We seem to be buying ourselves a warrior caste and I don't think that's good for society.

Scholar Morris Janowitz worried about the implications of a military separate from its society, and two surveys show they may be coming true.[13] A 2020 survey found that more than half of post-9/11 veterans believe those Americans who did not serve "should feel guilty."[14] And, a set of 2019–2020 surveys of West Point cadets found "some justification for Janowitz's fear that professionalism, especially when premised on the military's separation from society, could breed attitudes among military personnel antithetical to democracy" because cadets privileged military qualifications—even for traditionally civilian roles like the secretary of defense—and they knowingly supported "following orders over respect for the democratic institutions they will soon take an oath to protect."[15]

This divergence between the military and society is worrying. Through satire, *Duffel Blog* also conveyed many of the same elements that came up in these serious discussions. For example, one masterful *Duffel Blog* piece, titled "I Would've Joined the Military Too if I Didn't Think It Was Beneath Me," managed to touch on almost every stereotype and misunderstanding civilians have about the military in fewer than 400 words. The civilian—quick to say "thank you for your service"—lacks basic knowledge about the military; presumes that those who serve "didn't have other options or weren't smart enough to do something else like go to college and get a regular job;" thinks all veterans have post-traumatic stress or have killed someone; assumes that anyone in the military is "really into guns and killing people;" and holds that only "farmers or people in the South" choose to serve.[16] The article's popularity suggests that it resonates with a wide variety of military audiences.

The resonance of the crisis of caring means there are few opportunities to facilitate dialogue about the many costs of the post-9/11 wars and their impacts on military-society relations. As one senior general officer explained, veterans need a place, like the American Legion Post after the Vietnam War, where such conversations are possible and safe—a place where, as he put it, "they're not going to get asked questions they don't want to answer." Like so many others discussed in this book, this is not a new issue. In the wake of World War II, Americans were uncertain about how to engage those who returned from the war. Government-sponsored pamphlets warned that returning veterans might have difficulty finding jobs or be aggressive because of their time at war.[17] However, the crisis today may be even more acute, as the barriers to understanding where the U.S. military is deployed and where it is fighting continue to rise. As the Defense Department's official casualty list outlines, throughout the post-9/11 wars, U.S. troops have died or been wounded in places across the Middle East, Asia, Africa, and the Western Hemisphere.[18] Outside of the obvious locales like Iraq and Afghanistan, the list includes places like Seychelles, Sudan, Philippines, and Kenya. The U.S. public may face more Niger-like situations going forward, in which a family finds that a loved one has died in combat in a country few knew even hosted U.S. operations.[19] Moreover, the crisis of caring makes America more vulnerable to those who seek to do harm, particularly given questions about American willingness to support an overseas conflict of a different magnitude than the post-9/11 wars have been, such as with China or Russia. A continued dearth of dialogue coupled with continued disinterest will only exacerbate the crisis of caring.

It is dismaying but accurate to acknowledge that, for most of the American public, the post-9/11 wars have been largely cost free. No one has paid explicit taxes to support American military interventions. Many have not experienced personal loss. And few think about, let alone understand, why the United States is waging war where it is doing so. To be sure, the character of the post-9/11 wars, grounded in various and sundry adversaries around the world, has enabled secrecy over deployments and activities, facilitating public ignorance. Our approach to war has allowed, and in some cases perhaps required, civilians to remain apathetic.

But the lack of wartime consequences for society carries consequences for military-society relations. As former Marine officer-turned-author Phil Klay aptly put it, "If you think the mission your country keeps sending you on is pointless or impossible and that you're only deploying to protect your brothers and sisters in arms from danger, then it's not the Taliban or al-Qaeda or ISIS that's trying to kill you, it's America."[20] In other words, the tragedy of the Clausewitzian social trinity is real.

Remedying the crisis of caring can occur a few different ways, all grounded in serious and sustained dialogue. It should include (1) communicating to the American public why national security affairs matter; (2) shaping a message of caring and acceptance; and (3) in some cases, requiring an element of sacrifice—in time or in taxes, most likely—on the part of the people. Undergirding that dialogue must be a recognition that the public has an obligation to care—not just superficially but deeply, and not out of ignorance but from familiarity. These are difficult goals to achieve, but there are means of making at least incremental progress.

One construct that may be helpful, for example, was developed by a psychologist who focused on finding a way for veterans to talk and for civilians to listen. In her work, veterans were allowed to talk for hours, whereas civilians were asked to listen. The civilians would open up the conversation by saying that, as "an American whose government sent you to war, I take some responsibility for listening to your story, so *if* you want to talk about your experiences at war and since coming home, I will listen for as long as you want to talk, and I will not judge you."[21] This construct can facilitate dialogue, particularly by satiating civilian concerns about saying the wrong thing and by alleviating military concerns about the individual's interest in having a meaningful conversation.[22]

Over the last two decades, few in American society have served or done much to inform where and how the military has waged war. Civilian apathy, coupled with the power of strategic inertia as the military has repeatedly run toward the same problems, has fueled resentment on the part of those who serve. As the narrative takes hold that society does not care, the American people's relationship with their military may grow ever more precarious.

4

The Military's Relationship with Its Overseers

The Crisis of Meaningful Civilian Control

"We're probably raising Powells."

The last two decades of war have transformed the cracks that have always existed between the military and the civilians who formulate national security policy—most of whom are in the executive branch— into a chasm. A *crisis of meaningful civilian control* afflicts the military's relationship to the government, the third leg of Clausewitz's social trinity. The manner in which civilian political leaders have made decisions about military interventions, which has often been done with little strategic clarity, has, on the whole, represented a failure of civilian control of the military. Absent meaningful civilian control, the military has resorted to framing conflicts in its own ways, further fomenting the crisis. This is illustrated in four patterns of behavior: some in the military's tendency to blame civilians for failures rather than to conduct serious introspection; the resurgence of the Powell Doctrine; the popularity of

the "best military advice" concept; and military efforts to minimize civilian oversight in crucial arenas.

The crisis of confidence and the crisis of caring both interact with
and shape the crisis of meaningful civilian control. The first has meant
that civilian leaders have repeatedly sent the military to deal with problems it could not reasonably solve on its own. The second, in which the
public elevated an increasingly alien military over other forms of public
service while largely abdicating its own civic duty, has made the military feel increasingly isolated but means it hasn't had to face the costs
of strategy failures abroad. Aggravating each of these legacies of war—
harming the military's inability to understand its purpose and inhibit-
ing the public's ability to shape what is being done in its name—impedes
civilian control of the military.

In the U.S. system, there exist multiple institutional lenses for examining civil-military relations in general, and civilian control of the
military in particular, because civilians oversee the military through
both the executive and legislative branches of government. The president is the constitutionally declared commander in chief. Congress is
given the "power of the purse"—the ability to disburse funds—and the
right to authorize the use of force. The secretary of defense is the civilian "overseer in chief," manifesting oversight as the only civilian in the
chain of command (besides the president) and engaging with the U.S.
military daily on an extensive range of issues of enormous significance
to national security. This role is, therefore, critical for understanding the
crisis of meaningful civilian oversight.

Regardless of which lenses or theories one uses to examine civil-
military relations, the entire concept of civilian control of the military is
imbued with tension.[1] Some question if there truly is a crisis in meaningful civilian oversight and, more broadly, in civil-military relations. There
is, traditionally, little anxiety about a military coup within the United
States (even if tongue-in-cheek gifts like posters from the 1964 film *Seven
Days in May*, which imagines a fictional coup attempt, do occasionally
transit the Pentagon). Scholar and retired Major General Charles Dunlap
warns that "crisis" is an old trope that "never materialized."[2] Scholar Peter
Feaver is similarly skeptical. Recalling a conversation during a bumpy

period of civil-military relations in the mid-1990s, Feaver reminds us of his European colleague's quip: "In my country, we aspire to reach the depths to which you say you have sunk in the United States."[3] Yet Feaver acknowledges there are "challenges" and sees merit in the "paradox" in which scholarship of civil-military relations in the United States focuses on such concerns even though the problems often are quite small. Feaver sees productive utility in this worrying, which enables such problems to, ultimately, remain contained.[4] Other scholars, like Risa Brooks and Lindsey Cohn, and numerous practitioners, like the 2018 National Defense Strategy commissioners, are much more concerned.[5] Another indicator of these problematic dynamics is illustrated by a 2020 survey that found nearly 70 percent of post-9/11 veterans believe that "civilians who have not been to war should not question those who have."[6] While "crisis" may not be the term that resonates with everyone in this community of civil-military scholars and practitioners, it is undeniable that something in the civil-military relationship is adrift. These dynamics exist along a spectrum—they are not binary—and even those holding divergent views would, nevertheless, concur that civil-military relations have drifted into problematic territory. The strength of civilian control and the manifestation of civilian tensions with the military has not struck the appropriate balance. Natural tensions have created a gap. Norms that have been undone have exacerbated this gap and need to be reestablished.

While the post-9/11 wars have not resulted in a civil-military relationship crisis along the lines of General MacArthur during the Korean War—who was, ultimately, relieved of command by President Harry Truman for his unwillingness to accede to civilian guidance—one can and should expect healthier relations. Moreover, there exist particular challenges in managing these tensions inherent to extended periods of conflict, like the post-9/11 wars, since "in wartime in particular civilians are often too insecure about their knowledge, too fearful of public opinion, and too overawed by their military's expertise to exercise much control at all," whereas the military faces unprecedented pressure to show progress and to account for losses.[7]

Military leaders—like the commanders of the wars in Iraq and Afghanistan over the last two decades—have repeatedly expressed confidence in their ability to accomplish the tasks given to them by the political leadership. The dearth of examples of senior officers acknowledging that the military's "can do" culture often has been at odds with what they were being told to do is striking. As victory has proven elusive, the military's assignment of blame to external factors like bad political decisions or insufficient resources—admittedly real problems, of course—has inhibited its ability to take sufficient ownership for the current state of affairs. If the military leadership has made insufficient effort to speak hard truths to the civilian powers, then it is incumbent on them to accept some responsibility for the course of the post-9/11 wars. Wholly ceding ownership of failure to civilians is wrong—and, ultimately, itself a failure of duty.

BLAMING OTHERS: A "STAB-IN-THE-BACK" NARRATIVE

Over nearly two decades of conflict, the crisis of meaningful civilian control has manifested in disproportionate blame for strategic missteps placed at the feet of civilian policymakers, leading to the hollowing out of civilian credibility with the military. As one former senior civilian official explained, the military has inherited "cynicism in multiple directions" that includes "a challenge with being truthful to itself." Another former senior officer lamented that "the military isn't ready to . . . accept that some part of our failure is due to lack of its own efforts." In his opinion, the military has accepted that it should have done a better job planning for the post-conflict phase in Iraq, but it has not acknowledged its other mistakes in the post-9/11 wars. "Isn't it our responsibility to help translate military outcomes into political ends? We failed to do our share of that here," he declared.

The unwillingness to conduct meaningful introspection was pointedly captured in one former senior officer's argument that the military has a "stab-in-the-back narrative" focused on blaming civilian leaders for their lack of commitment and for micromanaging the conflicts. Few narratives could be more familiar to students of military history than blaming the politicians and civilians for getting in the way of military victory. For example, the "stab-in-the-back" theory of defeat was adopted by many German veterans following their loss in World War I, and it was popular in the U.S. military during the Vietnam War.[8] I recognize that, as scholar Jeffrey P. Kimball underscores, such references can be "inflammatory." As he accurately points out, however, "It seems safe to hypothesize that such legends are common responses to defeat in war."[9] In the case of the Vietnam War, in particular, those who propagated this narrative believed that victory would have occurred "if the correct strategy had been followed and if certain of the civilian strategists had . . . allowed the U.S. military to fight the kind of war they were most experienced with."[10] Simply put, one should not be terribly surprised by the military blaming others, but it is, nevertheless, concerning.

The upbraiding largely falls on civilian leaders. The Army's study of the Iraq War, for example, holds few punches in castigating civilian officials like Secretary of Defense Donald Rumsfeld; in contrast, military leaders come across as largely blameless.[11] The military is "quick to blame other leaders like [Coalition Provincial Authority chief Paul] Bremer and Rumsfeld," explained one senior officer. This blame transcends those who have fought in the post-9/11 wars themselves. For example, while discussing the Iraq War at a military service academy, I heard young cadets recount the senior officials they blamed for the Iraq war, including Secretary of Defense Donald Rumsfeld, Deputy Secretary of Defense Paul Wolfowitz, and Under Secretary of Defense for Policy Douglas Feith. None named a single senior military leader. Given that most of them had been kindergarteners in 2003, this narrative was clearly one they had inherited from others rather than developed through lived experience. Like the "stab-in-the-back" narrative itself, of course, destructive inherited narratives are not new. Following the Vietnam War, former Marine James Webb—a future Reagan administration official and U.S. Senator—exacerbated civil-military tensions by helping infect the post–Vietnam War generation of servicemembers with disdain for those outside the military. In his view, the public wrongly blamed the military for defeat. In his view, the military leadership should have excoriated civilians for a number of wartime sins, including dereliction, micromanagement, misunderstanding, and poor decisionmaking.[12]

This dynamic of blame extends throughout the Obama years, as well. As one senior retired general officer lamented, "the senior military realized under the Obama administration they should be seen and not heard." One general officer explained that he saw Obama administration officials as "suspicious of the military . . . like [they thought] it had been given too much latitude and deference, and it resulted in strategic overreach."

A different senior retired general officer erupted in anger when discussing the Obama administration, explaining that "the military was deliberately marginalized by people who didn't want it to have a voice." He went further, claiming that "nobody even cared to win" and lambasting civilian Obama administration leaders for allegedly "cry[ing] crocodile tears at Walter Reed [Medical Center] but not car[ing] about the outcome" of the wars. While surely exaggerating the case, his vitriol was conspicuous, and his accusations represented a dangerous impugnment of the motivation and competence of the civilian leaders with whom he had worked. He diagnosed the Bush administration as "blind to the complexities and risks of action" and the Obama administration as "blind to the risks of inaction," remarking that "it's extraordinary the extent to which there was self-delusion [among the civilian leaders] in these wars." He feared that contemporary civilian officials, like those of the Vietnam era, were "looking for what Lyndon Johnson was looking for: military advice that conforms to their predispositions." More specifically, another retired senior general officer said, "I've been astounded by how much bitterness I sense from the military about the Obama administration," underscoring that he found that "the military—the senior leadership down to the mid-grade officer corps—is very suspect of the civilian leadership."

One often-cited driver of this suspicion is President Obama's 2011 decision to withdraw from Iraq. While the Obama administration leadership saw the Bush administration's agreement with the Iraqi government on withdrawal as binding, that approach meant the Obama administration would bear any subsequent blame (or take the credit) for following through with it. As ISIS erupted across Iraq and Syria and the security situation in Iraq declined over the years that followed, some military leaders grew frustrated with civilian decisionmakers. Indeed, a former senior civilian official underscored that the decision to withdraw is "often characterized inaccurately in part because of what happened afterwards."

To be very clear, much of this blame is well deserved. Civilian leaders have the authority and the responsibility to make decisions—best described by scholar Peter Feaver as the "right to be right," but also the "right to be wrong."[13] Throughout the post-9/11 wars, there have been many examples of them making the wrong decision, of course.[14] As one former senior general officer underscored, "Ultimately, the civilian leadership owns the decisions, but they make those based on best military advice." While his statement is prima facie accurate, it also is a rather subtle reminder that the military leadership has weighty responsibilities, as well. Failing to exercise those responsibilities, particularly due to distrust of civilians, can have dangerous consequences for the responsible use of force. Civilian leadership is an enduring reality for past, present, and future military leaders, so engaging it productively—even amid dysfunctional and potentially catastrophic decisions—remains critical.

"LIKE VIETNAM, WE'RE PROBABLY RAISING POWELLS"

This third crisis is colored by the resurgence of the Powell Doctrine in the post-9/11 wars, which came up often in my interviews, and has a concerningly constrained view of what constitutes meaningful civilian control. The Powell Doctrine stemmed from Colin Powell's perplexing service in the Vietnam War. His first tour in Vietnam ended early because, he was told, the conflict was going well. His second tour was colored by the My Lai massacre investigation. His thinking was further refined by two key events: Operation Just Cause, the U.S. military operation to depose Panamanian dictator Manuel Noriega, and Operation Desert Storm, the Persian Gulf War. As he described both during and after his service as chairman of the joint chiefs of staff (CJCS), Powell believed that the United States must possess "a clear political objective and stick to it. Use all the force necessary, and do not apologize for going in big if that is what it takes. Decisive force ends wars quickly and in the long run saves lives. Whatever threats we faced in the future, I intended to make these rules the bedrock of my military counsel."[15]

He underscored the criticality of capturing American public backing for war, arguing that the failure to align each leg of Carl von Clausewitz's social trinity—the military, the government, and the people—in support of the Vietnam War led to defeat.[16] Conversely, he argued that the Persian Gulf War was Vietnam's antithesis. In his view, the "best part from my perspective is the way in which the American people saw this operation," which he explained as commanding broad American support despite prewar concerns over "tens of thousands" of potential American casualties.[17]

While Powell is quick to emphasize that "the so-called Powell Doctrine exists in no military manual," and argues that it is not composed of "rules," neither he nor other senior military leaders have hesitated to write about or discuss it.[18] Powell's immediate successors as CJCS, General Hugh Shelton and General Richard Myers, indicated their support for the key elements of his doctrine.[19] Major Mike Jackson, deputy director of the Modern War Institute at West Point, recounted how during his time as "a cadet in the mid-to-late 1990s, the Powell Doctrine was essentially gospel at West Point."[20] Indeed, in his retirement speech one year before the September 11, 2001, terrorist attacks, CENTCOM Commander General Anthony Zinni discussed the multitude of challenges that the U.S. military faced, including al Qaeda and Saddam Hussein, and expressed his fear that the U.S. military would have difficulty responding to these challenges and then "bitch and moan . . . dust off the Weinberger Doctrine and the Powell Doctrine and throw them in the face of our civilian leadership."[21]

Despite its popularity, the Powell Doctrine suffers from some flaws that limit its utility in conflicts like the post-9/11 wars. First, it offers an incredibly limited conception of conflict. Powell's emphasis on "using all the force necessary" and his use of terms like "decisive force" leaves too little room for the importance of deterrence before and during conflict and escalation throughout it.[22] By dismissing the potential political-military importance of gradual escalation in coercing adversaries—as Powell put it during discussions about Bosnia, once civilians "tell me it's limited, it means they do not care whether you achieve a result or not"—he thrusts policymakers into the untenable position of binary all-or-nothing military campaigns rather than nuanced ones appropriately scaled to a particular conflict and its unique political context.[23]

Looking at the Persian Gulf War and Powell's recommendations for using overwhelming force, one scholar wondered if this view "may in itself have contributed to there being a Gulf crisis in the first place." Particularly worrisome, the scholar posits that "this focus on war-fighting strategy led the U.S. military to underestimate the value of limited military action as a deterrent to war in the first place" rather than launching a full-blown conflict.[24]

In immediately pushing for such an enormous force commitment during the Persian Gulf conflict, one wonders if Powell was testing the civilian leadership's seriousness rather than deftly aligning resources with strategy. Given the unremarkable shows of force and lack of deterrent moves by the U.S. military before it initiated the massive mobilization of half a million troops to the Middle East, it is entirely possible that the Powell Doctrine stood in the way of policymakers taking deterrent steps that could have avoided war in the first place. Regardless, the doctrine's emphasis on using the various tools of statecraft separately from the threat to use force also ignores the complementary impact the former can and should have with the military.[25] Although Powell described his doctrine in 2017 as "classical military doctrine," it clearly is anything but.[26]

Second, the doctrine's persistent desire for "a clear political objective" before using force dismisses that such objectives often evolve during conflict.[27] It is an unrealistic standard and presents a catastrophic starting point for healthy civil-military relations, particularly given the character of the post-9/11 wars. As scholar Eliot Cohen described, "the result . . . is a military posture that is prepared only for all-or-nothing operations, likely to provide civilian leaders with only the harshest of military choices, or indeed none at all."[28] Indeed, Powell described the Gulf War as "the only time in my career, or in, frankly, most of American military history, where a chairman [of the joint chiefs of staff] can say to the president of the United States, I guarantee the outcome. And the reason I could guarantee that outcome is that the president gave us everything we asked for."[29] Ironically, then-national security advisor Brent Scowcroft believed that Powell's massive request for personnel and assets was "deliberately large with the hope that the President would reject them and there'd be no operation." He advised President Bush to give Powell everything he requested—not because he believed it was needed, but because he thought it would be the only way to get the military on board.[30]

The civil-military implications of his doctrine are loud and problematic, stemming not just from binary views on the use of force but also its tendency to shape binary views on the proper roles and responsibilities of civilians and military personnel that severely impedes the former's meaningful control of the latter. As one scholar explained, "There is a definite sense of 'us' and 'them' that permeates Powell's views on statecraft and the use of military force. His 'us' is definitely his extended family—the armed forces of the United States. Powell's 'them' are his civilian masters, including the President, the Secretary of Defense, the Secretary of State, and their advisors, experts and academics."[31]

What is most meaningful about the Powell Doctrine, however, is its resurgence during the post-9/11 wars. If this book's Dickensian "ghost of wars past" is Vietnam, then my interviews made clear that the Powell Doctrine remains a "ghost of wars present." One senior general officer warned that, given the character of terrorism, "it's hard to shoehorn the Powell Doctrine in where we are today." Still, he contrasted the wars of today with the Gulf War, which "had objectives, accomplished them, and went home," and identified the Powell Doctrine as a preferable approach to the use of force. One senior officer snapped, "Like Vietnam, we're probably raising Powells: I went to war and I did everything you asked and I fought honorably, but dammit, what do you want me to do?" In his view, the last two decades of war "will create a leader—like the Powells that said we are not going to fall into that again."

One retired senior general officer said his peers use language like "Colin Powell, [when he said] stay out of that kind of thing." In line with the Powell Doctrine, one senior general officer explained that "there's this fallacy of limited war." He judged that the United States should not get into a conflict "unless our vital national interests [are] at such a threatened state that we're prepared to make a long-term investment." Similarly, diplomat Kael Weston quotes a three-star general officer reflecting on his top lesson from serving in Iraq, a lesson that sounds about as impractical as the Powell Doctrine: If "you are not going to stay, don't go."[32] Based on his experience with the most senior military leaders, one former senior official feared they planned to "win big and get out" in future wars, in line with the Powell Doctrine. An overreaction toward the Powell Doctrine as a part of the legacies of the post-9/11 wars could, thus, inform war planning in a dramatic way.

While there is no contemporary survey research that explicitly examines the military's views of the Powell Doctrine, there have been a few illuminating proxy surveys. In 2004, 45 percent of mid-grade military officers supported "decisive force," a key element of the Powell Doctrine.[33] In 2011, nearly the same percentage of post-9/11 veterans supported the employment of "overwhelming force" against terrorism.[34] And in 2016, more than half of veterans supported key elements of the doctrine, such as using force "quickly and massively," but "only in pursuit of the goal of total victory."[35]

There are a number of implications of the Powell Doctrine's resurgence in the military. Looking back, it may have made it more difficult for military leaders to consider limited objectives for the wars in Iraq and Afghanistan given that commanders consistently developed ambitious campaign plans and requested additional resources. One former senior general officer concurred, saying the military "only understand[s] the big approach to war" and could not envision a different type of conflict. Today, it shapes how the military is learning from the post-9/11 wars. The Army's study of the Iraq War, for example, indulges in Powell Doctrine-esque rhetoric such as propagating the notion that the United States's wartime objectives were static.[36] Looking forward, it may feed the military's obsession with achieving tactical and operational goals as opposed to strategic-level successes. Since waging war is a political instrument, the military's conduct always should be subservient to the political goal. Operational victory means little unless it results in a strategic success. The military's judgment must, therefore, serve the political objective. This will prove difficult if the Powell Doctrine also encourages an "us-versus-them" mentality in the military that encourages greater mistrust of, or skepticism toward, the civilian leaders who send troops to war.

Scholar-practitioner Frank Hoffman, a self-proclaimed skeptic of the Powell Doctrine, tried to apply its criteria as a frame through which to analyze the post-9/11 wars because of its continued resonance. In doing so, he found serious flaws: fuzzy objectives, misplaced enthusiasm for clear victory, and the fading drumbeat of public disinterest. His argument, that the doctrine does, ultimately, "serve a useful purpose . . . to ensure the fundamental questions about purpose, risk and costs were addressed up front" is particularly compelling given the gut-wrenching costs of nearly two decades at war.[37] For the record, Hoffman does not say that the doctrine has succeeded in doing so but, rather, that it can be useful in facilitating proper scrutiny of strategy. Steve Leonard, the "Doctrine Man," is an advocate of referencing the Powell Doctrine for a similar reason. He sees it as a tool for asking the right questions: "not a checklist, but a menu for critical analysis and strategy formulation."[38]

Might a new set of views replace the Powell Doctrine? In his analysis of the *Washington Post*'s "Afghanistan Papers," journalist Greg Jaffe recalled that the last time the U.S. military was unable to attain victory, in the Vietnam War, "its new religion became the Powell Doctrine."[39] One senior official was skeptical that we will see the development of an alternative, however, as the Powell Doctrine became accepted in large part because the military itself accepted its defeat in the Vietnam War. In his view, "for the next chairman of the joint chiefs of staff to suggest a Powell Doctrine, he would need to acknowledge that Iraq and Afghanistan were failures; the military isn't ready to do that." Similarly, a senior general officer said that "there have not been the decisive conclusions to these conflicts that will set in stone a break with the past and allow us to start fresh in the future." To follow Jaffe, after two decades of inconclusive conflict in the post-9/11 wars, we do not know whether the military will become Powell Doctrine fundamentalists, strategic agnostics, or converts to some new doctrinal religion. We can, however, hope that the most effective proselytizers will preach greater awareness and understanding of how one fights and, hopefully, why meaningful civilian control is crucial.

A FIVE-SIDED TOWER OF BABEL:
UNTANGLING CIVILIAN AND MILITARY ROLES AND RESPONSIBILITIES

One of the major reasons for the crisis of meaningful civilian control is a mess of authorities, guidance, roles, and responsibilities among the organizations and people who manage violence.[40] Such a convoluted swirl—exacerbated by personalities—has bedeviled the United States throughout the post-9/11 wars. A cacophony of strategic guidance across the Department of Defense, ultimately, impedes meaningful civilian control because it makes it harder to determine which guidance is superior; easier to cherry-pick convenient justifications for preferred policies; trickier to cut through convoluted and confused dialogue over intent and efficacy; and safer to engage in bitter bureaucratic knife-fighting than otherwise.[41] This confusion over roles and responsibilities can be well understood by examining the office of the secretary of defense (OSD). While it is the epicenter of steady civilian oversight of the military inside the Pentagon, its purpose is poorly understood.

The secretary of defense, like the president, manifests civilian control. "The Secretary (of Defense) is the principal assistant to the President in all matters relating to the Department of Defense" and provides "authority, direction, and control" over the Department of Defense, according to U.S. law.[42] In establishing the position of secretary of defense, President Harry Truman understood the criticality of having a senior member of his cabinet wholly consumed with military affairs. He created it "to enhance the powers and effectiveness of his own office; by shifting military coordination to a supersecretary and a chief of staff, Truman hoped to free himself for more immediate concerns" and to strengthen the civilian role in the chain of command.[43]

In practice, the secretary of defense is the most senior civilian who engages the U.S. military on a daily basis and on an extensive range of issues. In day-to-day operations, the secretary is the civilian "overseer in chief." Of course, the secretary of defense alone cannot manage the Department of Defense—as I have written elsewhere, "oversight requires an organization, not an individual"—but he is not expected to do so.[44] The secretary of defense exerts civilian control with and through his staff. Meaningful civilian control requires civilian oversight, which I define as "watchful and responsible care" over the formulation, implementation, and assessment of national security affairs.[45] The OSD must exercise robust oversight to make civilian control by the secretary of defense possible. OSD's purpose is to "assist the Secretary of Defense in carrying out the Secretary's duties and responsibilities and to carry out such other duties as may be prescribed by law."[46] OSD staff cover a wide range of issues on behalf of the secretary of defense that have shaped the U.S. approach to the post-9/11 wars, including research, engineering, acquisitions, policy, personnel, readiness, intelligence, and budgeting, among others.[47]

By informing the secretary of defense on these issues and shaping the department's policies, OSD staff help the secretary facilitate the alignment of political ends and defense resources in strategic ways. To be clear, OSD is not a separate power center in the Department of Defense. Rather, it is "the management and advisory team" for the (ultimate) boss: the secretary of defense."[48] Scholar Charles Stevenson's book on the secretary of defense provides the most thorough description of the responsibilities of OSD personnel: "They are tasked to develop and promulgate policies to support U.S. national security objectives; to oversee DoD plans and programs; to develop systems to supervise policy implementation and program execution; and to serve as the focal point for DoD participation in other security community activities. In short, they are extra sets of arms and legs, eyes and ears, and authoritative voices for the secretary and other senior officials."[49]

As one former senior civilian official explained, "It isn't just a single voice—not just the secretary of defense or the deputy secretary of defense—where oversight gets executed. The Department is far too big of an enterprise. There has to be lieutenants."

Without a capable and informed staff, no individual has the wherewithal to do the secretary of defense's job decently, much less effectively.[50] In line with Deborah Avant's work on principal-agent theory, "principals must think hard about how to select appropriate agents and monitor them to ensure that they act as the principal prefers."[51] Such "appropriate agents" in the context of the Defense Department must have the capabilities and expertise to guide how the military implements secretary of defense-level intentions. To take one example: the under secretary of defense for policy (USDP) plays a critical role in supporting the "overseer in chief." Over the years, this position has been refined by Congress, including most recently in the Fiscal Year 2019 National Defense Authorization Act, which stated these responsibilities include "overall direction and supervision" over the National Defense Strategy, global force posture, and force development, in addition to guiding and reviewing war plans.[52] Issues like how to manage, employ, and develop the military, and how to treat U.S. allies, partners, competitors, and adversaries around the world, are fundamental to meaningful civilian control.

INTERNAL DYNAMICS HEIGHTEN CRISIS

Across nearly two decades of conflict, the dynamics inside the Pentagon heightened the crisis of meaningful civilian control. The balance of power swayed between the office of the secretary of defense and the joint staff. It is useful to first recall that the Goldwater-Nichols reforms, which made the CJCS the "principal military advisor" to the president and to the secretary of defense, empowered the joint staff, as did creating a vice chairman role. As one former senior civilian official reflected, however, this "inadvertently undermined civilian control and blurred the distinctions between the Secretary's and Chairman's responsibilities," which exacerbated dynamics between OSD and the joint staff.[53] This did not condemn OSD to impotence, however. For example, Donald Rumsfeld—who had famously tense relationships with senior military leaders—entered the George. W. Bush administration as its secretary of defense; he was quoted as exhorting, "I want to reinstitute civilian control of the military!"[54] Unsurprisingly, Rumsfeld's team in OSD held a lot of relative power and had a rocky relationship with the joint staff. This dynamic is most colorfully described by journalist Dana Priest, who wrote that they "weren't willing to take anything for granted. If you said the sun was up, they raised the blind and said, 'Let us see.'"[55]

Later in the post-9/11 wars, under the tenure of Secretary Robert Gates, which spanned the Bush and Obama administrations, relations between the office of the secretary of defense and the joint staff were markedly different. To be sure, civil-military tensions still existed. Gates recounted in his memoirs how frustrating it was to get CJCS Admiral Michael Mullen to support him on rebalancing the military to focus on non-state conflict. Mullen, who served in that role from late 2007 through late 2011, did not agree with Gates's decision to include in the defense strategy language that rebalancing would *require assuming some measure of additional, but acceptable, risk in the traditional sphere.*[56] Instead, he sought to issue strategic guidance that ignored the issues of terrorism, the Iraq War, and the Afghanistan War; this was bureaucratically contradictory, since it was "the opposite of what he and I had been telling Congress," according to Gates, and politically insensitive, since he planned to release it just before the 2008 presidential election.[57]

This represented a rather dramatic violation of scholar Peter Feaver's description of civil-military roles, in which the "military quantifies the risk, the civilian judges it."[58] During Mullen's tenure as chairman, moreover, tensions bubbled as Mullen sought to enhance the CJCS's stature. Gates believed that Mullen "felt the role of the chairman had been diminished over a period of years, and he was determined to strengthen it and make the chairman a much more publicly visible senior military leader."[59]

In spite of these tensions and occasional blips, however, Gates's tenure is seen as a zenith in relations between these two entities that has not been attained since. "I believe the last time there was true balance was when Gates was there," lamented one former senior official, who defined "balance" as having capable and confident senior civilian leaders willing and able to execute meaningful oversight. A few former senior officials discussed what conditions allowed Gates to strike this balance between the civilian and military leadership. First, the secretary of defense had a substantial background in national security affairs. Second, he had both President Bush and President Obama's full support to run the Department of Defense in line with his vision. Third, he actively managed dynamics between the office of the secretary of defense and the chairman of the joint chiefs of staff.

While Secretary of Defense Rumsfeld met these thresholds to varying extents, his approach to management alienated key constituencies. One former senior official said that Gates told his team that both OSD and the joint staff formed "one staff that supports me" and he wanted everyone to "play nice." For example, under his leadership, the under secretary of defense for policy and the vice chairman of the joint chiefs of staff signed a memorandum of understanding to facilitate collaboration between them and their staffs. In doing so, explained another former senior official, they hoped to develop better policy by better staffing the secretary of defense and the chairman of the joint chiefs of staff. Overall, as a final former senior official explained, "The biggest factor in all of this is leadership and having a secretary of defense who knows how things are supposed to work."

In the years since Gates's departure, tensions have grown between the office of the secretary of defense and the joint staff for a multiplicity of reasons. Indeed, they have grown so acute that one former senior official compared it to the brief and (infamously rocky) professional relationship between Secretary of Defense Les Aspin and CJCS Powell. After both Aspin and Powell departed in 1994, new Secretary of Defense William Perry and new Chairman of the Joint Chiefs of Staff General John Shalikashvili gathered their senior leadership teams and declared that "this is dysfunctional, does not serve our country, and will change." They made it clear that the secretary of defense and CJCS would now be one another's "closest counterparts." They warned that "anyone who can't get with the program will be thanked for their service" and then fired. According to this former official, the dynamics between the joint staff and the office of the secretary of defense changed for the better "within one week." Unfortunately, as of January 2021, there has been no similar senior civilian and military leader reckoning despite growing dysfunction that serves the nation no better now than it did in 1994.

Multiple former senior officials emphasized that the secretary of defense must play a crucial role in pushing past these tensions to be effective. They argued that the secretary is uniquely positioned to inform and actively manage civil-military dynamics. "The biggest factor in all of this is leadership and having a secretary of defense who knows how the system was designed, how things are supposed to work—what good looks like," explained one former senior official. Change only happens in the Defense Department, as one emphasized, "if the secretary himself rides herd and fires people." A third former senior civilian official emphasized that the under secretary of defense for policy's roles and responsibilities "can't be exercised if the secretary doesn't want them to be—or if the secretary isn't attuned to making it possible for the under secretary to do that." But if the secretary is unwilling to make it clear that OSD staff speaks for him or her, then the system goes awry. "If the secretary doesn't set that tone and guard it and protect against infringements where he or she sees that happen," then the joint staff will dismiss or ignore the civilian staff. Using colorful metaphors to describe their frustration with the secretaries of defense who failed to set that atmosphere, one former senior official exclaimed that the "fish rots from the head," and counseled, "if no one is guarding the henhouse, the fox is going to have a field day."

The CJCS plays a crucial role as well, of course. Chairmen throughout the post-9/11 wars have varied considerably in how they approached the role and their interaction with senior civilian leaders. For example, General Richard Myers was known for taking a more quiescent and constrained view of his role. General Martin Dempsey had a more defined professional vision: he described his job as being "the dash," as in the punctuation mark, bridging political and military affairs.[60]

More recently, General Joseph Dunford, a well-respected, professional, and accomplished military leader who served as chairman from 2015 to 2019, "came in with a very distinct agenda for what he believed should be the purview of the joint chiefs of staff," explained one senior officer. As chairman of the joint chiefs of staff, General Dunford sought to increase the chairman's power, including working with Congress to gain more authority to allocate and transfer forces.[61] Under the rubric of "global integration," which Congress mandated as the chairman's role in 2016, Dunford played a more meaningful leadership role across the military services and the combatant commands—and, in particular, in adjudicating their differing priorities.[62] The ostensible reasoning that Dunford sought this authority was to make the Defense Department better able to contend with contemporary and future wars, including the changing speed of communications, emerging domains of warfare, and expanding global challenges—although other possible justifications include his desire to escape civilian micromanagement and overcome key civilian leadership vacancies.[63] It is, of course, not only the joint staff who can or should adjudicate inter-combatant command debates.

Throughout the tenure of Secretary of Defense James Mattis, from 2017 through 2018, the six-month tenure of Acting Secretary of Defense Patrick Shanahan, and the two-month gap before Secretary of Defense Mark Esper was sworn in, civilian control declined over critical defense processes, including war planning, managing ongoing military operations, and building the future military. Over the same period, the chairman of the joint chiefs of staff enthusiastically embraced more influence over these issues. In short, Mattis and Shanahan shirked their responsibilities to uphold meaningful civilian control of the military.[64] In late 2018, a congressionally-mandated bipartisan commission of former senior civilian and military officials assessed civil-military relations in its quadrennial review of national defense strategy.[65] As the resulting report of the National Defense Strategy Commission warned, "civilian voices have been relatively muted on issues at the center of U.S. defense and national security policy."[66] The commissioners' effort was particularly notable, since previous iterations had not raised this issue.[67]

For years under the Trump administration, the formal processes for senior civilian appointees, including the secretary of defense, to review war plans did not occur. Simultaneously, the joint staff increasingly encroached on this responsibility. For example, the chairman adjusted the war plan review process so that multiple opportunities for the secretary and other senior civilian appointees to review plans, known as in-progress reviews, were eliminated, while the chairman himself played a greater role in a process increasingly adapted to his needs.[68] In 2018, the chairman released strategic guidance in which OSD is largely absent in its staff function and in which the secretary of defense appears only marginally in relation to topics that are core to that position's responsibilities as established in Title 10 of the U.S. Code.[69] The National Defense Strategy Commission, which, of course, understood that war plans that disregard the political aspects of conflict do not work, reiterated the crucial role played by senior civilian officials in war planning. They also, apparently, felt that this role was threatened, because they urged senior civilian officials to *exercise fully their Title 10 responsibility for preparing guidance for and reviewing contingency plans.*"[70]

As previously mentioned, over the same period, Chairman Dunford also sought greater authority to shift operational forces around the world.[71] The National Defense Strategy Commission expressed its strong dissent, declaring that, "bluntly, allocating priority—and allocating forces—across theaters of warfare is not solely a military matter. It is an inherently political-military task, decision authority for which is the proper competency and responsibility of America's civilian leaders."[72] And deliberate or not, "when the chairman sees the civilian role as very circumscribed, his subordinates will pick up on that and adopt that posture," explained one former senior civilian official. While Dunford's approach helped "balance . . . and say no to the combatant commands," according to one retired senior general officer, a different senior officer told me that his tenure as chairman was also marked by a period of "emotionalism" and the "us vs. them dynamic" between OSD and the joint staff described earlier. While the chairman's writ has expanded in recent years, the joint staff still should be cautious of infringing on the secretary's mandate to lead strategic planning in the department.

Secretary of Defense Mark Esper, for his part, tried to uphold the position's responsibilities; for example, by actively managing the Pentagon through regular, secretary of defense-hosted senior leader forums to review progress on priorities and to oversee implementation of the National Defense Strategy.[73] He also publicly acknowledged the dearth of critical war plan reviews conducted by his most recent successors. While he left them unnamed, Esper was clearly referencing his immediate predecessors, Secretary of Defense Mattis and Acting Secretary of Defense Shanahan. Indeed, as Esper publicly declared in summer 2020, under his leadership, "the Department is updating key war plans for the first time in years."[74] Nevertheless, his loss of influence with President Trump grew clear throughout the second half of 2020, particularly on issues like military base names and the role of the military domestically, resulting in questions about whether he had become a lame duck—questions that were answered when he was fired just after the 2020 presidential election. Clearly, the gap for future senior civilian leaders to fill is substantial.

There is no doubt that personalities also played a key role in deepening the confusion over civilian roles. "I don't think the reason that the power balance has gotten out of whack over there is because all of a sudden the civilians got stupid," remarked one former senior civilian official. Another former senior civilian official observed that "the erosion of goodwill and trust seems much more significant today . . . [before Mattis and Shanahan] it didn't have a depth to it like now." Similarly, one general officer feared that "too many in uniform believe they have insight due to their operational experience or special insight that makes their political military advice greater than their civilian counterparts. That's not accurate. To me, that's dangerous." Of course, personalities also can help cut through the confusion. For example, retired Marine officer Robert Work's efforts as deputy secretary of defense during the Obama administration to refocus the department on high-end conventional conflict demonstrate that meaningful civilian oversight, when exercised by the right civilians, can shift the course of national security.[75]

While congressional involvement has helped clarify roles and responsibilities, it also has made them more complex and difficult. Title 10 is littered with overlapping responsibilities for the chairman of the joint chiefs and other senior civilian and military leaders, including those of the secretary of defense, the under secretary of defense for policy, and combatant commanders.[76] These overlapping responsibilities foment clutter and duplication at best, and considerable confusion and conflict at worst.[77]

Throughout the post-9/11 wars, tensions grew, decreased, and then grew again between senior civilian and military leaders over the most fundamental issues of how to wage war. In the Bush and Obama administrations, and first half of the Trump administration, shifts in the power balance between OSD and the joint staff—particularly over understanding roles and responsibilities, and aggravated by personalities—often made the issues over which they wrestled even thornier. The consequences of this for democratic control of the armed forces and the military's relevance to larger foreign policy campaigns are profoundly worrisome.

"BEST MILITARY ADVICE": THE RETURN OF HUNTINGTON

One example of the crisis of meaningful civilian control is illustrated in the term "best military advice,"[78] which took hold among the military leadership throughout the last few years of the post-9/11 wars.[79] While the phrase initially came into widespread use just after the September 11 attacks and was occasionally employed by CJCSs General Richard Myers, General Peter Pace, Admiral Michael Mullen, and General Martin Dempsey, it skyrocketed across the Pentagon during the tour of General Joseph Dunford, who frequently used and, therefore, popularized it.[80] For a few years, the phrase infused the joint staff and combatant commands—and their PowerPoint slides and their interagency memorandums—becoming so pervasive that it even made that critical leap into a well-recognized acronym, BMA, as James Golby and I have discussed elsewhere.[81] The term was not defined in law, so it is most generously described by then Chairman of the Joint Chiefs of Staff General Dunford as "professional, competent, and apolitical" military judgment informed by geopolitics and national interests.[82]

As a concept, "best military advice" is a natural outgrowth of civil-military relations scholar Samuel Huntington's theory of objective control. Huntington draws a firm line between the purview of civilians and the purview of the military. The maintenance of these separate spheres epitomizes Huntington's approach. Although this is appealing in its clarity, to military personnel who hate the idea of civilian "meddling," it is, nevertheless, misguided and, ultimately, unhelpful.[83] Scholar Michael O'Hanlon notes how responsibilities cannot be easily separated for military and civilian leaders; they "must of necessity encroach on each other's policymaking territory."[84] In practice, objective control places significant constraints and limits on the ability of civilians to monitor and control the armed forces.[85] That, in turn, can influence how military and civilian leaders understand their responsibilities in wartime. This is worrying, as scholar Risa Brooks warns:

> Huntingtonian cultural notions can lead to an inadequate sense of ownership among military leaders over the strategic outcomes of their operations. If military leaders offer their advice and civilians do not provide the recommended resources or otherwise heed their recommendations, then military leaders can skirt responsibility for strategic failures. Rather than seeing themselves as mutually accountable for a war's outcome, military leaders influenced by Huntington norms may contend that civilians lost the war because they did not give the military what it needed to win. Alternatively, if military leaders achieve their mission's objective, they may count it as a success, whether or not it contributes to achieving larger strategic or political objectives in the war.[86]

In line with Brooks's warnings about Huntington's approach, "best military advice" is unhealthy for civil-military relations and effective strategic dialogue. "Best" implies that it should not be questioned—a curious implication given the principle of civilian control in the U.S. system. Its insinuation of superiority and its binary approach to engagement impede effective debate, as does its often-false suggestion of a unified military voice. Unitary "military" views to the secretary of defense do not represent advice, not least because unitary military views do not exist.[87] They, instead, represent a narrow and often unrealistic understanding of national security policymaking, colored by repeated and dynamic engagements among a wide variety of actors. In that vein, "best military advice" can be particularly problematic when it is used as an excuse to not share important information with civilian policymakers.

Outside the CJCS's private and personal views being given to the secretary of defense, his or her independent perspective would surely benefit from civil-military discourse before they are provided. Simply put, disagreements should be aired openly rather than dismissed using "best military advice" as a bureaucratic power play. Above all, "best military advice" is an attempt to draw a thick line between the use of force on one side and politics on the other. That is both a fundamental and dangerous misunderstanding of the purpose of violence as a tool of statecraft, as well as impossible to achieve.

Others, particularly those in the military, hold more positive views of the phrase "best military advice." Some see it as a construct that, rather than overwhelming civilians, acknowledges that military advice should be based on deep expertise and rigorous analysis. According to this view, "best military advice" is a defense mechanism against civilian micromanagement and offers clarity on what the military can (and, theoretically, cannot) deliver. Others suggest it is a way for the military to play its role in the policymaking trenches while avoiding political minefields. One general officer, for example, tried to outline how "best military advice" evolves as circumstances and decisions do. He described that "BMA shifts to a compromise position based on other aspects of government . . . from a purist standpoint, BMA . . . has to evolve to that and has to be in lockstep with civilian leadership."

These positive interpretations contrasted vividly with the negative attitudes toward "best military advice" held by the civilians I interviewed. They overwhelmingly brought it up in frustration, and often in reference to the military limiting civilian control. To take one example, a former senior official recalled how then Chief of Staff of the Army General Mark Milley would publicly say that the Army needed to be larger—contrary to Secretary of Defense Ashton Carter's public statements—and when approached by a senior official about these comments would explain that he was merely offering "my best military advice." But Milley had discussed the Army's end-strength with the secretary of defense and the president, and the civilian leaders had made the decision to go with a smaller number based on a specific force planning construct. The senior official relates that he pushed back: "You can't go out and say we need a 1.24 million man Army." But Milley believed that the force planning construct—which envisioned a single large war at a time—was wrong. The Army needed to be prepared for war with Russia and North Korea simultaneously.

This engagement demonstrates one pernicious aspect of "best military advice." Milley was effectively saying that he had given his best military advice, it was disregarded, so the consequences would be wholly on the senior civilian leadership. As another former senior civilian official snapped when this topic came up in an interview, "We've been listening to BMA for 17 years and how's that got us?"

Huntington's return through the vehicle of "best military advice" is notable. His approach is taught in U.S. professional military education.[88] Recent surveys of West Point cadets found support for what three scholars termed a "conflicted Huntington model."[89] While nearly three of four cadets surveyed agreed that civil-military collaboration resulted in the best outcomes, they also overwhelmingly adhered to the notion that "military leaders should expect to receive clear guidance about goals and objectives at the beginning of the planning process." The latter is particularly worrisome because it dismisses the iterative nature of national security policymaking. Although only around half of the cadets believe a fundamental element of Huntington's argument—"the concept of separate spheres and a clear division of labor"—it is, nevertheless, a staggering number who, ultimately, adhere to the notion that civilians should stick to a limited set of defense issues.[90] Overall, Huntington's return through the vehicle of "best military advice" reflects the confusion and uncertainty that has plagued the post-9/11 wars, particularly over civil-military roles, responsibilities, and missions. The tension it inspires between civilians and their uniformed counterparts appears to be antagonistic rather than productive.

COMMENCING REPARATIONS: RETHINKING ADVICE AND OVERSIGHT

To fix this crisis of meaningful civilian control, both the military and civilians need to take five key steps. Restoring relationships requires serious efforts to rebuilt trust, to set common expectations, and to stop catastrophizing—that is, to stop constantly revisiting their lowest moments. The military can broadly define advice, and civilians can ensure they have the appropriate expertise and capabilities; both must do their part to facilitate consistent dialogue and foster an atmosphere of collaboration, trust, and transparency to mend and tend relations.

First, the military should more broadly conceptualize the advice it gives civilian leaders.[91] Advice should not simply include recommendations—*do this* or *don't do that*—but, instead, run the gamut of realistic options and assessments. These options should be discrete, paired with detailed costs and benefits, and rigorously assessed. "Military advice should be policy-driven and politically informed," as James Golby and I have written previously. That involves demonstrating the military's cognizance of the guidance set by civilian leaders. One particularly thoughtful and realistic example of such advice comes from former CJCS Martin Dempsey. He responded to a letter from Senator Carl Levin inquiring about military options for Syria—a particularly thorny issue from both a policy and a political perspective—by offering nuanced insights over a series of potential options.[92]

By suggesting thoughtful and considered observations, military leaders should recognize that the advice they give ultimately informs a broader set of considerations by civilians. Civilian politicians like the president and the secretary of defense will weigh options, not based just on Department of Defense priorities but including broader issues and dynamics, as well. Simply put, politics matters. Perhaps civilians did not do a good job helping the military to understand that perspective, but politics, nevertheless, played a role in these decisions.

That view—which will resonate with a student of Clausewitz—is obvious. Two new books offer good examples of how the senior political leader's perspective is different from the senior military leader's view. In President Obama's memoir, he recounted a conversation with General David Petraeus about the balance sheet of continuing the war in Iraq. Petraeus was unable to explain to Obama what circumstances would enable the military to conclude its mission and when those might come to fruition. Obama explained, "I couldn't blame Petraeus for wanting to finish the mission. If I were in your shoes, I told him, I'd want the same thing. But a president's job required looking at a bigger picture." Unlike Petraeus, whose mandate was obviously limited, Obama was responsible for looking at balancing across global security threats, mounting economic challenges at home, and the impact on the force writ large.[93] Similarly, in former Chairman of the Joint Chiefs of Staff General Martin

Dempsey's memoir, he recalled a difficult conversation with President Obama over the draft defense budget in 2014. The joint chiefs had recommended a larger defense budget than the Obama administration had signaled support for—one week before the midterm congressional elections. Obama called Dempsey, perturbed that the timing could give the impression that the administration did not sufficiently support the military and, therefore, could influence the election. "It hadn't even occurred to us that our memorandum would be interpreted in the context of the midterm elections," explained Dempsey, who was chagrined for belatedly recognizing that "for us [the joint chiefs], the [defense] budget had become a singularly important issue; for the president, it was one of several equally important issues."[94]

Second, civilian officials need to have the relevant expertise, not just simply the will, to enable a meaningful decisionmaking process. As one former senior official explained, "Civilians have to show their value proposition . . . if they want to have a voice in these debates and have those voices be taken seriously, they have to have the expertise to be seen as a credible contributor. They have a responsibility to add value and bring something to the table." Richard Kohn put it well in his advice to senior civilians: "Know the military: the people, the profession, the institutions, the culture and its needs, assumptions, perspectives, and behaviors in order to permit proper and informed decisions on the myriad of issues that decide peace and war."[95] In a similar vein, scholar and former senior Pentagon official Kathleen Hicks explained the need for civilians to demonstrate to military personnel that they have "enough knowledge that they can't be gamed but also enough knowledge that maybe you could trust them with the real facts."[96] Scholarly and experiential exposure can deepen this crucial education on how military personnel conceptualize the spectrum of conflict and cooperation.[97] Janine Davidson recommends that the civilian side better educate itself on practical national security affairs, both through academics and experiential opportunities.[98]

Unfortunately, the personnel hiring system exacerbates these challenges. Former Secretary of Defense Rumsfeld noted that, during his tenure, the Pentagon "operated with 25.5% of the key senior civilian positions vacant."[99] Similarly, former Under Secretary of Defense for Policy Eric Edelman recounted that, in his experience as under secretary, the office of the secretary of defense was "being held together by paper clips and band-aids and bubblegum," with too few personnel, low retention rates, and difficulty finding competent new hires. He contrasted this with the joint staff, an institution he saw as "large, very capable" and growing.[100] Exercising meaningful civilian control was inevitably trying given these personnel challenges, which were aggravated by the volatility, exhaustion, and high operational tempo that characterized the post-9/11 wars. All these challenges surrounding civilian hiring and retention in the office of the secretary of defense invariably contributed to the joint staff's interest in playing an outsize role in policymaking.

Third, both military and civilian leaders can facilitate consistent dialogue and actively encourage this approach at all levels. Major General William Rapp, commandant of the U.S. Army War College, implored that they "have the responsibility to listen to each other and probe the answers they hear."[101] Advice cannot be an excuse for failing to coordinate or share materials with one another, or to squelch debate. They should become comfortable with relying on informed dialogue to understand and, therefore, appropriately shape national security affairs. "Civilians often look at military options to help illuminate [policy] options; military leaders often do not understand that," explained one civilian official with deep experience among senior military general officers. But for those who subscribe to Huntington's objective theory of control, "relations between civilians and the military in advisory processes" are often "essentially transactional, rather than collaborative."[102]

To help military leaders see this perspective, critical issues related to civil-military relations should receive greater emphasis in professional military education. The core curriculum at the U.S. Army War College, for example, spends little time on the subject. It examines neither issues of partisanship nor the relationship between the military and society. And while it offers an elective course that focuses specifically on civil-military relations, only about 2 percent of eligible students sign up for it.[103]

Civilians, in general, should recognize that civil-military dialogue, including the implementation of decisions, is iterative and should encourage regular assessment of the effectiveness of such dialogues to better exercise effective oversight.[104] Civilians in the Pentagon, in particular, should be aware of each military service's specific norms, values, and beliefs, as these differences will influence their ability to engage with and oversee military affairs.[105] For example, one former senior official warned, "There's this magicians union [in which] you're never going to get the military to criticize one another to civilians even when they are screwing up . . . no one will talk out of school." Civilians, therefore, need to emulate Secretary Gates, who would "figure out the code words or 'tells' that would let me know whether these men were putting on a show of agreement for me when, in fact, they strongly disagreed."[106] No senior civilian national security leaders will be able to do so effectively absent a deep and textured background in national security affairs.

They also must understand the military's desire for clarity and its can-do attitude, which exists even when it is impractical. "Civilians bathe in ambiguity. For the military, especially the Army, 'Jomini is driving the car,'" cautioned one civilian official, drawing upon the reputation of famed military theorist Baron Antoine-Henri Jomini, well known for promising success on the battlefield through exceedingly precise and scientific rules.[107] One senior general officer, recognizing this, explained that "sometimes, we're accused of being overly optimistic. We have to watch that. That has to be on the table with civilians."

Hicks recommends adopting "incentive structures" to reshape the dialogue around these military characteristics, but also wryly warns, "You learn over time that the reality is that the real refrain from the military is often 'give me guidance—no not *that* guidance.'"[108] She smartly suggests that civilians should not "focus too much on that friction, and the distrust it creates," at the expense of "how you build out better solutions and answers."

Fourth, both civilians and their military counterparts should make a hearty effort to encourage an atmosphere of transparency to begin filling what Brooks terms the "gap of trust" between them.[109] Providing sage advice to the military, Kohn bluntly observes that "many, and probably most, civilians come into office without necessarily trusting the military, knowing that they have personal views, ideologies, ambitions, institutional loyalties, and institutional perspectives and agendas."[110] While civilians are not compelled to follow military advice—as General Goldfein underscored, "Not one civilian leader that I've ever worked with or for has ever had to raise their right hand and say they will take my advice"—they should, nevertheless, demonstrate their willingness to hear and respond to it.[111]

Finally, civilians should do their utmost to convey meaningful guidance. It should clearly state prioritization, resources, and risks. A worthwhile checklist for assessing the strength of guidance includes asking if it is focused on something important that is either new or dictates a change; is clear, if it is implementable, and whether it contradicts itself or inadvertently contradicts other guidance.[112] In the wake of the Chilcot Commission's investigation of how the United Kingdom became embroiled in the Iraq War, the British Ministry of Defence published a "Chilcot Checklist" to facilitate decisionmaking on the use of force. Many of the questions it lists also have broad relevance to the United States in considering decisions related to the post-9/11 wars, including: "Why do we care?; What is happening now?; What might happen next?; What should we do?; How do we ensure action is lawful?; What does success look like?; What do we need to deliver?; How should we do it?; How will you monitor performance?; and, Is the policy working?"[113]

Manifesting oversight is tricky under the best of circumstances. No serious scholar or practitioner of civil-military relations would argue that a deputy assistant secretary or assistant secretary of defense should tell the CJCS how to do that job effectively. However, as the secretary's staff, it is exactly that individual's responsibility to ensure the secretary's guidance is understood as intended and is promulgated and implemented across the Department of Defense. As scholar Peter Feaver describes, civilians in places like OSD serve as "extensions of the executive branch principals" and operate as "police patrols" who vigilantly keep an eye on their military counterparts.[114] As one senior officer cogently said in an interview, the real question is "who gets to call the shot and at what level?" Senior military leaders believe they "move left or right because of the president or the secretary of defense, not because a deputy assistant secretary of defense would say move left or right . . . so until I hear that coming out of somebody higher at this organization, I'm not going to change." As one senior officer underscored, "I have never ever heard a four-star [general officer] dismiss civilian control of the military but I know that initial belief—if we were calling this shot or that shot, it does eek away at the idea—hey, the civilian gets to call the shot." This individual then quickly emphasized that even "if they're an idiot . . . they still get to call that shot." In other words, one would be hard pressed to find a senior leader in the U.S. military who seriously opposes civilian oversight or is not a staunch believer that orders come from the civilian president and the civilian secretary of defense. The secretary, however, cannot be expected to exert meaningful oversight if he or she does not have the staff to do so.

To alleviate the crisis of meaningful civilian control, the most senior civilian and military leaders must be willing to do their utmost to make this a reality. Acknowledging the divide, being respectful and empathetic, and emphasizing collaboration are the crucial initial steps.

CIVIL-MILITARY CRISES OVER TWO DECADES OF WAR

The result of the three crises discussed over the last three chapters is that the relationships between the military, the American people, and the civilian overseers of organized violence are increasingly fraught with tensions. These represent a deep and troubling set of legacies from America's post-9/11 wars, many of which manifest in dysfunctional patterns of civil-military affairs.

Unless and until civilian leaders recognize these patterns and deliberately tackle them, the legacies of the post-9/11 wars will grow more acute. Over the past two decades, civilians have not clearly articulated what the role of force should be, which has given the military outsized influence. However, the military, left largely on its own, has been unable to achieve conclusive results in the post-9/11 wars. Society—and many civilian policymakers—nevertheless, give it a pass, because the military is dealing with challenges that most Americans do not understand or want to confront themselves. This lack of accountability inevitably shapes the military in a deeply paradoxical way: while the military is

lauded by many outsiders and subsequently thinks it has the best answers on how to win the post-9/11 wars, it has, nevertheless, been unable
to sufficiently understand, prepare for, or execute these conflicts over
the past two decades. This paradox, in turn, has a profound impact on
civilian control and oversight given that civilian voices are deemed less
credible and are, therefore, more easily dismissed. This is a pernicious
outcome, not least because civilian voices will be crucial for revitalizing
the military. A civil-military maelstrom, ultimately, harms many—above
all, American democracy.

5

How the Military Goes to War

"You were not sitting back in your chair . . . ever."

The post-9/11 wars have heavily influenced how the U.S. military thinks about going to war. In three key areas—planning for war, paying for war, and perceiving war—the military has developed new habits, norms, and expectations based on its experiences over the last two decades. These may, but more probably will not, be appropriate for future conflicts. Reflecting on how the United States went to war over the last two decades offers a hearty reminder that going to war is not a story written solely in the field but, rather, one that is coauthored—and often stymied or propelled—in headquarters, as well.

PLANNING FOR WAR

"Our most reckless course would be to dwell on old threats," warned Secretary of Defense Donald Rumsfeld six months before the September 11, 2001, al Qaeda's attacks that killed more than 3,000 people.[1] He was underscoring the exceptional nature of a decade bookended, it would turn

out, by the collapse of the Soviet Union at its onset and the 9/11 attacks
at its close—a decade during which the United States did not appear to
have a serious threat. During that period, the national security apparatus was consumed by relatively small challenges in places like the Balkans and Somalia. Under Rumsfeld's leadership, the pre-9/11 Pentagon
pulled together a draft defense strategy that called for a radical transformation of the military to deal with high-end conventional challenges.[2]
But as the new threat of countering transnational terrorism—and, soon
after, invading Iraq—emerged, Rumsfeld's transformational ambitions
receded. The nascent effort to reconfigure and refocus the U.S. military
was largely abandoned.

To best understand how war planning—which is among the most
sensitive issues for civilian and military leaders—suffered throughout
the post-9/11 wars, it helps to understand how the process should work
in theory.[3] Based on guidance from the president and the secretary of
defense regarding the potential conflicts that might plausibly erupt in
places where U.S. national security interests are at stake, a deliberative
and time-consuming process should commence. The relevant combatant command (or commands, as the case may be) should pull together
potential approaches for winning those conflicts. Representatives from
the joint staff and the office of the secretary of defense should poke and
prod these alternatives at varying levels. At some point, the secretary of
defense—responsible for war planning under Title 10—should approve
the plan. It does not stop there, though; critical plans should be reas-
sessed on a regular basis.[4]

Civilian oversight is fundamental to this process, as it is a crucial lever
in governing U.S. management of violence. It is specified by the Constitution, which declares the president the sole commander-in-chief and gives
Congress the power to declare war and to support parts of the military—
and U.S. law assigns the responsibility to oversee war planning and force
development to the secretary of defense, key ways of manifesting civilian
control.[5] However, ensuring that this oversight meaningfully occurs is a
long-standing challenge across the Defense Department.

To offer one particularly egregious historical example, during the
Cold War, the joint staff deliberately prevented senior civilian leaders

from reading annex c of the Joint Strategic Capabilities Plan, which specified that nuclear strikes on the Soviet Union would automatically be accompanied by strikes against the People's Republic of China—terrifying, to say the least.[6]

Secretaries of defense are usually sensitive to this challenge. Indeed, during his 1994 confirmation hearing to become secretary, William Perry said that war planning would be his top priority.[7] As Perry understood, it is an issue rife with high-stakes political-military consequences that demands persistent oversight by and critical input from civilians. Failure by senior civilian leaders to oversee war planning heightened the crisis of meaningful civilian oversight throughout the Trump administration.

War planning also is invariably influenced by the personalities involved—and the legacies those personalities subscribe to. Before the 9/11 attacks, Robert Gates—who would go on to serve as secretary of defense in both the Bush and Obama administrations—criticized what he saw as a military approach to war planning scarred by the baggage of previous wars. In one illustrative interview, he warned that military planners "are so accustomed, after Vietnam, to civilians wanting to use military force that any time a President demands a contingency plan to consider, the military puts together a force that is so overwhelming that the President will balk at the cost and at the disruption and everything else and not do it."[8]

While this is, undoubtedly, an exaggeration, that Gates believed it and was so open about this belief should force all national security practitioners, military and civilian alike, to take note. Unsurprisingly, Secretary of Defense Gates was renowned for his obsession with conducting regular reviews of war plans.

The rapid shift in strategic focus following the September 11 attacks kicked off a period of intense, and often chaotic, war planning.[9] After minimal debate, Congress voted nearly unanimously to pass the Authorization for the Use of Military Force Against Terrorists.[10] Planning began immediately within the Pentagon, where there were no off-the-shelf plans for an Afghanistan contingency. Rumsfeld tasked General Tommy Franks, commander of U.S. Central Command (CENTCOM), to prepare a war plan to destroy al Qaeda's sanctuary in Afghanistan. Franks requested two months to fulfill the tasking but Rumsfeld gave him days.[11] The team at CENTCOM rapidly began building a war plan to brief Rumsfeld and President Bush. Over the next year or so, the same hectic planning process would expand to include a broader war on terrorism and Iraq.

According to journalist Tom Ricks, tensions in planning for the Iraq war—which complicated and was complicated by the ongoing war in Afghanistan—were concentrated primarily in disagreements over the proper size and shape of the invasion force as well as the role played by the civilian leadership in formulating plans.[12] However, it is worth underscoring that there remains some debate regarding how detailed pre-9/11 war plans for an invasion of Iraq actually were, the extent to which these existing plans were modified or ignored, and, if they were, by whom.[13]

Even within the military leadership, making war plans for Afghanistan and Iraq proved a bumpy process. General Franks was unenthusiastic about including the joint chiefs in Afghanistan planning. His deputy commander for CENTCOM, Lieutenant General Michael DeLong, attested that "for Franks, briefing the Joint Chiefs was merely a formality."[14] DeLong underscored that most of the chiefs wanted to make parochial contributions that would only benefit their own services' equities.[15] He argued that the planning for Iraq faced similar pushback, although CJCS Richard Myers raised other issues, specifically the importance of planning for post-conflict stabilization operations, which Franks was uninterested in. Given the catastrophic course of the early occupation, this calls Franks's judgment into serious question (as does his infamously cruel leadership, as well as his desire for fantastically optimistic, rather than realistic, assessments).[16]

Many have criticized Franks's rejection of serious planning for post-conflict stabilization; that is an accurate but incomplete assessment given that Rumsfeld gave guidance in this vein.[17] A particularly insightful report by RAND scholars, for example, argues that he "saw major combat operations during Phase III as fundamentally distinct from Phase IV stability and reconstruction requirements, and as the military's primary task," which meant that CENTCOM focused overwhelmingly on major combat operations.[18] Indeed, a draft CENTCOM briefing prepared for President Bush explicitly stated, "We don't do windows," a punchy reference to post-conflict stabilization.[19] The Army's official study of the Iraq War also notes that war planning was highly classified and heavily restricted, which precluded other senior military leaders from usefully contributing to it.[20]

Nevertheless, as one senior military leader reminded, "It is engrained in us: if you're going to execute the plan, you must be a part of the planning process." Even as war plans were finalized, they often suffered from "PowerPointitis," meaning they were poorly developed beyond the bullet-point requirements of a slide deck, resulting in a lack of clarity and exacerbating confusion among the senior military leaders charged with executing them.[21] Moreover, receptivity to lessons already learned from the Afghanistan war seemed slim.

For example, in late August 2002, a U.S. Army War College-convened dialogue with senior Army leaders assessing how the fight in Afghanistan war had proceeded reached overwhelmingly critical conclusions regarding the lack of strategic-level guidance, the dearth of long-term planning, and the frequent operational ad hocery. The War College held a similar dialogue a few months later—focusing on the potential war with Iraq—and ominously warned that similar mistakes were being made. The conveners found little enthusiasm for their work among the senior leadership.[22]

The influence of civil-military tensions in planning for war also stands out over these two decades. According to the joint staff's official directive, the post-9/11 war planning process was characterized by limited options and minimal flexibility. In particular, it underscores that war planning during the run-up to the Iraq War felt "cumbersome" and plagued by fallacies.[23] In 2005, Secretary Rumsfeld responded by establishing a new process, Adaptive Planning and Execution (APEX), which sought to inject dynamism through regular reviews of draft war plans.[24] Some saw this deliberate and rigorous planning process as time-consuming micromanagement, but it did provide regular opportunities for senior civilians to engage and debate options, disentangle their pros and cons, and offer guidance. Rumsfeld, thus, pursued a heavy-handed approach to war planning (and, indeed, in most of his interactions with the military). As then CJCS Richard Myers recounts, during one war plan briefing, the combatant commander told Rumsfeld, "I'm here to have you approve my OPLAN," to which Rumsfeld responded, "No, General. You're here to have me *improve* your plan."[25] While one of Rumsfeld's senior appointees claims that Rumsfeld's favored approach in war planning was to "nudge" senior military leaders rather than to dictate, his infamous "snowflakes"—his ideas, questions, or recommendations on any number of topics, which littered the Pentagon by the thousands during his time as secretary of defense—lend more credence to Myers's account.[26] Rumsfeld's tendencies, particularly when coupled with his abrasive approach, ended up adding additional friction to an already confused effort.

Acute trouble between the military and the civilian leadership compounded this friction. In his memoir, Rumsfeld recounts his frustration with senior military leaders failing to share their objections to the Iraq War, specifically citing a January 2003 meeting with President Bush in which CJCS Myers, Commander of CENTCOM Franks, and Army Chief of Staff Eric Shinseki reportedly kept quiet. "I assumed and expected that they would speak up if they had reservations—indeed, it was their duty to do so," explained Rumsfeld.[27] One should be appropriately skeptical of this post-facto exculpatory rhetoric, of course, particularly because the senior military leadership may have found their opportunities to offer dissent circumscribed. However, just before the Iraq War kicked off, President Bush met with senior military leaders to directly gauge their support; all concurred with his approach.[28] Scholar and retired Lieutenant General Jim Dubik found real flaws in the war planning dialogue after the September 11, 2001, attacks, particularly surrounding the Iraq War. Deeming it "broken," he explains that those who were willing to offer different views were ignored or punished and the dialogue resembled a "facsimile" focused on "compliance with the plan rather than a dialogue around adapting the plan to unfolding realities."[29]

This fledgling dialogue was surely further undermined by the military and political leadership's unwillingness to use accurate words to describe the post-9/11 wars. General Stanley McChrystal, who commanded the war in Afghanistan, criticized leaders for avoiding the word "'war' . . . it was always 'the problem' or 'the situation' or 'the conflict.'"[30] Civilian leaders noted the same tendencies, often with disquietude. "Words like decisive defeat . . . it's not clear to me what that ever meant," explained one former senior civilian decisionmaker reflecting on Pentagon war planning debates in the wake of the September 11, 2001, attacks. Without clarity on what the U.S. military was doing, or even supposed to do, in the post-9/11 wars, amorphous guidance was far from helpful and, ultimately, undermined the military's ability to execute the civilian leadership's vision. For any number of reasons, in the years following the 9/11 attacks, the dialogue inside the Pentagon on war-waging was problematic. As chapter 4 details, it remains so, contributing to the crisis of meaningful civilian control.

Looking forward, Dubik offers sage advice to preclude a broken planning dialogue in the future: "War-waging dialogues require protected space" in which the parties thoughtfully and iteratively engage in war planning.[31] Such an environment would benefit from having capable civilian and military leaders who operate transparently and with a genuine commitment to collaboration. It is especially needed in five places: within the Pentagon; in Congress; between the Pentagon and the White House; and among the Pentagon, the White House, and Congress. However, as of early 2021, none of these actors has seriously sought it. Congress, for example, has failed to reassess the 2001 Authorization for the Use of Military Force (AUMF). Other than passing an AUMF focused on Iraq in 2002, and outside a brief moment following the 2020 killing of Iranian Revolutionary Guard Corps leader Qassem Soleimani, Congress has been unable or unwilling to seriously debate the use of force over much of the last two decades, even though it has managed to approve much of the funding for it. Politics and parochialism make protected dialogue particularly difficult, but it remains critical.

PAYING FOR WAR: "IT WAS LIKE AN OPEN BAR"

In the aftermath of the September 11, 2001, attacks, the U.S. military found it relatively easy to fund its war, setting a precedent for the post-9/11 wars of minimal dialogue between security leaders and the American public, coupled with robust resourcing. Within days, the Defense Department requested $20 billion in emergency supplemental funding. "Congress basically gave us a blank check," declared one senior civilian defense official from that period. "It was like an open bar," quipped one officer. Another compared the free-wheeling spending atmosphere to "buying prime rib on the credit card." In pulling together its initial request, the Pentagon's comptroller explained that the military services saw this as an opportunity to fulfill many needs; they sent him lists that "include[d] everything but the kitchen sink in their estimated requirements."[32] A third military officer wondered about the cascading effect of these lavish budgets on those who serve in the future, already worrying that they might now assume that funding will always flow freely and easily.

This rapid infusion of wartime resources without hard questions and associated cuts to domestic spending was historically anomalous for the United States, which has generally adjusted entitlement spending in line with wartime needs.[33] However, neither the Bush administration nor Congress pushed to raise taxes, and neither made real cuts to domestic spending to offset defense outlays.[34] It was, therefore, the first time in U.S. history that Congress "increased nonsecurity spending and cut taxes while also appropriating large sums to fight a war."[35] While official government rhetoric underscored that the wars would be long, the American public was not asked to immediately chip in, as it had in the other major wars of the twentieth century. "Unlike in past wars, there were no bipartisan calls for patriotic sacrifice," observes one scholar.[36] While there were occasional debates in Congress about establishing a war tax, including around the Iraq surge decision, they were unsuccessful.[37] These dynamics may reinforce the views of skeptics like Gordon Adams, who warned in 1981 of an "iron triangle" between the Defense Department, Congress, and defense contractors addicted to using public resources for war.[38]

The cost of the first seventeen years of the post-9/11 wars often is estimated at $1.5 trillion.[39] Much of this budget was restricted to supplemental packages that were soon referred to by the anodyne name "overseas contingency operations." Funding schizophrenia posed a challenge to those hoping to control spending, as the overseas contingency operations account could be manipulated much more creatively than the primary budget. Indeed, some argue that the wars have actually been much more expensive, as the $1.5 trillion figure does not tally some important things. According to Brown University's Watson Institute for International and Public Affairs, the cost of the post-9/11 wars—including the bills for homeland security, veterans affairs, and additional equipment and personnel—is actually $6 trillion.[40] This is a relatively reasonable estimate. For example, long-term healthcare for wounded warriors—a clear result of direct warfighting but not included in the lower estimate—was priced at $160.4 billion as of 2015.[41] The financial opportunity costs of being at war for so long may, therefore, have wider-spread long-term impacts across America than many acknowledge.

Since these funds were largely restricted to theaters of active combat like Iraq and Afghanistan, they were, generally, not fungible for the other nonterrorism-related challenges on which the U.S. military focused during the post-9/11 wars. This meant that "you should be training for Russia and China, but you're training for Iraq and Afghanistan" because that is where the money is, one former senior defense official explained. The military's ability to prepare for other contingencies besides fighting terrorists and insurgents was minimized by this operations-focused funding in the period after September 11, although, in more recent years, the "overseas contingency operations" account has become a seemingly bottomless bucket for paying various military bills, such as deterrence initiatives in Europe. Notably, when sequestration hit, as discussed later, its funds were exempt from the caps, which inevitably incentivized the migration of military budget requests into it, with pernicious consequences for the broader defense budget.

While the post-9/11 wars received an initial funding windfall, budgets grew bumpier after the first decade or so of conflict. Following the 2008 financial crisis, the Defense Department experienced what former Pentagon comptroller Robert Hale calls "nearly constant budgetary turmoil."[42] Over the ensuing years, a number of budget-related events wracked U.S. defense spending, including tens of billions of dollars in sequestration cuts, multiple government shutdowns, congressional reliance on continuing resolutions, and massive reprogramming requests.[43] Profound budgetary uncertainty plagued this period, which resulted staff and leadership spending thousands of hours preparing multiple budgets, planning for potential shutdowns, and negotiating wiggle room for the use of existing funds. Critics of the Obama administration frequently argue that it did not sufficiently fund the military, and many in the military hold the administration responsible for the defense budget cuts that occurred during its years in office. But as former Secretary of Defense Ashton Carter reminds us in his memoir, "Every federal budget proposed by the Obama administration but one called for *higher* levels of Pentagon spending than Republicans in Congress ultimately approved."[44] Moreover, although the Defense Department occasionally would receive higher budgets over the years, those funding levels were often a surprise, and future funding levels remained uncertain—making it harder to confidently make major investments (figure 5-1).

A particular issue in this period worth addressing is sequestration, the shorthand mechanism for the Budget Control Act of 2011's caps on defense and nondefense discretionary spending that forced equal cuts across all accounts if Congress failed to abide by its spending caps. This originated in a dispute about the debt but ended up having a real impact on defense spending. While sequestration was deliberately constructed by Congress under the assumption that it would never come to fruition—a classic "poison pill" to force political agreement on spending reductions—that assumption was proven inaccurate in 2013, and it threatened to recur repeatedly over the following years. Although sequestration was Congress's brainchild, President Obama and his team received blame from others for allowing it to occur. Then Secretary of Defense Leon Panetta claims he "fought as hard" as possible to prevent its implementation, and he blames both Congress for its unwillingness to lead and President Obama's White House for the cabinet's largely ineffectual response.[45] "President Obama bore some responsibility, as well, not for concocting the sequester, but rather for failing to lead Congress out of it," he argues.[46]

Sequestration cuts meant reduced facility maintenance; furloughs or layoffs of more than half a million civilian personnel; halts or reductions in training across the military services; and the cancelation of military exercises, including with allies and partners. Some spectacular examples

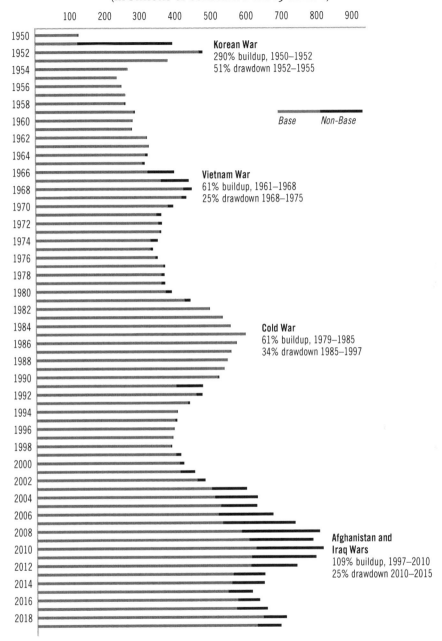

FIGURE 5-1. DOD Budget Authority: A Historical Perspective
(in billions of constant FY2019 dollars)

Korean War
290% buildup, 1950–1952
51% drawdown 1952–1955

Base   Non-Base

Vietnam War
61% buildup, 1961–1968
25% drawdown 1968–1975

Cold War
61% buildup, 1979–1985
34% drawdown 1985–1997

Afghanistan and
Iraq Wars
109% buildup, 1997–2010
25% drawdown 2010–2015

Sources: Congressional Research Service analysis of Department of Defense, Office of the Under Secretary of Defense (Comptroller), National Defense Budget Estimates for FY2020, table 6-8: DOD Budget Authority by Public Law Title (FY1948–FY2024), table 2-1: Base Budget, War Funding and Supplementals by Military Department, by P.L. Title (FY2001–FY2020), May 2019; Department of Defense, FAD-809 table, January 1978; Congressional Budget Office, supplemental appropriations reports from the 1970s–2000s; Office of Management and Budget, historical tables, table 10.1: Gross Domestic Product and Deflators Used in the Historical Tables: 1940–2024.

included delaying the 2013 USS *Truman* carrier strike group's deployment to the Middle East and canceling two of the Air Force's Red Flag
exercises, among the most sophisticated high-end combat training exercises the United States conducts with partner militaries.[47]

The opportunity costs of the time and attention spent planning and
making these cuts is immeasurable. Across the Defense Department apparatus, untold numbers of staff were put in the unenviable position of
planning multiple budgets simultaneously, which was time-consuming,
frustrating, and confusing. The morale-crushing impact of sequestration affected every corner of the Pentagon, and what made the cuts particularly pernicious was their inherent unpredictability. Decisions about
funding, or not funding, ongoing conflicts struck at the most sensitive
issues for the U.S. military. More than half a million civilian employees at the Defense Department were not permitted to go to work. One
senior official recounted the immediate emotional impact of sequestration in 2013. To shield the troops in Afghanistan, the Army needed additional funds, but the Navy didn't want to give any up and was "pissed," as
he described it. The senior official chastised the Navy leadership, saying
that "this is not the Army's war; this is the nation's war that the Army is
fighting." Nevertheless, some servicemembers managed to find humor
in the sequestration-related budget challenges that plagued the military.
Duffel Blog, as usual, nailed it with headlines like "Budget Cuts to Bring
Military Spending Down to Pre-Civil War Levels" and "Budget Cuts
Force Defense to Downsize Pentagon to a Square."[48]

In sum, over the course of the post-9/11 wars, the funds flowed, but
sometimes more slowly and less reliably. Their justification became fuzzier, politics seeped in, and the public remained largely disengaged, contributing to the crisis of caring. Save for the real and perceived threats
posed by sequestration to its ability to plan for the future, the military
generally received the funds it requested to fight these wars—albeit less
so to prepare for future wars. The U.S. public did not have to make any
immediate financial sacrifices for these wars, no doubt enabling its disinterest and disincentivizing oversight—a particularly ironic outcome
because the overseas contingency funds were initially developed to increase transparency and predictability in war funding. As scholar Sarah

Kreps inquired, "If individuals no longer saw the costs of war, would they be less politically engaged with the cost, duration, and outcome? [Her research] suggests that the answer is yes."[49] More forcefully, scholar Jonathan Caverley argues that the public pays little in blood and treasure for conflicts, like the post-9/11 wars, that involve fighting terrorists and insurgents, and "supporting a capital-intensive military doctrine, and small wars of choice [therefore become] rational policies for the average voter."[50] Invariably, the approach taken for funding the post-9/11 wars has informed how the military thinks about going to war; the lessons it leaves reflect what occurs when a disinterested public largely keeps its checkbook open and asks few questions.

PERCEIVING WAR: WHAT WAR LOOKS LIKE

Before the post-9/11 wars started, a former senior official explained to me that there existed a "false sense of security, like [the threat was] a gnat buzzing in our ear." Most of the U.S. military had limited experience in long-duration combat environments. Despite fighting around the world in the 1990s, the military of the year 2000 was, at its core, a peacetime force. But in the wake of the September 11, 2001, attacks, the U.S. military responded with a "sense of urgency 24/7," as one senior military officer described it. It was, he said, a period in which the military worked so hard that "you were not sitting back in your chair . . . ever."

Those who have waged war over the last two decades often carry a few embedded expectations about the future. Many are unable to conceptualize wars that result in hundreds of thousands of casualties. They also may be skeptical that conflicts can have a clear ending, or any ending at all. To them, war is inevitably interminable.[51] Its incessant drumbeat bleeds into ambient noise. That noise has a severe impact on the military itself.

As we explore these impacts, it is worth keeping in mind that, during the post-9/11 wars, the U.S. military has possessed overwhelming and ahistorical advantages over its adversaries. These are illustrated by the existence and proliferation of forward operating bases (FOB) and by operational military advantages.

While not all the troops lived on a large FOB, hundreds of thousands did.[52] FOBs looked like a piece of America awkwardly plopped down in a foreign country. They were, also, exceptional in the history of war. As a U.S. Army War College monograph described, FOBs became "refuges from danger, places of renewal for physical needs, a respite from the mental stress of battle, and, finally, a means for soldiers to stay connected with the world."[53] Moreover, thanks to FOBs and the substantial logistics pipelines that enabled them, "American forces in Iraq and Afghanistan have been by far the best-supplied U.S. troops ever to go to war," as scholars Nora Bensahel and David Barno remind us.[54] Those stationed on FOBs who rarely left this sanctuary were given the derogatory nickname "FOBbits." One jarring example of the scale of FOBs is offered by a retired senior general officer who noted that, in 2004, there were more U.S. troops "inside the wire" at Balad Air Base in Iraq than in all of Afghanistan.

A good example of a FOB is Camp Leatherneck, a U.S. military base in Afghanistan that at its height housed 40,000 troops and contractors. Nicknamed Camp Pleasureneck by some troops, one military officer said it represented "everything the Marine Corps should not be when it deploys."[55] FOBs often had plentiful food options, gyms the equal of anything back home, hot water, air conditioning, shops for expensive goods like televisions, contractors running amuck, and regular internet access. "It was haves and have nots," explained one officer as he distinguished between life on a FOB and the experience of troops in more remote areas of Iraq or Afghanistan. Further out, troops were "raising chickens and eating them," but on the FOB, troops drank fancy coffee drinks at cappuccino bars, ate steak and shrimp dinners, and finished meals with ice cream sundae bars.[56]

The creature comforts available at a FOB, unsurprisingly, had an impact on the troops stationed there, as well. Many could be in regular communication with their families and struggled with how to meaningfully connect with them, compartmentalizing aspects of their experiences on deployment even as they wrestled with issues on the home front.[57] One soldier argued that the "entitlement" of life on the FOB "affected our ability to handle stress . . . and the performance of soldiers."

He was struck by how the troops on his FOB would become stressed when hot water wasn't available, when the internet was blocked due to a casualty (to ensure the family was informed first), and when they were not able to speak to their families or watch Netflix.

The FOB narrative, however, represents only a piece of the U.S. military's changing perception of war. Another perspective can be found in the experience of those chicken-raising frontline servicemembers, nearly always soldiers and Marines, who lived in more austere conditions and experienced more incessant combat. They relied heavily on the extensive fire and air support, and the rapid medical evacuations, that the FOBs enabled. Doing so meant they developed habits and expectations of what other parts of the force could provide for protection, particularly in more remote locations.[58] The presence of such dramatically different experiences of war, even between personnel from the same occupations of the same services in the same general places, can help explain some of the generational dynamics in the post-9/11 wars, as well, discussed further in chapter 8. In particular, some military leaders may be particularly sensitive to creature comforts (or the lack thereof) when in command of infantry units in these environments if their previous experiences had been quite different.

The experience of combat in the post-9/11 wars was often shaped by the fact that the U.S. military held singular operational advantages, including unimpeded logistics and communications; air superiority; and the ability to find, fix, and finish nearly any target practically anywhere in the world. "What separates us from others is our ability to project power over long distances . . . to put force on the ground in Afghanistan, a landlocked country 8,000 miles away: it's a capability that no other country has," explained one former senior Defense Department official. These wars involved "largely permissive environments," emphasized another former senior Defense Department official, and the military "didn't have to fight for control of these domains." A general officer quipped, "We basically have been gods on the battlefield; we could go anywhere we wanted and do anything we wanted . . . fly around low, slow, do stupid things and they still work." Agreeing, one officer said the military got "spoiled by communications architecture, supplies, logistics, and the creature comforts," while another officer rued that these advantages have led the military to inherit "a sense of entitlement in what war is going to be like: we believe we can know everything on the battlefield and we have grown commanders [accordingly]."

Taken together, these operational advantages are best summed up by a general officer who argued that they inculcated "the culture of one-way war: we shoot and nobody shoots back." The inherent assumptions in this perception of war are profoundly dangerous. They can result in the belief that only when there is total military superiority—the possession of overwhelming operational advantages—should military operations be launched. This mindset is unhelpful at best, and potentially dangerous, because it squelches dialogue on which elements of superiority are most meaningful. One should be wary of putting the concept of superiority on so high a pedestal as to render real debate meaningless.[59] And above all, one would do well to recall that military superiority at the operational level throughout the post-9/11 wars did not deliver spectacularly successful results at the strategic level. Regardless of whether this was due to the character of these conflicts; the specific enemies encountered; the battlefields on which they were waged; the strategies pursued; or the civilian or military leaders who led these wars—or some combination of these elements—military superiority was clearly insufficient to achieve victory by itself. Part of the legacy of the post-9/11 wars, therefore, may be a military that, while learning to wage unconventional warfare, inadvertently developed a mindset that may inhibit its ability to fight competent conventional adversaries.

EXQUISITE CAPABILITIES: A FEATURE AND A BUG

Throughout these wars, the U.S. military also found itself relying on exquisite capabilities. It developed twin obsessions with precision and with shadows, best exemplified by two capabilities: special operations forces (SOF) and drones.[60] Each presented its own features and bugs, but, above all else, each became a crutch that made it easier to go to war more quietly and more precisely following the initial invasions of Afghanistan and Iraq. Indeed, both capabilities disrupted how the United States has fought. As one senior policymaker explained, the "problem of warfare historically is typically destroying the enemy once found . . . with terrorism, we have exactly the opposite problem and we've solved it . . . [we developed] an other-worldly lethality in finding and killing small numbers of people who don't want to be found and killed."

Since long before the post-9/11 wars kicked off, SOF have faced the challenge of being simultaneously misunderstood and mythologized. Much of the misunderstanding comes from confusion over how and in what ways SOF differ from and complement conventional forces.[61] After the 1980 Operation Eagle Claw debacle, when eight U.S. military personnel died attempting to rescue U.S. hostages in Iran due to a bungled command and control architecture and a lack of jointness across the U.S. military (among other reasons), Secretary of Defense Harold Brown leaned forward to support the formation of a counterterrorism-focused joint special operations force. Most notably, he made the decision to empower them based on limited input from other senior military leaders.[62]

Nevertheless, as one senior defense official recounted, SOF "were considered marginal" until Secretary of Defense Rumsfeld dramatically elevated and resourced them. In September 2001, they were unable to rapidly and effectively inform war planning to the extent Rumsfeld wanted them to be able to do, so he sought to empower SOF as much as possible.[63] For example, he authorized U.S. Special Operations Command (SOCOM) to become the global coordinator for terrorism.[64] Moreover, the al Qaeda Network Execute Order, the key Defense Department guidance on targeting al Qaeda after the September 11 attacks, gave SOCOM unparalleled powers to operate around the world and independent of the regional combatant commands.[65]

As the post-9/11 wars began, few appreciated how heavily SOF would, ultimately, be used. Their budgets soared, doubling within a few years, and they deployed around the world, particularly to the hot spots of Afghanistan and Iraq.[66] As of 2018, SOF were deployed to approximately 100 countries. Since they operate mostly in secret, SOF can be easily employed without most Americans or civilians in host countries having any cognizance of their presence or their mission.

Yet, the ways in which SOF have been employed over the last two decades is cause for serious concern. They have become "fungible," as one general officer explained, because formations like Navy SEALs, Army Rangers and Special Forces, and Marine Raiders were used interchangeably. Indeed, some interviewees rued misguided decisions to send Navy SEALs to places like Fallujah, Iraq, and the mountains of Afghanistan. An understanding of SOF's capabilities also was not always clear to those on the ground: "What the fuck am I going to do with these guys . . . . this is not their thing," complained one Marine who could not understand their purpose nor how they might be useful—and was surely demonstrating some parochial bureaucratic frustration, as well, given that SOF have become known for their comparative jointness forged by training and deploying together. Indeed, some have argued that the depth of their cooperation across services is better than cooperation within services, although there are fears that this jointness may be diminishing.[67] Still, this begs the question: What are SOF good for?

The simple answer is that they have overwhelmingly focused on finding and killing targets during the post-9/11 wars. This is a crucial mission, to be sure, albeit one that has come at the expense of their traditional focuses on waging unconventional warfare and working by, with, and through partners. "Nobody envisions special operations forces in anything besides counter-terrorism," sighed one general officer. Another military officer recounted that they were "somewhat hamstrung" from focusing on other types of missions because the "political leadership always wants them to get the bad guy." While these elite forces can execute a wide variety of missions, they, increasingly, are seen through this single "find and kill" aperture and are spending less time on their other missions—not least because of how well they have engaged in counterterrorism operations.

Moreover, the heavy reliance on SOF has taken a heavy toll on the special operations force. It's routine to hear about special operators with six, seven, or eight deployments.[68] These incessant deployments have resulted in a highly experienced force. "When you look at the ribbon racks of special operations forces, they look noticeably different than everybody else: we look like North Korean dictators," one senior special operator told me ruefully. They have also, however, resulted in an exhausted and spent force. In 2016, for the first time in U.S. history, the overwhelming majority of U.S. troops killed in combat were in special operations. This, from a force that comprises just 5 percent of the entire military personnel.[69]

SOF are, as named, special. They ballooned in the post-9/11 wars—more than doubling since 1999—but it is worth recalling the pride the special operations community takes in confidently declaring the "truth" that they "cannot be mass produced."[70] More than perhaps any part of the U.S. military, they possess bespoke capabilities.[71] The tipping point at which further expansion will come at the cost of the quality of the force is unclear, but at some level of growth and tempo of operations, the pool of special operators will be exhausted—both literally and figuratively. Indeed, a 2019–2020 review organized by the commander of SOCOM found that SOF were privileging combat experience as "the ultimate expression of competence" over "leadership, discipline, and accountability."[72] Responding to the review and the subsequent letter to the force issued by senior SOF leaders, some active-duty special operators vented their frustration over the criticism. "The military tells us to be savages, but now they want us to be choirboys," one of them slammed.[73] His response is particularly troubling, as an undisciplined and unruly force would violate the fundamental values that have characterized the U.S. military.

Going forward, the post-9/11 wars have confronted the special operations community with an existential question: On which missions should it focus? Invariably, policymakers will want it to continue hunting and killing terrorists. They likely will want it to play an outsized role in working with partner military forces, as well, given their specialized training and experience. But, as the military increasingly focuses on competing with China and Russia, SOF can and should play a role, given their historical focus on waging unconventional warfare. Future decisionmakers should consider the comparative strengths that these forces possess in certain types of conflicts and focus on exploiting those advantages rather than turning to them as an easy-button solution for any challenges that arise. Civilian policymakers and the military leadership will continue to face the age-old riddle posed by SOF, which is best encapsulated by scholar Alice Hunt Friend: "SOF capabilities are a . . . solution in search of a problem."[74]

Like SOF, unmanned aerial vehicles, known as drones, also became a heavily-relied-upon tool in the post-9/11 wars, and their influence on how the U.S. military goes to war is dramatic. Before exploring this, however, the language deserves a brief explanation. The Air Force pushed hard for drones to be referred to as "remotely piloted aircraft," or RPAs. Drone missions require human involvement at every key step, including purchasing, operating, and maintaining them. The Air Force, therefore, feared that using the term "unmanned" would encourage "misperception," as former Air Force Chief of Staff General Norton Schwartz explained.[75] One scholar found in her research that the "tail" for drone operations is long both in time and in personnel, and often severely underestimated by decisionmakers, lending some credence to General Schwartz's argument.[76]

Drones provided not just unparalleled reconnaissance abilities but also unparalleled attack capabilities. Thanks to them, it was "now easier for the United States to carry out killing operations at the ends of the earth than at any other time in its history," according to one journalist.[77] At first, the United States employed them sparingly, but soon the sortie rates skyrocketed. What had been a handful of drone strikes in Pakistan in 2005 grew by 400 percent in 2010.[78] And while such drone strikes became a near-regular occurrence in the wars of Iraq and Afghanistan, they bled into other conflict zones, as well. There were roughly "10 times the number" of strikes under President Obama's administration as under President Bush.[79] According to the Obama administration, it conducted 473 strikes from January 2009 through December 2015, during which the United States killed 2,372 to 2,581 combatants and 64 to 116 noncombatants.[80] However, these numbers are almost assuredly flawed given the difficulty of accurately assessing civilian casualties. In four countries, for example, the U.S. military claims that there have been approximately 100 or so civilian casualties, whereas nongovernmental organizations estimate that there have been nearly 11,000.[81]

Drones were not only cheap and effective at monitoring and killing—

particularly the influential and effective terrorist operatives known as "high value targets"—but also altered decisionmaking dynamics, particularly by enabling micromanagement.[82] They provided the opportunity for civilian and military leaders to watch operations minute by minute. It became like "battle porn . . . people want to watch the guy die," one officer disturbingly recounted. He particularly found this to be the case for the senior military leaders with whom he interacted, and he was concerned about the implications. From a safe distance, they satisfied their desire to participate in combat by watching others kill.

That dynamic, which is inherent in modern command and control architecture, applies to civilian national security policymakers as well. After numerous interviews with Obama administration officials, former policymaker and scholar Loren DeJonge Schulman found that drones altered decisionmaking dynamics in meaningful ways: they "both enable micromanagement and are themselves ripe for micromanaging—a practice that emphasizes the tactical over the strategic."[83] Because national security policymakers have limited time and attention, moreover, their tendency to prioritize the intelligence gleaned from, and the use of, drones has larger implications. In particular, drones have, like SOF, become a convenient solution to myriad challenges with potentially pernicious consequences for both statecraft and the effective management of force given the ability to wield them under the radar.

Those tasked with monitoring and launching drone operations also often have a unique experience of war. Air Force drone operators, for example, were generally not deployed overseas and, instead, commuted from home each day and were, therefore, at war on the home front in a way that most were not. Quoting one former operator, "I'd literally just walked out on dropping bombs on the enemy, and 20 minutes later I'd get a text—can you pick up some milk on your way home?"[84] While there are some changes ahead—for example, at Air Force Special Operations Command in Florida, drone operators now wear special uniforms to remind both themselves and those around them that they are at war—there is certainly more progress to be made.

Although fights over drone capabilities were painful throughout the Air Force, they were also crucial. "The 'Predator civil wars' was one of the most productive things we ever did. We took 10 years grappling with meanings," explained one operator who underscored that the Air Force is now much better prepared for the technology advances ahead.[85] Another officer put it more bluntly, saying that drones "went from [a] red headed stepchild to something that is almost respected now, entirely because of war." It provided operational capabilities for the Air Force that didn't exist before and could even shift the power balance in inter-service rivalries. For example, when the *Harry S. Truman* aircraft carrier was pulled out of the Middle East due to sequestration, drone strikes were used, instead, to kill Mohammed Emwazi (better known as "Jihadi John").

Respect for drone operators, however, is not yet universal. Former Air Force Chief of Staff General Schwartz recounts the knotty tale of trying to get a new medal for them, which represented the first new combat award in more than seven decades.[86] It was rescinded after complaints about its level, but the secretary of defense and the Air Force, nevertheless, issued new recognitions of the contributions of drone operators in 2016 and in 2019. There also, inevitably, will be more changes ahead. As one younger operator explained, the "older generation always saw Predators and Reapers as a tax they had to pay, and finally they can be rid of," but for his generation, "that partnership became a new story."

Increasingly, drones are now seen as complementing rather than competing with traditional platforms, likely because they have proven their utility and received the buy-in of senior leadership. Scholar Mark Cancian put it best: looking at the debate on RPAs, he bluntly declared that for "the Air Force, this revolution is over."[87] They have accepted that these capabilities are here to stay. The key questions will be how and why they are used rather than if or whether.

Going forward, other exquisite capabilities will, undoubtedly, inform the military's operations and how policymakers employ them. Offensive lethal autonomous weapons, which manage to be both widely and wildly misunderstood, appear to represent the next evolution.[88] They may enable better targeting of adversaries and offer decisionmakers new and different options in conflict.[89] The post-9/11 wars may, in fact, have delayed their production by focusing resources on operations rather than research. More notably, and aside from the last few years, the wars distracted the Department of Defense from giving serious and focused attention to the raft of ethical and operational questions they raise.

It is easy to say that humans rather than machines will make the important decisions in an artificial intelligence-infused national security system. Perhaps it is also lazy, because the availability of lethal autonomous weapons may reshape the management, employment, and development of military force with unexpected consequences. While the Defense Department has pledged humans will always make the ultimate decision about killing another human being,[90] there are, nevertheless, serious questions about what that means if artificial intelligence enables a weapons system that can "independently compose and select among alternative courses of action to accomplish goals based on its knowledge and understanding of the world, of itself, and of the local, dynamic context."[91]

That last issue—the context of the conflict—is particularly relevant, as policymakers will be more inclined to empower machines to make decisions under some circumstances rather than others.[92] For example, increasing delegated authority in the Western Pacific during a high-intensity war between the United States and China is distinct from delegating similar authority to conduct a targeted killing in a populous Pakistani city. When speed plays an outsized role, such as in a scenario requiring heavy missile defense capabilities, or when connectivity is limited so a system cannot consult a human for additional guidance, decisionmaking authority may be further devolved to machines, but anything that risks detaching the operational-level employment of lethal autonomous capabilities from consideration of its strategic-level consequences is inherently dangerous.[93]

The ethics of these capabilities, moreover, are dizzying. To be sure, the Defense Department is making crucial progress to promulgate principles of ethical use that are "responsible, equitable, traceable, reliable, and governable," per the Department's Defense Innovation Board.[94] Nevertheless, given expectations that U.S. adversaries may be less encumbered by such dilemmas, will the U.S. military be stuck choosing between operating ethically on the battlefield or losing a war? While some may hope war will become "bloodless" with such technological advancements, it is, perhaps, foolhardy to assume it also can achieve its ends under such circumstances.

Above all, national security policymakers must be cautious of believing they have absolute control over both autonomous systems as well as the course of their development—beliefs that the post-9/11 wars seemed to provide. Indeed, as a deputy assistant secretary of defense, I oversaw a review of Defense Department policy on autonomy in weapons systems and, throughout that process, often found myself, and others, clinging to a past that may no longer resemble the future.[95] Our ability to conceptualize the potential futures—both positive and nefarious—of these capabilities was imperfect and, to be frank, frightening.

FIGHTING THROUGH TACTICS: AD HOCKERY IN COUNTERING ROADSIDE BOMBS AND PROVINCIAL RECONSTRUCTION TEAMS

While political leadership warned within days after the September 11, 2001, attacks that, as President Bush explained, the war would be both "sweeping" and "sustained," the Defense Department's organizational approach was, nevertheless, exceedingly ad hoc.[96] As one retired senior general officer explained, "If you were to ask in January 2002: do we need to reorganize because we're going to be in this fight for 18 years, we might have done something different." Rather than making meaningful organizational adaptations to better fight the war, the Defense Department improvised through off-the-cuff processes—and often only when there was heavy pressure from the most senior civilian leadership, as demonstrated later. This was because, as the U.S. Army's study of the Iraq War describes, "the short-war assumption" plagued leaders.[97] Two examples merit exploration: the response to roadside bombs in conflict zones and the effort to coordinate civil-military efforts in the field. They demonstrate that a key organizational inheritance of this ad hockery is a tendency to change only under duress, and often too little, too late, and absent strategic reassessment.

Roadside bombs "accounted for up to 80% of soldier casualties" in Iraq by late 2006, but the Pentagon's bureaucracy took few meaningful steps to counter them until Secretary of Defense Robert Gates took a personal, heavy-handed approach to force it to do so.[98] These bombs, known as explosively formed penetrators (EFPs) and improvised explosive devices (IEDs), had horrific effects. One soldier described the experience of facing a roadside bomb in Iraq: "Boom, flash, chaos . . . I can only say this because I didn't get blown up. When . . . it's your patrol or your guys . . . those minutes after are horrible. What happened? What did I do wrong? And . . . I'm gonna go out tomorrow and have to do this again. And the next day. And the day after. It's its own torture."

During interviews for this book, junior officers recounted similar experiences. In one group interview, all four officers reported they had been hit on their first patrol. Many had daily engagements with roadside bombs, and one faced more than 800 IEDs in a single deployment. For the first few years of the threat, servicemembers took creative approaches driven by severe desperation to protect themselves and their vehicles, including filling them with sandbags and adding scraps of metal, or "hillbilly armor."[99] This usually was far from effective. In spring 2007, I visited Camp Arifjan, a sprawling U.S. base in Kuwait, and walked around the "boneyard"—a vast expanse of destroyed U.S. military vehicles that went as far as the eye can see. It was chilling.

Yet the Pentagon bureaucracy did not prioritize its response to these roadside bombs. When a senior Army general blamed the defense industry for being unable to quickly produce many more mine-resistant vehicles, he was quickly contradicted by the manufacturer, who underscored that the Pentagon had not requested that they do so.[100] One Marine, recounting his 2004 deployment to Iraq, explained that some "families were raising money . . . to get body armor shipped to the Marines because that hadn't come online fast enough to meet the needs of the IED-laden environment." To the chagrin of many, after hearing troops complain about serious problems with their equipment, Secretary Rumsfeld infamously quipped, "You go to war with the army you have, not the army you might want or wish to have at a later time," and then reminded his audience that armored vehicles were imperfect.[101] His response aligned well with the fledgling efforts by much of the rest of the senior military and political leadership in the Pentagon. As the threat continued and evolved during his tenure, scholars David Barno and Nora

Bensahel pointedly demonstrate that "institutional adaptation to this new challenge was a complete and utter failure."[102]

The real change came early in Secretary of Defense Robert Gates's tenure. Gates read in the newspaper that mine-resistant, ambush-protected vehicles, known as MRAPs, were saving considerably more Marines due to their "V"-shaped armored hull than the vulnerable Humvees (High Mobility Multi-Purpose Wheeled Vehicles) normally used to travel around Iraq. Gates quickly asked his civilian and military advisers about purchasing as many as possible, but most did not want to do so given the budgetary impact it would have on more sophisticated systems intended for conflicts beyond Iraq and Afghanistan.[103]

Gates was not deterred. He declared that MRAP purchases would be "the highest-priority Department of Defense acquisition program," and established a task force to brief him twice a month on the status of MRAP procurement.[104] Egregiously, even the Army's official history of the Iraq War whitewashes the Army leadership's role in pushing back against Gates's efforts. Instead, it takes a sterile approach, underscoring the budgetary tension in purchasing MRAPs compared to a more sophisticated capability that could be used in other conflicts, and asserts that "funding both priorities [was] impossible."[105] Simply put, as one former officer assessed ruefully, Iraq and Afghanistan were not seen by many military leaders as "the main effort" and, instead, they were "something to be engaged in while simultaneously preserving force structure for other fights still to come." The focus for many remained on future fights rather than on those where the force was currently engaged.

This view held in interviews with general officers, as well. One retired general officer criticized the MRAP program as an example of how "we've made a whole lot of tactical decisions by strategic decisionmakers." Perhaps this different assessment of the criticality of Gates's personal intervention is due to the dramatically different wartime experiences of general officers than more junior officers. As one officer explained:

> A lot of these generals don't realize they fought this war from a TOC [tactical operations center]. But they don't get the mental anguish. It's just different: when you're a battalion or brigade

commander, you feel like you're the master of the universe. When you're in that position, you don't think about those things. It's different when you're walking or driving and don't know if I'm going to get blown up.

From his perspective, senior military leaders may have been more responsive to the threat posed by roadside bombs if they had experienced them more intimately. Their rare encounters, particularly compared to junior and mid-grade officers, meant they did not internalize the imperative of countering this threat. This fierce intergeneration tension cannot be dismissed.

Gates's singular efforts paid off. While time-consuming—he spent three years forcing MRAPs on the Army, and even visited the Wisconsin plant that built the vehicles—he, nevertheless, succeeded in pushing a recalcitrant system into action, and the deployment of 27,000 MRAPs saved countless American lives in both Iraq and Afghanistan.[106] The issue was an emotional one for him. Recounting meeting a soldier at Walter Reed hospital who survived because of MRAPs, Gates explained, "I managed to keep my composure—barely."[107]

It is hard to imagine that servicemembers who went through this experience have much sympathy for the bureaucratic inertia that resulted in such a delayed response. The system took too long to support them in combat, and they likely take with them skepticism over its ability to yield vital capabilities in a timely manner in future wars. While there exist real problems in Gates's willingness to sidestep traditional processes—it both undermined the Defense Department's systems and reduced the longevity of many of his efforts—it is hard to imagine the Pentagon bureaucracy responding to this threat in a timely manner absent his personal intervention. As scholar Sharon Weiner found, "the MRAP was delayed because the services had already decided to invest in other vehicles regardless of whether they were appropriate for current or future combat operations."[108] Similar to Robert Komer's infamous indictment during the Vietnam War—that efforts to win using standard operating procedures were ineffectual—bureaucracy continued to do its thing in the post-9/11 wars.[109]

Bureaucracy also did its thing to derail civilian contributions to the war effort. A good example of this was a new construct established in Afghanistan in 2002 and then exported to Iraq to facilitate civil-military coordination in the field: provincial reconstruction teams (PRT), a name changed from joint regional teams based on President Karzai's view that "warlords rule regions; governors rule provinces."[110] Their clunky manifestation, however, made the military believe it was at war alone, and the lack of civilians forced the military personnel on the PRTs to dabble in diplomacy and development, thereby deepening the civilian-military divide.

Unfortunately, the PRT concept was plagued both by confusion over its purpose and insufficient resourcing.[111] Although PRTs spread across Afghanistan, they overwhelmingly consisted of U.S. troops, with very small representation of U.S. diplomats and U.S. aid workers. These numbers barely improved over the years. As then Secretary of Defense Donald Rumsfeld wrote in a memo, by late 2006, "the percentage of non-military personnel in the Afghan PRTs had increased from 2 percent to a disappointing 3 percent."[112] Yet Secretary of State Condoleezza Rice would not require foreign service officers to serve in Iraq or Afghanistan even though she had the ability to do so; indeed, she expressed her perturbation when General George Casey explained that there were not enough diplomats in Iraq in front of President Bush.[113]

Above all, this capacity imbalance between civilian agencies and the military furthered an unhealthy dynamic. Civilian personnel often felt misunderstood, unsupported, and perceived as subordinate to the military rather than as equal partners in reconstruction. Military personnel often were frustrated that their counterparts were junior, had limited clout with their respective agencies, and did brief tours.[114] Lamenting how few foreign service officers were stationed at her PRT in Afghanistan, one military officer said, "I worked with three different State Department officers in ten months, and that was frustrating and really unfortunate."[115] In Iraq, although the surge increased the number of PRTs to fourteen, the goal of 450 civilian personnel based in those PRTs was never achieved, and many of the civilians who did show up were either Defense Department civilians or contractors rather than foreign service officers or development personnel from the U.S. Agency for International Development (USAID).[116] This also fostered resentment and frustration at senior levels of the Defense Department and the Army.[117]

The ad hoc establishment and management of PRTs also demonstrated that the United States had failed to remember and apply lessons from a similar but more successful effort from the Vietnam War: the Civil Operations and Revolutionary Development Support (CORDS) program. CORDS represented civil-military cooperation and integration in the field at its best, because large numbers of capable civilians were incorporated into a construct under a single chain of command.[118] Indeed, senior civilian adviser to Secretary Rumsfeld Marin Strmecki underscored that PRTs were "an echo of them [CORDS], but without the full system that made CORDS work."[119] CORDS worked because they empowered one individual to command all relevant U.S. personnel. They even included a civilian ambassador in the military chain of command, and went so far as to assign military personnel evaluations to foreign service officers.[120] Given the vital role these ratings play in shaping military personnel careers, this last point underscores just how seriously CORDS civilian leaders were empowered. Similar empowerment was absent from the PRTs. Retired Brigadier General Brian Copes outlined a fundamental challenge PRTs faced: senior general officers "should answer" to the State Department in guiding PRTs but "you would be hard pressed to find a military commander willing to relinquish control."[121] Unfortunately, as was often the case in the post-9/11 wars, historical lessons were tossed aside in favor of often-convoluted and ad hoc approaches.

Throughout the post-9/11 wars, the military's views about going to war were shaped in key areas. While in many ways the military found itself with the upper hand in the wars, particularly in terms of resource prioritization and operational capabilities, it also often found itself on its own—invariably contributing to and exacerbating the crisis of caring and the crisis of meaningful civilian control. The legacies for how it plans wars, pays for wars, and perceives their character will unavoidably inform how it prepares for and wages war in the future—issues explored in more depth in chapter 6.

6

How the Military Wages War

"Every service fights its own war."

As the previous chapter's discussion of special forces and drones began to explore, fighting for nearly two decades has shaped the U.S. military's expertise in and understanding of warfare. Much of the force has specialized in unrelenting and inconclusive conflicts against terrorists and insurgents. Each military service, however, has undergone a bespoke transformation on the basis of its idiosyncratic experience; to abridge James Jones's *The Thin Red Line: Every Man Fights His Own War*, "every service fights its own war."[1] These experiences also have colored how different parts of the military view one another, and they have influenced the balance of power between the services and the combatant commands (COCOM). This will shape how the military wages war in the future—and in potentially unexpected ways.

BALANCING ACROSS THREATS

To understand some of the defense choices made during the last two decades of war, it helps to have an appreciation of what Kathleen Hicks terms the "iron triangle of painful trade-offs."[2] As she aptly describes, the challenge for the Defense Department is "to maintain a reasonable balance among three factors: preparing to be ready today (readiness), preparing to be ready tomorrow (investment), and sizing the force (structure)."[3] The bigger the force is, the more it costs to keep it ready and to keep it modernized. A large force with insufficient funding for readiness or investments is a hollow force. It may look powerful on paper, but it is not capable of effectively waging war. To add even more complexity, there exist multiple triangles: one for the entire U.S. military and one for each military service. For example, the entire U.S. military may now be shifting its focus toward great power competition and preparing for future great power conflict in line with the 2018 National Defense Strategy, but portions of it will need to remain focused on threats like terrorism and other challenges familiar to the post-9/11 wars.[4] Taken together, this geometry precludes radical change—even in the face of serious threats—and makes it particularly difficult to reallocate resources.

There are no perfect solutions to these "painful trade-offs." Instead, senior Defense Department officials must bet and hedge across them in line with implementing strategic guidance. They must be cognizant of opportunity costs and how to balance priorities in response to changing threats. Doing so can best be conceptualized as a matter of implicit judgment rather than mechanical allegiance to an ordinally ranked "1 to x" list of priorities. They may seek to make meaningful, not marginal, change, but doing so entails picking bureaucratic winners and losers and is, therefore, both daunting and taxing. This, in turn, requires awareness of which sides have been neglected, the consequences of that neglect, and a willingness to adjust to ensure there is no chronic damage. For example, while the 2018 National Defense Strategy prioritizes competition with China and then Russia, it also underscores that the U.S. military cannot ignore the Middle East and must consider how best to take risk in that region.[5] Of course, given these dilemmas and the costs of resolving them, requesting more money to increase each service's overall budget—growing the triangular pie so that each service can take a bigger bite—is often the easiest (and also the intellectually laziest) response.[6]

EACH SERVICE TELLS A STORY

Understanding the impact of fighting wars for nearly two decades requires a deep examination of each military service's specific experiences. Some of a service's story can be attributed to its historical experience, some can be attributed to its role in specific post-9/11 wars, and some can be attributed to its leadership.[7]

Sensitivity to each of these factors matters. As West Point professor Elizabeth Samet cautions, "The universalizing of wartime experience ignores differences in rank, branch, and service culture; in the nature of the conflict; in the duration of combat service; in the length of a military career."[8] Similarly, as one official underscored, "There's a battle within the military on what the . . . baggage should be." He hastened to emphasize intra-service differences, as well, describing them like "rings on a tree." Each one tells its own story. This chapter offers a textured diagnosis of each service's inheritance and how it may be addressed. The impact on individual military personnel is explored in the next chapter.

The U.S. Army: "Putting Your Young Men in the Mud"

The U.S. Army, the oldest and, traditionally, the biggest military service in the United States, was overwhelmingly on the front lines throughout the post-9/11 wars. Before these conflicts kicked off, the relatively few and small size of most conflicts involving the United States over the preceding decades meant that "most people in the army didn't have operational experience," according to one senior general officer. This changed rapidly. Of the nearly 3 million service members who have been deployed for the Iraq and Afghanistan wars, the Army provided the largest contribution.[9] In the first decade of the post-9/11 wars, for example, soldiers represented more than half of the U.S. military deployments to the primary war zones.[10] And early in the wars, particularly in Iraq, the Army was able to achieve some important victories.

However, the Army faced real challenges as civil war and insurgency soared, and it grew understandably resentful of Washington's unwillingness to counter the Iranian-supported clients who fomented violence that killed more than 600 American military personnel and wounded untold others.[11] At the broadest level, there is a compelling argument that two decades of waging wars without achieving conclusive strategic victories shaped the Army more profoundly than any of the other military services (table 6-1).

Some argue the Army came out of these wars in better shape than the Air Force, Marine Corps, or Navy. Certainly, it appears to have come out healthier than it did from the Vietnam War, a conflict in which "the Army was broken and sought to heal itself . . . [it] had wounds that would take a long time to heal," as General Stanley McChrystal described.[12] One general officer underscored that his generation "grew up being inculcated in how the Army destroyed itself in Vietnam [so] in everything we did, there was this voice that said: don't screw this up a second time." The Army took a number of steps early in the post-9/11 wars to avoid hollowing out the force, as had occurred during the Vietnam War, such as rotating units rather than individuals and preserving the noncommissioned officer corps. It maintained its ballast and did not see the indiscipline or severe hollowing out that had occurred previously.

Yet others argue that the Army, nonetheless, has emerged in grim shape. In particular, it became severely unbalanced. Its end-strength (the Army term for capacity, or the number of soldiers in the force) grew during the height of the post-9/11 wars, and it understandably prioritized winning on the battlefield at the expense of long-term modernization programs. But as the wars started to ramp down a decade ago, Army leaders proved reluctant to make personnel cuts. Over the last decade, they continued to prioritize maintaining and growing end-strength, which exacerbated not just the previous decade's repeated deferral of modernization but also a series of poor capability investment choices, like the failed Crusader artillery system and Future Combat Systems.[13]

Whereas, historically, the Army's personnel numbers have been cut

TABLE 6-1. Characteristics of Deployment by Service and Component

	Army		Navy		Marine Corps		Air Force	
	Active	Reserve	Active	Reserve	Active	Reserve	Active	Reserve
Deployments	1,049,771	503,507	506,423	43,375	351,704	46,918	497,186	194,946
Service members	608,166	371,871	31,8479	31,996	225,691	39,179	262,214	92,543
One Deployment	50.0%	67.2%	49.9%	60.4%	53.3%	74.1%	46.4%	40.1%
>1 Deployment	50.0%	32.8%	50.1%	39.7%	46.7%	25.9%	53.6%	59.9%
Number of Deployments								
1	50.0%	67.2%	49.9%	60.4%	53.3%	74.1%	46.4%	40.1%
2	29.8%	24.4%	31.0%	24.1%	33.9%	19.1%	27.1%	26.4%
3+	20.2%	8.4%	19.1%	15.5%	12.8%	6.8%	26.5%	33.5%
Deployment Length (months)								
Mean (SD)	9.93±3.82	9.08±3.40	5.98±2.56	6.54±3.39	6.69±2.82	6.91±2.90	4.72±2.06	3.14±1.92
Median	11.4	9.7	6.1	7.0	6.7	6.9	4.3	2.8
Total Time Deployed (months)								
Mean (SD)	9.43±4.15	8.79±3.65	5.78±2.51	6.21±3.50	6.60±2.72	6.60±2.89	4.42±2.04	2.77 ±1.79
Median	11.1	9.5	6.1	7.0	6.7	6.9	4.2	2.1

Source: Marlene Gubata and others, "Accession Medical Stands Analysis and Research Activity 2013 Annual Report," AMSARA Department of Epidemiology, Preventative Medicine Program, Walter Reed Army Institute of Research, May 29, 2013, https://apps.dtic.mil/dtic/tr/fulltext/u2/a580689.pdf, p. 8.

between wars, particularly for cost-savings and based on a view that personnel can be surged in wartime more easily than materiel,[14] efforts by senior civilian leaders to scale down the size of the Army in recent years has met with severe resistance from an Army leadership that, instead, pushed—and continue to push—for a larger force. General Mark Milley, former chief of staff of the Army and currently the CJCS, declared that he and his predecessor "fought hard" against those who sought to make the Army smaller.[15] Much of their effort was based on trauma from the post-9/11 wars, particularly from when the Army was forced to enact a "stop loss" order that kept soldiers in involuntary service beyond their commitments because the force was too small to wage the Iraq and Afghanistan wars simultaneously.

Others argue, however, that this push against prioritizing Army modernization was, instead, because these wars were not seen as "the main effort" but, rather, "something to be engaged in while simultaneously preserving force structure [Army end-strength] for other fights to come," as one former officer criticized. Regardless of the reason, two former senior policymakers howled, the Army "lost a generation of modernization" because of its emphasis on personnel, and when it did make investments in the force, those platforms were "the same thing the Army bought in 1980."

The decision to preserve the Army's size at all costs is a product of how the Army perceives itself. One officer described how "the story of the Army is that from the beginning, people get it wrong and they downsize us, but then war comes and we have to do all the things they said we're not going to have to do . . . the constant story is 'I told you so.'" In his view, the book *This Kind of War* by T. R. Fehrenbach, a masterful history of the Army experience in the Korean War, explains the Army's perspective most aptly: "You may fly over a land forever; you may bomb it, atomize it, pulverize it, and wipe it clean of life—but if you desire to defend it, protect it, and keep it for civilization, you must do this on the ground, the way the Roman legions did, by putting your young men in the mud."[16]

Every officer in the Army "feels this quote in his marrow . . . in your soul, you think you will always have to have a muddy boot on the ground," this soldier told me. It is ingrained in the Army ethos. It also suggests a sentimentalized sense of superiority within the Army regarding its role in war that characterized many of the Army interviews I conducted. This superiority also may travel to the Marine Corps, as well, since at least one Marine—then Secretary of Defense Mattis—quoted it when asked for his views of a potential U.S. war with North Korea.[17]

Coupled with the inconclusive victories of nearly two decades of war, other steps the Army took heightened this inherited neuralgia. Some specialties focused on missions that differed from their capabilities, like the artillery branch. One retired senior general officer criticized the artillery for not living up to its "King of Battle" motto. However, that was invariably tied to the character of the post-9/11 conflicts; artillery personnel played a much smaller role compared to the infantry during the counterinsurgency fights in Iraq and Afghanistan. As one non-infantry Army captain lamented, "We were the red-headed step-child . . . all the love went to the infantry."[18]

The Army and the Marines also increased waivers for recruits who had felonies or misdemeanors on their records. At the height of the post-9/11 wars, the Army granted these waivers to nearly 20 percent of new recruits, a sign of desperation that validated the concerns of those who sought to keep the Army as large as possible for as long as possible.[19] And the Army minimized opportunities for its leaders to reflect on their experiences (and, thus, learn from the wars). As one general officer noted, the Army "waived a lot of education requirements to keep officers and NCOs in the fight."[20]

Moreover, the Army grew "tired," as a different general officer lamented. He was echoing Secretary of the Army John McHugh's very first meeting with incoming Secretary of Defense Leon Panetta in 2011. As Panetta recalls, McHugh said, "'Mr. Secretary . . . the army is tired' and he explained [it] had lost more soldiers than any other service during the Iraq and Afghanistan wars, and it was showing the strain."[21] Samet observes how her cadets became downtrodden as the wars hit their nadir.[22]

This enervation reflected a growing aversion within the Army leadership to taking operational risks. As one soldier explained, fighting in the post-9/11 wars "built in me this belief that the most important thing is saving a U.S. soldier's life" rather than successfully completing the mission. In that vein, a general officer complained that "everything was 'ask for permission'" rather than being sufficiently empowered to take risks. Perhaps most worryingly, the Army has been described as "aggrieved [and] the martyr," according to one officer. One retired senior general officer explained the Army's perspective as believing "we're owed some more support . . . we were carrying the heavy load . . . you have to help restore us and make us whole," but he sympathetically argued that this "argument will go nowhere; it's understandable but unpersuasive."

Although the Army has done a slightly better job of learning lessons from the post-9/11 wars than it did after the Vietnam War, it still has taken problematic steps. In 2005, for example, it suppressed a study by the RAND Corporation about post-war Iraq—a story that itself took three years to come out. The study, reflective of the usual rigor and analysis that characterizes RAND's work, was heavily criticized by Army leaders and buried after its publication. This likely was due to a combination of factors, including senior Army leaders' perturbation over the criticism and, more notably, their fear that the study would elicit a harsh reaction from Secretary of Defense Rumsfeld.[23]

More than a decade later, then Chief of Staff of the Army Raymond Odierno, who believed the Army had suffered because it was unwilling to examine its role in Vietnam, sponsored another study on Iraq. This, too, lingered unpublished after his retirement as other senior Army leaders grew concerned that its findings were too controversial.[24] Some senior Army leaders were worried that it was too unkind to their peers, although it is, ironically, much kinder to Army leaders such as General George Casey than other accounts. Others thought it should "focus its conclusions more on military operations instead of policy," and some historians expressed concern over its research methods.[25] However flawed the study may be—and to be sure, it is extremely flawed, given its laser-like focus on faulting Washington bureaucrats rather than taking a serious and disciplined look at how the Army and its leadership contributed to the war's execution and outcome— it, nevertheless, represents an important first step for the Army to reconcile the legacy of these wars.[26]

More steps, of course, are necessary, lest life imitate the *Duffel Blog*'s art. Years before the Army finally published its Iraq War study, *Duffel Blog* mocked the Army's unwillingness to acknowledge the lessons learned from the post-9/11 wars, satirically quoting then Secretary of Defense Chuck Hagel as reporting that "we expect [the Army] to completely eliminate and/or discourage the retention of any human memory of either Afghanistan or Iraq by fiscal 2016."[27]

Going forward, the Army's officers will need to adjust to a security environment devoid of constant strenuous deployments, one that still includes some need to counter terrorists and insurgents and is, potentially, punctuated by large-scale conventional conflicts. Its dilemma over prioritization of threats will continue to be vexing and likely will focus on heavy maneuver operations in Europe and Korea, although that may be made slightly easier should the situation in Pyongyang shift in a positive direction.[28] As Samet explains, "For a generation of officers who have spent their entire careers commuting to war, peacetime would feel anything but normal."[29] She found that many West Point cadets were unclear about how to judge success in the Army, both personally and professionally, given that the force still saw "combat experience as the paramount validation" and they had been "conditioned since their first day in uniform as new cadets—well before, for the many who define themselves primarily as a post-9/11 generation—to become veterans of particular wars," an opportunity which would be limited to many of them over at least the near-term.[30]

One former soldier recalled being struck by meeting ROTC cadets in 2016. As he described it, "There was no talk of [deploying] to solve something or to end something . . . it was to participate, to do their part, [and] to get their combat patch," which he decried as losing sight of the mission. While this tendency is not anomalous, it does represent an expectation that likely will be unmet for many, with negative repercussions. Similarly, one retired senior general officer recounted how his children who serve in the Army today don't really understand what it means to be in an Army that isn't at war: "My kids poke me on this: how could you be in the Army for so many years and only be in combat for a few days here and there? How could you stand being in an Army that wasn't at war? They are baffled about why anyone would want to do that." Unless and until the Army finds a way to answer such questions, it will struggle to move past its post-9/11 wars' inheritance.

"The Marine Corps Has an Identity Crisis"

In many ways, and like in many previous wars, the U.S. Marine Corps made an outsized contribution relative to its small size to the post-9/11 wars. The heavy reliance on ground combat and on task organizing (or, designing a force for a certain mission) played to the Marine Corps's strengths. The cultural predisposition of the Marines—to be the toughest force around and to push as hard as possible regardless of the price—stood in stark contrast to the Army's more deliberate organizational approach to resourcing the wars. The Marines have a "'can do' attitude," emphasized one senior officer, and that pushed the service into a key role during the wars. More deeply, however, the Marines's fear of being excluded or sidelined bureaucratically shaped their approach throughout these conflicts.[31]

The Marine Corps jumped directly into the post-9/11 wars. Wartime deployments became routinized, although they also were generally shorter than Army deployments. One general officer emphasized that "30 years ago . . . it was a big deal to get a unit ready to go on board ship to rotate to the Mediterranean or Okinawa [and] you focused almost a year's effort preparing for the deployment next year." But after nearly two decades of continuous deployments, another Marine explained, the Marine Corps has become "very good at task organizing and deploying forces in a different way than in the past." Similar to the Army, Marine officers and NCOs became highly professionalized as they cycled through deployments.

One senior general officer highlighted the benefits of accumulated combat experience across the force, noting that "we've got another 15-20 years and we'll still have combat veterans leading the Marine Corps," which will, thus, shape "discussions . . . investments, and training" for generations. This substantive firsthand experience in combat, he believed, probably will make them both more willing to shake the system when necessary to support Marines in the field and imbue in them a sense that wars can go on exceedingly long.

However, the Marine leadership's desire to lead and own parts of the war, exacerbated by a wariness of relying on other services, had serious implications for the force. First, the Marines bore considerable casualties. Some interviewees questioned whether at least some of these were caused by the leadership taking unwise steps like insisting on their own area of operations in Marja, Afghanistan, and building an expensive aviation fleet plagued by mishaps. Second, the Marine Corps's comparative advantages vis-à-vis the other military services has grown fuzzy. "The Marine Corps has an identity crisis: it's crisis response, it's high end, it's low end," lamented one senior general officer. "Your average Marine was, in many respects, just interchangeable with the soldiers," explained a different general officer. Indeed, the Marine Corps's fundamental identity crisis is shaped by the fact that this ostensibly naval-oriented service spent a generation serving as a second land army. A third general officer underscored how the Marine Corps's role in Iraq and Afghanistan "clearly did damage to our relationship with the Navy, our identity as a sea service, and part of the maritime force," because the Marines were overwhelmingly focused on their ground capabilities.

All these views are echoed at more junior levels, as well; one mid-grade officer published a pleading piece, "Sir, Who Am I?" in which he delineated the multiple identities and responsibilities of today's Marine Corps and begged the incoming commandant to resolve them.[32] Given historic pressures to fold the Marine Corps into the other services—which remain an existential motivator for the Marines even today—this confusion over its purpose and relevance is particularly notable.

The iron triangle framework helps explain the Marine Corps's challenges during the post-9/11 wars. While some of its equipment was high quality—as one officer quipped, "Some of the stuff we carry you would be comfortable buying at REI"—it faced problems with capacity, capability, and readiness. To grow quickly from 175,000 to 180,000 Marines in 2006 to 202,000 by 2012, the Corps "started inducting necessarily a wider quality spread [and] it became a euphemism: 202K Marine," explained one officer.[33] He was politely explaining that the Marine Corps had lowered its standards to increase its recruiting numbers, which had serious implications for the broader force. Among the biggest crises for the Marine Corps became its aviation portfolio, which grew impracticably pricey and suffered from a number of accidents due to readiness challenges.[34] Perhaps most notably, the Marine Corps struggled to meet its mandate—to "be the most ready when the nation is generally least ready"—as the force underwent incessant rotations in high-operational-tempo environments for so many years.[35] "We deferred scheduled maintenance to keep stuff in the fight or at sea, [so] you now have a situation where [equipment is] less ready, costlier, less predictable, and when it does fail, it is catastrophic," warned one Marine.

While concern over operational risks was justified, it also veered into the impractical. One officer discussed how protective gear requirements grew from vehicles without armor during the first part of the Iraq invasion into requirements for Kevlar sleeves, Kevlar pants, special eye protection, and even combat diapers. The result veered into the tragicomic. He described how, given the scorching weather in Afghanistan, Marines who were already carrying 120 pounds of equipment did not want to wear a combat diaper, but that if they did not and were injured, he would be blamed. The result, like in the Army, was an emphasis in minimizing tactical and operational risks: "Any time a Marine got hurt, first report I got was to itemize all the protective equipment he was wearing . . . if I put none, I was a bad leader . . . the pressure there is don't friggin' get hurt." However, when compared to the Army's unwillingness to invest in MRAPs, as outlined in the previous chapter, the Marines's emphasis on investing in protective gear, despite its strained resources elsewhere, is striking.

Going forward, the Marine Corps will need to reconcile its surf-or-turf identity crisis while also rehabilitating its force. Given that the Marines have the highest turnover rate of any military service as a matter of force design, it may be best positioned to address the legacies of the post-9/11 wars, because a smaller percentage of the force will have experienced them.[36]

Above all, the willingness of Marine Corps Commandant General David Berger to release what can only be described as provocative commandant's planning guidance in 2019 represents the best opportunity for the Marine Corps to reconcile and rehabilitate. His guidance takes on every sensitive issue for the Marines, including ship numbers, presence, organizing constructs, capability investments, divestments, personnel changes, and operating concepts. In urging the Marines to return to their naval roots, Berger bluntly declared, "We cannot afford to retain outdated policies, doctrine, organizations, or force development strategies."[37] In 2020, he declared that the future Marine Corps would not focus on massive amphibious assaults, an assertion so dramatic that scholar Michael O'Hanlon underscored that it "is almost as if John Madden had just said that in the NFL, it will no longer be important to run the football."[38] The moment is ripe for the Marine Corps to tackle its inheritances; it is the furthest ahead of any of the services thanks to General Berger and the commandant's planning guidance, but its success remains to be seen.

The Air Force: "We Never Went Home"

In contrast to the other military services, the legacy of being embroiled in seemingly endless war does not begin on September 11, 2001, for the Air Force. Instead, its story starts with the Persian Gulf War and rolls right into the post-9/11 wars. The Air Force "has been in continuous combat operations since 1990; we never went home," explained one senior Air Force leader who described how Operations Northern and Southern Watch involved the Air Force securing Iraqi airspace from the end of the Persian Gulf War up to the beginning of the 2003 Iraq War.[39] More bitterly, a retired general officer asserts, "People forget that . . . that has taken a toll on the force."

This narrative suggests a melancholic view that the Air Force has been snubbed. Moreover, in facing an enemy that couldn't fight back over the last few decades, the Air Force became used to a certain type of conflict.[40] One retired general officer wonders, "Twenty years when I look back, did we misunderstand how lucky we have been to have air superiority?" Scholars Nora Bensahel and David Barno recount a telling exchange between a current and a former senior Air Force leader, in which the former discussed upgrading the biannual Red Flag exercise to face a more sophisticated adversary and the latter responded, "Oh, you mean *war*?"[41] The risk is that the Air Force will be insufficiently ready to fight in an environment where it faces a real threat.

The Air Force has, therefore, inherited some of the thorniest legacies of all. To be sure, much of this is self-inflicted rather than an inevitable consequence of the post-9/11 wars. It faced serious problems along all three legs of the iron triangle: capacity, capability, and readiness. Its capacity plummeted as older aircraft were retired and fewer, more expensive aircraft were purchased. The fighter force decreased by 50 percent, and overall airplane numbers and squadrons decreased by 30 percent despite creative reorganizations of fighter wings.[42] Many Air Force pilots received deep but circumscribed training that, like their operational experiences, focused overwhelmingly on close air support missions in support of ground forces. "We've worn out most of our equipment," lamented one general officer, although it is worth recalling that the Air Force managed to fulfill new equipment requests, like F-35A strike fighters, through overseas contingency operations funds even as it wanted to retire legacy platforms like A-10s.

On the personnel front, airmen were seen as interchangeable with ground forces in what were known as "in lieu of" deployments. These deployments involved airmen and sailors filling roles that would traditionally be filled by soldiers or Marines. At the height of the post-9/11 wars in 2007, the Air Force was filling more than 6,000 in lieu of roles, which represented nearly 25 percent of its CENTCOM deployments at that time, and it had deployed a total of 22,000 personnel since 2004 to fill this requirement.[43] The Air Force "declared its 'all in' policy," according to one senior official, because the ground forces were "fighting and dying . . . [and] the numbers they had were not enough, so its leadership came to the Air Force and the Navy and said, 'you guys have to take your turn.'" It was "an emotional argument," he underscored—"my guys are dying while your guys are playing golf"—but also hard to refuse. Because of this policy, "airmen were sent to do convoy security," explained one senior Air Force leader, and another general officer articulated how the Air Force became "so flexible that you could pull an individual airman . . . to do something for the joint force that someone else could have done."

The Air Force seemed to be caught between two heavily flawed options: to support the post-9/11 wars by hollowing out the force or to focus on future threats to the detriment of the current wars. In the end, the Air Force leadership was forced, against its strenuous resistance, to hollow out its force. Interestingly, one Army general officer compared the Air Force's inheritance to that of the Army during the Vietnam War: just as "the Army came out of Vietnam hollow," the "Air Force came out of this war hollow." Because the Air Force "did not live through what we lived through in Vietnam," they "rotated individuals over nearly 20 years . . . they did this with pilots, their backbone," he declared, although there is very little evidence that the Air Force sent many pilots on in lieu of assignments, which overwhelmingly consisted of enlisted personnel. Nevertheless, this had been a "self-inflicted wound," agreed another general officer, that infected the entire force for little service-level benefit, as it got little credit for its role in what were seen as primarily ground fights.

While the Air Force served in a "supporting" role for the Army and the Marines, who were the "supported" services, it did so at substantial costs and with minimal recognition. To be sure, there is much justification for this relatively minimal recognition; these wars simply did not affect the Air Force or the Navy the way they affected the Army and the Marine Corps. Yet airmen had a difficult time amid ad hoc and short deployments that exacerbated perceptions that their service's role was less critical than others. "We traded people we needed to think about the future to people who saw the elephant, loved the war for five years, then got worn out over five more," lamented one senior general officer. Failing to seriously focus on future threats has led many in the Air Force to question "why did I lose all this time," he explained—which is different from the ground forces, who, instead, question "why did I lose all these guys?" These issues paired in a discomfiting way with the summary dismissal of the Air Force's contribution to the post-9/11 by servicemembers from other services. The *Duffel Blog*, thus, struck painfully at an issue airmen wrestle with when it ran a piece in which the secretary of the Air Force declares that "the Air Force would limit future rotations to Afghanistan to a three-hour tour with free lunch."[44]

When the Air Force did try to focus on future threats, it was clumsy at best. The previous chapter addressed how it struggled with moving toward a more unmanned force. More significantly, the infamous debacle over the F-22 air superiority fighter from 2008 to 2009 demonstrated the Air Force leadership's clumsiness in designing the service's future structure. The F-22 was the most sophisticated fighter jet in the world, and the Air Force had hoped to build 381 of them. Then Secretary of Defense Robert Gates complained that "nearly every time" he met with the Air Force leadership, "it was about a new bomber or more F-22s," but as Gates reminds readers, "We had been at war for ten years, and the plane had not flown a single combat mission."[45]

More broadly, Gates "had a perception that the Air Force wasn't fully committed to the fight in Iraq and Afghanistan," explained General Norton Schwartz.[46] That frustration was further magnified by two separate and egregious nuclear mishaps in which nuclear weapons were mistakenly transported from North Dakota to Louisiana and nuclear parts were mistakenly sent to Taiwan—and no one higher than a colonel was blamed.[47] The result was Gates's decision to fire both the secretary of the Air Force and the chief of staff of the Air Force.[48] The firings were "like a scene out of a Tom Clancy thriller," explained General Schwartz, who was brought in as the new chief of staff of the Air Force after his predecessor's removal.[49] Notably, Schwartz represented the first Air Force chief of staff with a transport and special operations background, and he surely was selected as someone from outside of the "fighter mafia" in the hopes of shaking up the service at a critical moment. Not long after new leadership was in place, Gates decided the Air Force should purchase no more than 187 F-22s, given basing plans, costs, the fact that the Air Force was going to get more than 1,700 F-35s, the need for additional funding for drones, and, ultimately, his concerns about the F-22's utility in the current wars.[50]

Gates's decisions to fire the Air Force's top leadership and to shrink the F-22 purchase came up in nearly every single Air Force interview I conducted. Some interviewees remain bitter and frustrated, accurately pointing out how the security environment has since shifted to prioritize high-end conflict that will require more air superiority platforms; a former official described the Air Force's mindset as "the chickens that we told you would come have come home to roost." This, however, ignores both the perilous state of the wars in 2006 through 2008 and, as one senior official explained, epitomizes the Air Force narrative that "Gates screwed us." As another former official put it, many in the Air Force feel a "sense of frustration and resentment" because they knew the force needed more F-22s than it could realistically purchase.

Instead of the "I told you so" refrain that generally came up during Air Force interviews, one senior general officer gave a very different account that blames the service itself for some of its problems:

> The lesson that it should have taught us as airmen does not appear to be the lesson it did. It should have taught us about the need for diversity in our leadership cohort—people who bring different perspectives and can see other sides of a problem. When a significant portion of the Air Force's senior leadership cohort shares the same background and set of experiences, as it did in 2006, it shouldn't surprise us to find we may have trouble hearing what our boss is telling us; it is filtered through our own homogenous and flawed perceptions of the environment.

He went on to highlight how "381 F-22s" seemed like the Air Force's answer to every question Secretary Gates posed. While acknowledging that this was a caricature, he, nevertheless, noted that the Air Force tried to claim that the F-22 was the appropriate platform to satisfy Gates's priorities for fighting the post-9/11 war: ISR and close air support. He went on to explain:

> Our perception of the environment was that we needed 381 F-22s and that self-reinforcing narrative, without any dissenting voices in a homogeneous leadership cohort, caused us to miss what our boss was telling us. The lesson we should have learned out of that fiasco was we need to grow a more diverse senior leader cohort in the Air Force. Instead, 12 years down the path, we find that we basically replaced one set of pilots [in senior leadership] with a different set of pilots [in the same positions].

This senior general officer correctly identifies that the Air Force's inheritance from the post-9/11 wars goes far beyond a flawed iron triangle. Instead, it failed to learn lessons from arguably the most traumatic episodes the Air Force has faced in decades. According to him, this was fundamentally a leadership failure in which homogeneity undermined efficacy.

If he is right, then the Air Force must make colossal change going forward. Its decision to change promotion policies so that those airmen identified early in their careers as the best leaders do not have quite so automatic a path forward is a small but necessary step.[51] Its growing obsession over capacity is not, however. In late 2018, the Air Force took a page out of the Army and Navy handbooks by conducting a force structure assessment that called for its growth from 312 operational fighter squadrons to 386.[52] But a point solution to an evolving security challenge, one that merits new concepts and capabilities, is shortsighted.[53] The establishment of the Space Force also will present new challenges and competition to the Air Force in force management, force development, and funding, to say nothing of bureaucratic structures. In other words, the Air Force must rebalance across the entire iron triangle, which will require it to more compellingly tell its story about its critical role in the joint force.

"No One Turned to the Navy and Said You're the Key"

For the Navy, the post-9/11 wars had a minimal impact on day-to-day business, as it maintained its global focus more than the other military services. However, the Navy faced serious challenges in reconciling its wartime role given how detached it felt from most of the fighting. "No one turned to the Navy and said you're the key to solving ISIS or al Qaeda," emphasized one flag officer. Another agreed, saying, "we got this adversary . . . what should I do about it as a Navy guy? I don't really know how we should contribute." A third officer put it more bluntly, declaring that the "fight was not a predominantly Navy fight."

Despite its relative lack of direct participation in the post-9/11 wars, the Navy's iron triangle suffered, nevertheless. Ship numbers decreased from 316 in 2001 to 278 by 2008 before rebounding to 308 in 2019, reducing capacity in the capital-intensive force.[54] This decline in hulls is more dramatic when considered in the context of the Navy's overall loss of capacity since the late 1980s, when it had more than twice as many ships as today. The service's obsession with restoring ship numbers, particularly under the leadership of Secretary of the Navy Ray Mabus, which lasted the entire eight years of the Obama administration, impinged on the Navy's capabilities and readiness. Mabus was unwilling to cut any surface ships to invest in higher-end capabilities—even submarines that would be included in ship counts.[55] As Mabus confidently declared to then Secretary of Defense Ashton Carter, he was violating guidance from his boss to prioritize sophisticated warfighting capabilities: "In order to build some types of ships, I will not cut other ships, regardless of their function in the fleet."[56] As one former senior official colorfully described it, Mabus "essentially gave the finger to the president," given that the Pentagon was trying to implement the administration's guidance to shift toward higher-end capabilities.

Simply put, the force had grown smaller and less capable of fighting high-end conflicts since the Cold War. But for a long stretch that was particularly exacerbated by the post-9/11 wars, the Navy focused on the number of ships at the expense of its overall capability and their readiness. Its leadership regularly touted that the 2016 force structure assessment showed the Navy needed to grow to 355 ships.[57] But prioritizing capacity meant that ships were going out to sea without trained sailors or appropriate equipment. The ugly consequences came to a head with the 2017 at-sea collisions that took the lives of nearly twenty sailors.

Similar to the Air Force, the Navy insufficiently focused on the future—a dynamic informed, but not solely caused, by the requirements that arose from the post-9/11 wars. Rather, as one flag officer worried, "Did that preoccupation with this urge to fight make me unprepared to do what the nation really needs me to do?" The Navy's missteps, in other words, were driven in large part by its aimlessness during the post-9/11 wars.

This aimlessness proceeded from the Navy's feelings of detachment from much of the heavy fighting during the post-9/11 wars. This detachment, in turn, contributed to its hyper-focus on conducting global maritime presence and shaping operations over the last two decades, which it saw as its best way to prove its value. Such missions are designed to demonstrate U.S. capabilities to influence the actions of allies, partners, competitors, and adversaries. As one former senior Pentagon official explained, this focus had become "ingrained . . . in the Department of the Navy," which "tried to provide the same presence with a much smaller force than we did with a much larger force in the 1990s." Left unsaid was that the Navy's push for such a heavy operations tempo also may have been a way to justify its incessant requests for more ships.

This heavy operations tempo devastated readiness. As a flag officer noted, the Navy "didn't change our deployment schedules." "We treated the aircraft carrier like it was an Air Force base, parked it in the same spot . . . called it the boulevard, [and] flew the same mission over and over," explained another. Constant deployments coupled with the impact of sequestration resulted in a catastrophic readiness crisis that began in 2013 and then exploded in 2017 with four ship and aircraft mishaps. According to the subsequent readiness review conducted by then Fleet Forces Commander Admiral Philip Davidson, the heavy operational tempo was largely to blame, and had aggravated serious training, maintenance, and personnel shortfalls.[58]

Similar to the Air Force, the Navy also faced personnel problems due to the in lieu of policy. For a decade, so-called "individual augmentees" were pulled from across the Navy. By 2007, 46,000 sailors had shifted from their regular jobs to fill positions the Army needed for the broader wartime effort.[59] This approach meant that "sailors were pulled out of their primary warfare specialties . . . [and] sent to drive trucks in Iraq or run a mission in the mountains in Afghanistan," explained one retired flag officer. Many Navy leaders emphasized the long-term opportunity costs of this approach given the sailors' subsequent lack of experience in key areas. The same flag officer lamented, "We had highly trained sonar technicians who should've been looking for Russians and Chinese but were driving trucks in Afghanistan." In his view, it made no sense to "build a Navy to deal with terrorists in Afghanistan." Other flag officers also expressed dismay over the individual augmentees approach, stating the Navy is "still recovering" from it and noting that Navy personnel "are [still] doing the jobs of other personnel."

The Navy's personnel challenges over the last two decades of war have only grown more serious. The "Fat Leonard" scandal, in which a contractor bribed dozens of officers, including admirals, and received sensitive information in return, gutted Navy leadership in the Asia-Pacific over the last decade.[60] One previous chairman of the joint chiefs of staff described its impact in stark terms, explaining the Navy "lost a generation of officers" because of the scandal.[61] The Navy Special Warfare community has committed a string of misbehaviors in recent years, wiping some of the shine off an exalted community.[62] Numerous senior leaders have been removed for various reasons, including chief of Naval Operations nominee Admiral William Moran and Pacific Fleet commander Vice Admiral Joseph Aucoin.[63] And the most recent crisis plaguing the U.S. Navy, the firing of Secretary of the Navy Richard Spencer at the end of 2019, was so convoluted and confusing that it will surely take the Navy a long time to unravel what happened and its implications.[64] As is often the case, the *Duffel Blog* punchily treated these sensitive issues in its declaration that "the Navy has officially fired more captains than torpedoes over the last five years."[65]

Like their Air Force counterparts, senior Navy officer interviewees often expressed frustration and bitterness toward other military services, specifically (but not surprisingly) the Army. One said that before the post-9/11 wars kicked off, the Navy "took the Army unseriously" because they spent their time deployed to places like Europe rather than "on a ship, where there's no email and you're isolated." Another remarked that "now others get to see what it's like" to be away for long stretches of time that, given the Navy's lengthy deployments at sea, has long been de rigeur for sailors.

And the much-anticipated Army-Navy football game came up, as well. For most of the post-9/11 wars period, from 2002 to 2015, the Army suffered its longest losing streak since the beginning of the series in 1890. *Duffel Blog* sardonically described the losses as "an experiment to build officer resiliency for the military's next impossible war," describing fictional midshipman "pranking" their fellow soldiers "with 17 years of sustained land-based combat" so they would lose the game.[66] This mockery captured a serious issue and reflected both the unequal burden and prolonged duration of the land-based post-9/11 wars. They were yet another manifestation, albeit a minor one, of the difficulty of securing victory during the post-9/11 wars.

Going forward, the Navy must reconcile its severe imbalances across the iron triangle, prioritizing unmanned and undersea investments, and must recover from its leadership crises. Its recent, and strident, emphasis on transforming education across the Navy is an important start to the latter.[67] The Navy played a supporting role in the post-9/11 wars—a role that received minimal attention and often was viewed with contempt or criticized as insufficient. Absent meaningful steps to recalibrate, particularly in line with the joint force, the Navy may face serious challenges collaborating in future fights.

While each service has its own experience, some similarities emerge from their legacies. None are satisfied with their current capacity-capability-readiness iron triangles. All want additional resources. And without a real reckoning of the forces and the narratives they have inherited from the post-9/11 wars, they will not be able to effectively adapt to the future.

SHIFTING BALANCE(S) OF POWER:
MILITARY SERVICES VERSUS COMBATANT COMMANDS

Being at war for nearly two decades influenced the entire national security apparatus. Inside the military, the balance of power shifted to the combatant commands from the military services; over the second decade of war, the pendulum began to swing back. Inside the Pentagon, the balance of power swayed between the office of the secretary of defense and the joint staff, as described in chapter 4. And across the interagency, the State Department and its foreign service grew weak as the military filled their role time and time again, as chapter 9 will discuss.

Being at war for so long invariably influenced the military's key institutions. Some of these legacies are beneficial. For example, ongoing operations enabled consistent contact across the force in some areas. As one retired general officer argued, "I think we are inherently born joint now; that culture of service isolation is gone because the people who

FIGURE 6-1. Evolution of the Size of the Four Military Services Since 9/11

Number of Military Personnel

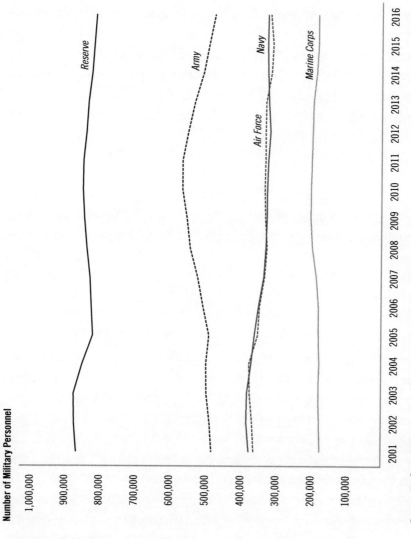

Source: Defense Manpower Data Center, Office of the Secretary of Defense, U.S. Department of Defense, www.dmdc .osd.mil/appj/dwp/dwp_reports.jsp.

grew up under that culture are no longer serving." Yet, there were notable examples to the contrary. As previously noted, the Marines insisted on having their own area of operations in Southwest Afghanistan; their unwillingness to share control with the Army diluted the impact of the troop surge and injected more internal disunity into an already complex conflict.[68] And, of course, the service rivalries discussed earlier demonstrate that all was not rosy across the joint force. Nevertheless, being at war for so long exposed many soldiers, sailors, airmen, and Marines to one another, and, at varying levels, forced them to work together and learn about the other services.

During the first decade of the post-9/11 wars, the military services lost attention and influence to the combatant commands—specifically U.S. Central Command. This reflected the 1986 Goldwater-Nichols legislation, which deliberately shifted power toward the combatant commands, and, specifically, the regional commands, which would focus on fighting wars, and away from the military services, which would focus on manning, training, and equipping for wars.[69] One retired general officer quipped that the combatant commands used to be seen as "stepchildren," but being at war meant they were briefing war plans to senior officials and directly requesting resources. He explained, "When you are at war, the folks who were sitting in the back row were now sitting in the front row." The combatant commands became "the most powerful," according to one former senior Pentagon official. "The COCOMs had all the pull," reinforced a flag officer. A general officer observed that "they've largely gotten what they wanted." A final former senior official questioned whether that was even possible: "The COCOMS are baby birds and are always going to want more."

Their frustration is understandable but reflects that the system was working as it was designed. Some tension between the military service and combatant command leaders is natural. One retired senior officer, for example, complained that while the COCOMs soared in influence, "the services just 'gave' at the office" to support COCOM needs. But this was exactly what the services were supposed to do in wartime. These dynamics were on display in the quarterly discussions Secretary of Defense Donald Rumsfeld convened for senior military and civilian leaders across the Pentagon. During those dialogues, as one former senior official rued, the military services became "a lonely voice that gets to speak up a little bit, once every quarter."[70]

A different interpretation of the services' role came from one former senior official, who bitterly complained that "the services, all of them, have been more than willing to let the COCOMs roll right over and not ask questions; it serves their purposes to show we don't have enough." Nevertheless, like Rumsfeld, Gates also was clearly perturbed with the service chiefs' perspectives. Just before he took over as secretary of defense, Gates recalled sitting in on a meeting with President Bush, Vice President Cheney, Secretary of Defense Rumsfeld, and the service chiefs. He angrily described their "seeming detachment from the wars we were in" and remarked that "not one uttered a single sentence on the need for us to win in Iraq."[71] Certain personalities also exacerbated these tensions. CENTCOM Commander General Tommy Franks, for example, is infamously known for complaining about the military services and even referring to the chiefs as "Title 10 Motherf—s."[72]

The overwhelming emphasis on prioritizing the post-9/11 wars largely resulted in gains for CENTCOM because it was responsible for hotspots like Afghanistan, Pakistan, and Iraq. Its personnel tripled within months of the 9/11 attacks.[73] Not everyone was enthusiastic about CENTCOM's elevation, however, as two sobering examples demonstrate. First, one retired general officer recounted the shocked faces of U.S. Pacific Command and U.S. Forces-Korea's leaders when personnel and capabilities were transferred from South Korea to CENTCOM; he said it was "unthinkable" to them, even though "not only was CENTCOM the highest priority mission—it was almost the only priority mission." Second, one retired general officer recounted a briefing with Army leadership in which they complained that "CENTCOM requirements are preventing the ARFORGEN model from reaching its full potential." (ARFORGEN was an Army force generation model designed to regain readiness.) He was dismayed and shot back, "Let me give you a different perspective: CENTCOM is fighting a war. Their goal is to win a war—not to ensure the ARFORGEN model reaches its full potential." In other words, differences of priority between the services and CENTCOM were often stark.

Indeed, former officials and senior general officers remember CENT-COM's growth during this period with stark language. It got "rich, fat, and powerful," according to one former officer; "the big man on campus," in the words of another. A former general officer described it as "the center of the universe," while another complained that it became "the place where things go and never come back." A different former general officer was harsher, describing CENTCOM as "the monster."

As CENTCOM rose in power and influence amid the post-9/11 wars, CENTCOM commander became "the most important job in the military at some point," according to one general officer. While that made a lot of sense given the importance of the wars in its area of responsibility, there was some concern about how CENTCOM's various leaders operated given the heightened attention they received. One former officer with significant senior-level joint experience described the frustration he saw among senior military leaders in Washington over how CENT-COM commanders operated across the broader Defense Department landscape. He offered an illuminating warning: "For years, the command and control broke down [between Washington and CENTCOM) . . . if you find that you're becoming a rock star as a general or a flag officer, something is wrong. When the press is hinging on everything you say and not what your boss says, that's a problem."

By the second decade of war, however, a slower operational tempo and sequestration had pushed some power back to the military services. And in recent years, the National Defense Strategy's focus on China and Russia has taken some attention away from CENTCOM, as well. For example, the Navy made a "modest reduction" in its deployments to the Middle East for a period since the National Defense Strategy was released.[74] But shifting prioritization toward U.S. Indo-Pacific Command (INDOPACOM) and or U.S. European Command is difficult given the many security threats that continue to run rampant across CENTCOM's area of responsibility. And given that the military services have been "removed from the operational problem set," as one former senior official described, it is important to question how and in what ways the services can ensure they are not "less able to think creatively about those issues" of particular concern, like preparing for future conflicts. Nevertheless, managing risk in the Middle East while calibrating to a more sustainable approach in CENTCOM is not impossible.[75]

As the balance of power shifts between and among the military services and the combatant commands, it may be timely to rethink the organizational structure dividing operational issues and manning, training, and equipping across the military. The relationship between problem owners and problem solvers has grown more tenuous over these past two decades of incessant conflict. The current construct has proven imperfect at best.

THREE TRAJECTORIES

Fighting costly yet limited wars for nearly two decades shaped the U.S. military along three trajectories: time, space, and the spectrum of conflict. Time refers to prioritization between present and future threats; space refers to prioritization of regions; and, spectrum of conflict refers to prioritization of certain types of warfare. Throughout this period, the U.S. military faced challenges in these three areas in key ways. Before exploring them, however, it is crucial to underscore two points that at first glance may appear contradictory but, in reality, are both true. First, focusing resources on the wars that the military was actively waging made strategic sense. Second, doing so invariably posed immense opportunity costs, as well.

Time

The past two decades can be loosely divided into three periods of time. Over approximately the first five years of the post-9/11 wars, Secretary Rumsfeld pushed the military to shoehorn his vision of transformation into contemporary conflicts in places like Afghanistan and Iraq. Doing so sucked readiness from key force elements as the military grew busier and busier in fighting contemporary adversaries. "We got into a battle-rhythm of sourcing the war," described one retired senior general officer, although acquisitions remained overwhelmingly focused on preparing for future challenges rather than winning the ongoing wars. During the next five years or so, Secretary Gates pushed the military to focus on the contemporary conflicts to a much greater extent than potential future wars, shifting key acquisition priorities to focus more on the near term. And over about the last decade, senior civilian leaders have mostly pushed for the opposite: an increasing focus on tomorrow's fights, occasionally punctuated by the need to respond to urgent challenges like ISIS.

The result was a military engaged in strenuous and seemingly endless fights that frequently rendered it unable to focus on the future. As one former senior civilian official explained:

> We used to have this idea that we'll return to full readiness when we're not fighting the wars. The military has tended to resent that they're always operating . . . why aren't you letting me do what I'm supposed to: train for the big wars? It's not my fault that we're not training for that; we are just busy. That has been built into the system for so long. People are still waiting to be off . . . as opposed to [acknowledging that] this is just how we operate.

Agreeing, another lamented that "our gear was running down, our force was getting tired, and I don't think we ever came to terms with what that meant for the military."

Both these comments illustrate the tension between the long wars and long-range priorities. Making meaningful change to slow down, to recalibrate, and to focus on the future was grueling. "There are other hands on the tiller saying, 'no, no, no: we need to drive to another mission," explained one former senior policymaker. The result was a stretched and struggling military.

Space

Overwhelmingly, the post-9/11 wars have focused on the Middle East and South Asia. These fights "really suck the attention and the oxygen out of the room," sighed one former senior policymaker, noting how hard it was for the Defense Department—and the broader national security apparatus—to focus on other issues. A myopic focus on terrorism began to shape the U.S. approach to many places around the world. As the terrorism fight expanded to include portions of Africa and Southeast Asia, the force largely studied places like Iraq and Afghanistan and languages like Arabic, Pashto, and Dari.

Europe received attention almost solely because of NATO's role in the Middle East and South Asia. The military began to see NATO, the most powerful military coalition on the planet, through the lens of the post-9/11 wars: as, first and foremost, a helpful tool for fighting al Qaeda and providing security in Afghanistan. A laser focus on the Middle East and South Asia, thus, came at the expense of Europe and the Asia-Pacific, which helped China and Russia grow into the chief threats they are today.

Spectrum of Conflict

The post-9/11 wars primarily focused on two types of conflicts: countering terrorists and countering insurgents. Large swaths of the U.S. military, therefore, stopped thinking about, or seriously preparing for, high-end conventional conflicts and nuclear conflicts, including related demands for deterrence and escalation management. In key areas, "we were creating holes in the force which made it extraordinarily brittle," explained one former senior policymaker. "Across all the warfighting functions, it wasn't just stuff we learned for Iraq and Afghanistan that we have to forget, but also all the stuff we didn't learn because we were there," described one officer who was notably skeptical that fighting insurgents for two decades would help the United States wage future high-end conventional wars. The U.S. military, a global force that has generally operated across the spectrum of conflict, had developed gaping holes in its staffing, training, and equipping—a result of its narrow focus on, and experience at, one end of the spectrum of conflict.

Nearly two decades at war have influenced how the U.S. military fights. Along key trajectories, within each military service and between the services and the combatant commands, the military has inherited numerous legacies that will shape how it confronts the next war's enemies. For it to prevail in the future, the military must acknowledge and, most critically, adapt to address them. Its temporal focus is slowly shifting toward future conflicts through prioritization of modernization and the preservation of readiness, while it also maintains a close eye on near-term threats.

Its geographic prioritization has remained stultified, however, as grand pronouncements about refocusing resources to the Asia-Pacific and Europe have largely not come to fruition. There is widespread concurrence across the defense community that the most serious long-term challenger to the United States is China, given its rapid military modernization over the past two decades in general and its demonstrated intent to reshape Asian security in particular, yet meaningful prioritization to meet the threats it poses over broader concerns in the Middle East concerns has been limited.[76] Across the spectrum of conflict, the greatest concerns for the future include nuclear war, high-end conventional war, gray zone conflicts, and terrorism. Without a sustainable and resilient approach to managing terrorism, the military will remain overly specialized in the wars of yesterday and, ultimately, unready for the wars of tomorrow.[77] Failure to acknowledge how fighting for two decades has shaped the military, in other words, will result in a force that cannot effectively propel itself into the future.

7

Who Serves in the Military

"It's a nearly sole source supplier."

Over nearly two decades of war, the composition of the U.S. military has shifted in meaningful ways. Relative to the U.S. population, the force is the smallest it has been in nearly 100 years. It has become an increasingly insular family business even as it also has undergone cultural changes with the repeal of Don't Ask, Don't Tell, the near-full integration of women, and debates over transgender troops. Many of these dynamics began well before the September 11, 2001, attacks, but being at war for nearly two decades has both heightened them and thrust them further into the open.

WHO SERVES . . . AND WHO DOESN'T?

More than 2 million U.S. military personnel served in the Vietnam War, and as it was ending, the president and Congress agreed to terminate the draft and move to an all-volunteer force (AVF). This decision fundamentally shaped the state of today's military.[1]

At the time of the AVF's creation, there were broad worries about the future composition of the force.[2] Many of those concerns have been proven wrong. Contrary to fears that those who joined the military would be poor and uneducated minorities, for example, the military post-9/11 wars "is as representative of the nation socioeconomically as racially . . . and like their peers in the American middle class, service members are generally well educated."[3] Interestingly, that finding applies across the force, including both officers and enlisted personnel, and stays true even when the Army lowered its standards at the height of the wars.[4] Similarly, despite expectations that the AVF would crumble during long and large wars, requiring the reintroduction of the draft, the AVF has remained cohesive over the last two decades. The post-9/11 wars have, therefore, demonstrated the AVF's feasibility as a wartime construct. As one retired general officer recalled, "Honestly, if you'd told me in 2001 that the AVF could persevere through 17, 18 years of deployments, and that their families would stay strong in the saddle with us, I'm not sure . . . but they have . . . it has also demonstrated resilience."

Such resilience has come at a price, however. The AVF was preserved by the fact that these were relatively small wars, meaning that a draft was never so militarily essential as to outweigh its political liability. However, the civilian and military leadership needed to adopt creative approaches to stretch the AVF across the battlefields of the post-9/11 wars, including "stop loss, involuntary reserve mobilizations, retiree recalls, retention bonuses, and contractor utilization"[5]

Some of these approaches posed real challenges to those who serve, including stop loss decisions that prevented personnel from leaving the military on their planned timelines, as well as involuntary mobilizations that minimized the degree of choice to which reservists had become accustomed. In another example, former Secretary of Defense Gates recounts in his memoir the wrenching experience of deciding to extend Army deployment tours from twelve to fifteen months in 2007. His junior military assistant told him that fifteen-month tours had outsized impacts on soldiers' families since it meant they might miss multiple special occasions, but his senior military assistant explained that "the troops were expecting this decision" and "they think you're an asshole for not making it."[6]

Moreover, other often-expensive approaches, like distributing bonuses to increase retention rates and relying heavily on contractors to do
jobs previously assigned to military personnel, helped the AVF endure.
Given all these dynamics, military personnel are more likely to have
been deployed and to have been in combat than their pre-9/11 war predecessors.[7]

Notwithstanding these efforts to preserve the resilience of the force,
the AVF has grown particularly insular over the post-9/11 wars, as scholars James Golby and Hugh Liebert assert.[8] Fewer than half of 1 percent
of Americans serve in the military—the lowest proportion of the population in nearly a century—as the force has shrunk and the population
has grown.[9] By 2015, 2.5 million American troops had served in Iraq or
Afghanistan by 2015, but less than a third of Americans had friends in
the military, let alone knew someone who had served in combat zones.[10]

Although military personnel are socioeconomically and racially diverse as a whole, they are increasingly likely to come from rural areas
and from the south—which one general officer described as the "southern smile." To take one sharp example, Fayetteville, North Carolina,
(population 209,000), had twice as many enlistees in 2019 than Man-
hattan, New York (population 1,600,000).[11] This dynamic is exacerbated
by a combination of history, geography, and base closures.[12] Military in-
stallations created in the reconstruction period following the Civil War,
coupled with the plentiful availability of inexpensive land in rural areas
and relatively mild weather to support year-round training, means that
the South boasts many big bases.

Above all, the military has become even more of a "family business," in the words of multiple general officers I interviewed. About a
decade into the post-9/11 wars, 80 percent of those in the military had a
family member who also served, including 25 percent with a parent who
served.[13] That the military has become a family business is exemplified by
a simultaneously heart-warming and jarring photo from General James
McConville's confirmation hearing to serve as chief of staff of the U.S.
Army. Behind McConville sat his wife, an Army veteran, his three adult
children, and his son-in-law—all wearing the exact same uniform.[14]

Throughout the interviews for this book, I was struck by the number of current and retired general officers who mentioned that their children are in the military. It was ubiquitous. One retired general officer noted that his son was leaving for his fifth deployment; another talked about how all of his children went to West Point; a third mentioned that two of his kids are planning to join the military; and still another general officer remarked that one of his children is currently deployed to a war zone. In one particularly powerful story, a retired senior general officer described how his sons would frequently run into friends from grade and high school when deployed to Afghanistan, because they had all gone to school together on the military bases where they lived with their parents. One officer who taught in a professional military education institution recalled that he used to poll students to ask how many had a family member in the military; it was "never less than 75%." Many of the interviewees were the children of military officers, as well.

The "family business" dynamic means that, for many U.S. senior military leaders, the costs of the post-9/11 wars were extremely personal. For example, General Raymond Odierno's son was badly wounded in Iraq; General John Kelly's son was killed in Afghanistan; and Lieutenant General Keith Walker's daughter was killed in Afghanistan.[15] While all these losses are heartbreaking, Kelly's became public in a dramatic scene when, as chief of staff to President Trump, he stood in the White House press room to explain the process used to inform military families that their loved one has died while serving. He explained this in a matter-of-fact tone, although he grew angry in defense of the president, criticized a member of Congress, and, by the end, was brimming with contempt as he lamented the state of American society.[16] This was a true tragedy: a retired senior general officer whose family had paid the ultimate price, and who had sought to avoid discussing that loss publicly, had it thrust into the national spotlight. Kelly's public display of his deepest wounds called to mind a modern-day Coriolanus; as Shakespeare's war hero-turned-politician declares, "I had rather have my wounds to heal again/ Than hear say how I got them."[17]

Two Dangers

The rise of the "family business" carries with it two key dangers rooted in the uneven distribution of burdens of the post-9/11 wars. First, relying almost wholly on one cohort could threaten the sustainability of the AVF if that cohort volunteers at lower rates. "What if the family stops telling them to join? It's a nearly sole-source supplier," worried one former senior civilian official. This concern is reasonable, particularly because of the heavy level of military involvement in the post-9/11 wars.

Regular deployments, coupled with intense activity at home stations, means that over the last two decades many servicemembers have felt like they were on an exhausting merry-go-round. For example, one retired general officer worried about the toll on families and the impact it could have on recruitment. He underscored that, for many troops, "the time that was supposed to be at home isn't really at home" due to a never-ending onslaught of commitments, which made it feel like there was little time to recover mentally and physically from deployments.

Others reflected on a generational divide within the force that has been exacerbated by experiences in the post-9/11 wars. One officer lamented the high divorce rate among soldiers in the combat-arms specialties, criticizing "the boomer generals [who] don't get" the need for "predictability and stability." Although some clearly do—as one recently retired senior general officer noted, "I was gone [as a young officer] much less often than they are now . . . that puts an extraordinary burden on families." And there have been few meaningful institutional fixes. Given the nature of the family business, such dynamics could impede recruitment and retention. Perhaps the Army missing its recruitment goal in 2018—for the first time since the height of the Iraq War—will shake the system into change.[18]

The second danger inherent in relying on the same cohort relates to the changing security environment. As one general officer described, "I find myself having to relearn my own craft every day because the demands of this environment are so different." Given geopolitical shifts and the likelihood that the wars of the future will look different from those of the last two decades, the U.S. military needs to recruit diverse and adaptable personnel. It means attracting people with diverse skill sets, such as in the cyber domain, regional expertise in Russian and Chinese affairs, and private-sector experience from places like Silicon Valley and other parts of the technology industry. It also means bringing in troops at different stages in their professional careers, and updating the "up or out" system to improve career flexibility.[19] Above all, it means attracting volunteers with varied life experience, something limited both by the geographic homogeneity of the force as well as the family business dynamic. Although the Defense Department has taken steps to diversify, they have borne little fruit thus far.

Indeed, the profession of arms itself may be shifting, as scholar Paula Thornhill underscores in her seminal work on the increasing permutations of the United States's use of force.[20] Making a more deliberate and concerted effort to bring in and incorporate different skill sets will be crucial for the military to adapt to new threats. Moreover, to the extent that high-intensity conventional conflicts are becoming more likely, the military's current demography could catastrophically concentrate casualties on the relatively small number of families that make up the business.

Taken together, the family business dynamic, therefore, poses real dangers to the AVF that, in the absence of serious study and adaptation, could become very problematic—not least because they contribute to the crisis of caring. As scholars from the Center for a New American Security found in their analysis of recruit quality, "The AVF model is quite brittle and overly susceptible to economic forces and public opinion trends, particularly in wartime."[21] If those who serve actively discourage their progeny from doing so, if the military fails to diversify, and if the growing gap between those who serve and those whom they serve does not get reversed, the AVF's future may be less bright than its present.

CULTURAL CHANGES

The U.S. military has undergone substantial cultural changes during the post-9/11 wars attendant to three developments in particular: the integration of women in combat; the repeal of Don't Ask, Don't Tell; and the opening to transgender troops. Each of these developments deserves study because they involved intense debates within the military as well as political fireworks and public brouhaha. Despite this, each, ultimately, has had only a superficial impact on the military's cohesion and ability to effectively to do its job.

Gender Integration

The integration of women into all parts of the military has been a tumultuous journey.[22] Like the effort to racially integrate the military, which faced resistance from military leaders and came about only thanks to Presidents Franklin Roosevelt and Harry Truman flexing their executive authority, the integration of women, in many ways, required the activism of senior civilian leadership. Some steps had been taken in the decades before the September 11 attacks, like allowing women to attend the military academies beginning with the class of 1980 and permitting them to serve in air and naval combat units, including flying fighter jets, in the 1990s. However, women remained prohibited from serving in units primarily focused on direct ground combat, resulting in uneven integration across the military services and branches.

Nevertheless, throughout the post-9/11 wars, more than a quarter of a million women deployed to Iraq and Afghanistan, many earning combat badges.[23] And during these long wars, the military experimented with female-centered constructs in Iraq and Afghanistan, which enabled access and security measures with partners that otherwise would have been impossible. One of the best examples is the creation of Female Engagement Teams, units comprised of female soldiers and Marines that focused on engaging Iraqi and Afghan women in the hopes that better relationships with them would provide clues about how to improve each country's security and stability.

In 2013, then Secretary of Defense Leon Panetta announced that women would be permitted to serve in units focused on direct ground combat. Given what he described as "the reality of conflict" since 9/11, he argued that it no longer made sense to categorically exclude women from such jobs.[24] Ironically, when he made that announcement, at least one future female senior general officer was already deployed in support of combat operations (Lori Robinson was in Southwest Asia and would go on to become the first woman to lead a combatant command), and more than a quarter of a million female service members had already deployed to combat zones.[25] Within a decade and a half of the 9/11 attacks, more than 800 female servicemembers had been wounded and more than 130 had died in the post-9/11 wars.[26] In 2015, Secretary of Defense Ashton Carter opened all 200,000 combat jobs across the military to women. Although some had expected a more gradual approach—for example, the Marines believed they would be granted an exception—there was little ensuing controversy.[27] Indeed, as then Secretary of Defense Ashton Carter explained, he "received almost no backlash from Congress after the announcement," which is essentially unheard of in major Defense Department changes.[28] The *Duffel Blog*'s coverage was characteristically quippy: "DoD To Save Funds by Paying Women 73 Cents on the Dollar."[29]

The impact of full integration on the military's capabilities has been minimal. Gender integration into the combat arms has gone smoothly, according to the sergeant major of the Army.[30] By 2016, more than 1,000 women had been integrated into previously closed specializations; by summer 2019, more than thirty women had completed Ranger training.[31] Greater integration will likely improve retention rates, as well, since more female servicemembers will find greater opportunities available in their military career. After years of study, the National Commission on Military, National, and Public Service announced in 2020 that women also should be included in the Selective Service System. This approach to inclusivity, it argued, is important not just for equality's sake but also because it would enable the government "to draw on the talent" of all its citizens.[32]

There remain real hurdles to integration. As scholar Rosa Brooks observes, "The overwhelming majority of new recruits are young and male . . . in that sense, the American military of 2012 still looks a great deal like the American military of the 1970s, the 1940s, the 1860s, or the 1770s."[33] Perhaps most worrisome, then Secretary of Defense James Mattis disparaged gender integration during his tenure. When asked about it in 2018, he underscored the lack of data on the impact it has had on the force, but also made a number of gratuitous statements that undermined the policy, including his declaration that gender integration was a "policy that I inherited" and his reference to female troops as "young ladies."[34] Nevertheless, it appears that those who serve are increasingly supportive of full gender integration. For example, one 2019 poll of active-duty servicemembers and veterans found that views on integration grow markedly more supportive with each generation, culminating in nearly 82 percent of millennials.[35]

This topic rarely came up in interviews. But when it did, most interviewees would acknowledge that, in the words of one retired senior general officer, "We came from an era of some good old boy things going on." Another senior general officer worried that integration and some promotion decisions were "driven by politics or political correctness" but emphasized that "if the person has the talent, then by all means [go ahead]." To best underscore the slow pace of female integration into the military's senior leadership, as of the end of 2019, the Air Force has had four female four-star general officers. The Navy and Army each have had one, and the Marine Corps has had zero.[36]

Don't Ask, Don't Tell

The repeal of Don't Ask, Don't Tell—the military's ban on gay servicemembers serving openly—was another notable change made during the post-9/11 wars. Historically, the military had not permitted gay servicemembers to serve openly, but implemented this policy haphazardly.[37] President Bill Clinton pledged a new course. His consideration of full integration fomented profound civil-military tension at the time, particularly given CJCS General Colin Powell's strident opposition to lifting the ban.[38] The result of these debates was the mid-1990s policy of Don't Ask, Don't Tell. Under it, gay servicemembers could not openly acknowledge their sexual orientation and continue serving.

During his very first State of the Union address, President Obama announced his intention to repeal Don't Ask, Don't Tell. The Pentagon began studying the issue in depth shortly thereafter. Then Secretary of Defense Robert Gates organized a senior group to examine how Don't Ask, Don't Tell could be overturned and what impact doing so might have on the force. As Gates recounts in his memoir, he was surprised to learn that, in a survey of 400,000 servicemembers and 150,000 service spouses, two-thirds were either unconcerned about repeal or thought allowing gays to openly serve would be good for the military.[39] In its foundational study on Don't Ask, Don't Tell, the RAND Corporation conducted a number of focus groups of serving military personnel and found that they "displayed virtually no hostility toward gay servicemembers . . . many participants said that they knew gay men and lesbians who were serving and respected their contributions to the unit."[40] These studies undermined arguments by some retired generals and admirals about the deleterious consequences of repeal,[41] as did CJCS Admiral Michael Mullen, who shocked many when he publicly declared his personal support for repeal during a Senate Armed Services Committee hearing.[42]

Congress repealed Don't Ask, Don't Tell in 2010, and the new policy formally came into being in September 2011. *Duffel Blog* ran a piece outlining how "public reaction to the event was mostly a chorus of shrugged shoulders and the occasional screaming that the military was 'ruined forever.'"[43] This pinpoints a critical truth: the reaction to repeal was muted. As then Secretary of Defense Gates observes, the Department of Defense "had turned a page in history, and there was barely a ripple."[44] The CJCS at the time, General Martin Dempsey, remarked, "What we were afraid of is [what] we didn't know."[45] In other words, such vehement opposition to gays openly serving was due to ignorance. Most tellingly, one senior officer I interviewed simply said that "when Don't Ask, Don't Tell was repealed nobody junior to me cared and nobody senior to me could understand." His observation suggests that openly gay servicemembers will merit even less acrimony as older generations move on.

Like gender integration, moreover, the repeal of Don't Ask, Don't Tell has had a minimal impact on the military's capabilities. A rigorous study of the repeal found that it "had no overall negative impact on military readiness or its component dimensions, including cohesion, recruitment, retention, assaults, harassment, or morale."[46] Notably, the authors also found that it "appears to have enhanced the military's ability to pursue its mission . . . we did identify data indicating that the new policy of open service has promoted greater honesty which, in turn, has enabled the troops to develop tighter bonds of trust."[47] The inclusive approach, in other words, has not harmed the military's cohesion but, instead, has improved it.

Transgender Troops

The issue of transgender troops has proven more complicated than gender integration and the repeal of Don't Ask, Don't Tell, largely due to the Pentagon's comparatively less consistent approach toward it. Historically, the Pentagon would not allow transgender Americans to join or continue to serve in the military. In 2015, however, the secretary of defense created a working group to examine the potential impact of reversing this policy. The Pentagon asked the RAND Corporation to study related issues, as well. The resulting report found that a few thousand troops identify as transgender out of more than a million who currently serve, and very few would seek surgery, costing a few million dollars at most.[48] Most notably, the RAND study examined foreign militaries that permitted open service by transgender personnel and found "in no case was there any evidence of an effect on the operational effectiveness, operational readiness, or cohesion" of the military.[49]

In light of these findings, the Obama administration announced in 2016 that the policy would be repealed and transgender troops would now be permitted to serve openly. One senior officer recalled his deployment during the repeal and sitting through the subsequently required transgender training; as he described, "no one cared," implying that it had no impact on his troops' cohesion or ability to fulfill their mission. However, the Trump administration rescinded this decision, resulting in widespread uncertainty for the status of the military transgender community.[50] Secretary of Defense Mattis's February 2018 memo largely disqualified transgender personnel from serving despite internal Defense Department data that found "40 percent" had deployed to combat zones and "only one" had to end their deployment early.[51] The military appears largely supportive of re-repealing the ban—one study found that two-thirds of active-duty military personnel supported transgender Americans serving—suggesting that the matter is far from closed.[52]

Given how briefly the transgender ban was repealed, its impact on the military's capabilities is unclear. Yet perhaps there is a lesson embedded in the Don't Ask, Don't Tell congressional hearings, during which the military leadership expressed overwhelming support for repeal. As then CJCS Mullen testified before the Senate, "No matter how I look at the issue, I cannot escape being troubled by the fact that we have in place a policy which forces young men and women to lie about who they are in order to defend their fellow citizens. For me, personally, it comes down to integrity—theirs as individuals and ours as an institution."[53] The military leadership would do well to heed his sage words as it builds the future force and ensures it is ready for the next war.

One often hears warnings about the dangers of the military being used as a social experiment. But, as scholars Jacqueline Whitt and Elizabeth Perazzo argue, "The American military has always been a social experiment, especially when determining who can and cannot serve and why."[54] During the Civil War, many Union draftees could pay instead of serving; during World War I, only certain immigrants could join; and during World War II, units were segregated by race on the basis of unproven assumptions about military effectiveness.[55] Whitt and Perazzo underscore that such warnings are "deployed selectively, namely against populations other than heterosexual, white, Christian, native-born cisgender men in the military."[56] Their research is a hearty reminder that who serves in the American military has changed over time—often with little relationship to how well the force operates in combat.

An important legacy of the post-9/11 wars is, therefore, a military that has new opportunities for those who serve but has also become more insular. Its efforts to diversify should be applauded, but many remain fledgling and some inspire skepticism—such as the Army's enthusiasm for expanding the pool of recruits by advertising at the annual Army-Navy football game.[57] Sustained focus and energy is needed to expose more of the public to the military, and to open more of the military to the public, because who serves will remain a crucial factor in mitigating the crisis of caring and determining the military's future effectiveness.

8

Who Leads the Military

"It's the fight. It's the fight. It's the fight."

Just as the post-9/11 wars shaped who serves in the military, they also shaped who leads it. In the early years of these wars, civilian leaders took a notably hands-on approach to selecting military leaders. But many senior leaders faced an environment characterized by confused accountability and frustratingly indecisive outcomes, influencing the crisis of confidence. Moreover, senior leaders also experienced deep and personalized losses, fueling a sense of grievance that further stressed civil-military relationships. Some micromanaged, while some were caught up by politicization or made worrisome ethical decisions. Almost all of them, particularly over the first decade or so of these wars, also had been imprinted, either directly or indirectly, by the Vietnam War and its aftermath. In combination, these factors shaped how they led. The legacies of the post-9/11 wars for the military's senior leaders differ dramatically from those of more junior officers, who may be increasingly skeptical about the utility of intervening abroad.

It is critical to recognize at the outset that many senior U.S. military leaders brought a wide range of positive leadership attributes to the post-

9/11 wars. These include a high degree of professional expertise, a willingness to work alongside others, and deep empathy for both their troops as well as civilian policymakers. Perhaps most importantly, they had a sense of responsibility for their actions as well as the actions of their troops. Indeed, the word "responsibility" and its synonyms came up more often than nearly any other word in interviews with current and former senior military leaders.[1] It was used in three main ways but always was underscored by a deep seriousness of what it meant to lead in wartime.

The first was in reference to the responsibility that military leaders had to give their all in executing the post-9/11 wars—to "squeeze every ounce of efficiency out" of both themselves and their troops, as one senior officer described it. The second was the responsibility for senior military leaders to help both the force and senior civilian leaders understand the character of wars being waged as well as wars that could occur in the future. This included the criticality of "not just saluting and doing things mindlessly," as one retired general officer explained, but also what a senior officer described as a willingness to engage in "debates and discussions . . . about who bears responsibility" for making serious decisions. The third way in which responsibility came up was the imperative to use military force appropriately. Underscoring the "overwhelming [and] massive power" of the U.S. military in the post-9/11 wars, one retired senior general officer emphasized that it had to be "used in a responsible manner." In a similar vein, a senior general officer highlighted the "great responsibility" that the military leadership has in shaping how force is employed. Simply put, many senior military leaders devoted much of their lives over the past two decades of war trying to do the right thing. That represents an important and positive element of the inheritance that must not be understated.

MILITARY LEADERSHIP IN WARTIME

In examining military leadership throughout the post-9/11 wars, it is useful to first consider the parameters and permutations of wartime leadership more generally. The U.S. Army defines leadership as the "activity of influencing people by providing purpose, direction, and motiva-

tion to accomplish the mission and improve the organization."[2] Studies
of senior military leadership typically focus on qualities such as "intellect," "energy," "selflessness," and "humanity."[3] Wartime leadership
would, of course, demand all of these elements. The type of war would
influence their relative importance, as well. For example, one scholar
underscored that ethics are particularly important in wars like the post-
9/11 conflicts, since counterinsurgency doctrine offers counterintuitive
approaches to the use of force, suggesting the heightened significance of
leadership traits that facilitate ethical warfighting.[4]

Strategic-level military leadership in wartime—normally the domain
of general and flag officers—particularly benefits from three additional
attributes. First, leaders must be willing to appropriately take initiative.
Take, for example, the efforts of Lieutenant General David Barno, the
second commander of the war in Afghanistan: when he saw the need
for a different U.S. response, he quickly began to work with his troops
to conceptualize a new strategic approach. Barno's leadership also illustrates the second attribute: senior military leaders in wartime must
engage in meaningful assessments, including perceiving changes in relevant metrics, and adapt in response to the shifting security or political environment. This combines two criteria for effective organizational
management: "absorptive capacity" and "adaptive capacity." Taken together, these elements refer to a leader's ability to usefully absorb information and make appropriate changes based on it.[5] They are epitomized
by General Raymond Odierno's 2006 Iraq War review, completed before
he took command of that war, which argued that a surge of troops and
a shift to counterinsurgency would be beneficial. It is not illustrated by
General McChrystal's view that he was just a "technician" in the 2009
Afghanistan-Pakistan assessment process.[6] Third, they should have the
ability to effectively interface with external actors who are not under
their command, including politicians, policymakers, allies, and partners. General David Petraeus's engagements with Congress regarding
Iraq from 2007 to 2008 offers a good example of this attribute in action.

More than anything else, however, the stakes in wartime mean that
both civilian and military leaders must prioritize and expect accountability. As the following section on "accountability soup" explains,

however, there have been disappointingly few positive examples of this attribute over the last two decades. A single fact is demonstrative: no senior military leader was removed for their operational handling of the post-9/11 wars.

THE LINGERING IMPACT OF THE VIETNAM WAR

In the post-9/11 wars, the military was led for a long time by general and flag officers shaped by the Vietnam War. The contours of that imprint are debatable—especially because every leader was unique. It is, nevertheless, clear that joining the military during the Vietnam War, or just after it had experienced the most spectacular defeat in its history, influenced their experience of their time in uniform. Given that the general and flag officers interviewed for this book extemporaneously brought up the Vietnam War nearly as much as the war in Afghanistan, that it continued to influence their thinking—decades later—is indisputable.

Numerous senior military leaders from throughout the post-9/11 period fought in Vietnam. This includes CJCS Richard Myers, the most senior military officer in the early years of the post-9/11 wars. Myers directly addresses how his tours in Vietnam shaped his approach to senior military leadership in his memoir.[7] His personal "lessons learned" primarily focus on civil-military relations; as he puts it, the "heart of the issue was that U.S. forces had developed effective tactics in Indochina, but our civilian leadership had ignored the principle that these tactics must advance from a solid strategic foundation."[8]

Chief of Staff of the Air Force Norton Schwartz recounts his service at the end of the war in Vietnam in his memoir, as well, and also discusses what it was like being a cadet at the Air Force Academy during the war. "Whenever a graduate died in the line of duty," Schwartz writes, "the name would be read in front of the entire cadet wing at lunch in Mitchell Hall. All three thousand cadets would stand and softly sing the third verse of the Air Force Song in tribute. By the time I graduated, there had been hundreds of such recitals."[9] More recently, one soldier recounted his experience as a West Point Plebe at the height of the wars in 2007: In his memory, it "felt like we had a moment of silence daily."

Other senior military leaders who served in the Vietnam War include General Tommy Franks, CENTCOM commander as both the Iraq and the Afghanistan Wars kicked off; General Peter Pace, who was vice chairman of the joint chiefs and later CJCS; Admiral Michael Mullen, who followed Pace as CJCS; General Eric Shinseki, vice chief and later chief of staff of the Army, who was injured in the Vietnam War; Admiral Gary Roughead, who served as chief of naval operations; General Jim Jones, who served as commandant of the Marine Corps and supreme allied commander, Europe and his successor, Michael Hagee; Admiral William Fallon, who went on to lead CENTCOM; and General John Jumper, who became chief of staff of the Air Force. And while he didn't serve in Vietnam, General George Casey, who led U.S. forces in Iraq and served as chief of staff of the Army during the Army's toughest period there, lost his father during the Vietnam War just after Casey became an officer. While posted to Iraq, "Casey wore one of his dad's medals around his neck as a reminder of the sacrifice."[10]

More senior military leaders who played pivotal roles in the post-9/11 wars joined the military in the wake of the Vietnam War or as it was ending, and were shaped by the post-Vietnam military. They include General Martin Dempsey, who commanded troops in Iraq and served as CJCS, as well as his fellow West Pointer from the class of 1974, General David Petraeus, who ran the wars in Iraq and Afghanistan, served as CENTCOM commander, and wrote his dissertation on how the Vietnam War shaped the Army's views on force.[11] It also includes graduates of the famous West Point class of 1976: General Stanley McChrystal, who led troops in the war in Afghanistan, as well as those who captured Saddam Hussein and killed Abu Musab al Zarqawi; Lieutenant General David Barno, who both directed the war in Afghanistan and trained the Iraqi opposition forces before the Iraq War began; General David Rodriguez, who was the deputy for the war in Afghanistan; and General Raymond Odierno, who led forces in Iraq and was chief of staff of the Army.[12]

On the Army side, it also includes General John Abizaid, who was CENTCOM commander from 2003 to 2007. From the Marines, it includes General James Mattis, who led troops in Iraq and Afghanistan and served as CENTCOM commander as well as secretary of defense;

General John Kelly, who led troops in Iraq; General John Allen, who led troops in Iraq and Afghanistan; General Joseph Dunford, who led troops in Iraq, commanded the war in Afghanistan, and served as commandant of the Marine Corps and as CJCS; and Generals James Amos and James Conway, each of whom led troops in Iraq and later served as commandant. In the Navy, Admiral Sandy Winnefeld led forces in Iraq and became vice chairman of the joint chiefs of staff.

While this list is far from exhaustive, it serves to illustrate how the overwhelming number of senior roles related to waging the post-9/11 wars were filled by soldiers and Marines; the relative scarcity of general and flag officers from the Air Force and the Navy is telling. The military privileged operational experience in wartime as it promoted leaders throughout the post-9/11 period. As one senior general officer explained, "The Services have a tendency to reward and promote those who perform well in a combat environment." Another retired general officer concurred: there is "an assumption [that] if you were a really good division or corps commander and you did a combat tour, you are now the perfect guy to be the G3 in the Army even if you never spent a day in the Pentagon. They [the Services] equate operational excellence with Title 10 excellence or strategic excellence."

This officer's observation underscores the devaluation of headquarters and senior staff-level experience. To take one example, the top three leaders at CENTCOM in 2018 had not had any real experience in either the office of the secretary of defense or on the joint staff because they had been rotating in and out of the war theaters, primarily in the Middle East.[13] One senior general officer worried about this dynamic; as he underscored, given the changing security environment, "We need people who can utilize their experience from a counter-terrorism fight to the high-end fight." A notable exception is General James Cartwright, who was appointed as vice chairman of the joint chiefs of staff in 2007. His transition was bumpy, however, partly due to his lack of operational experience in Iraq or Afghanistan.[14]

This senior military leadership had dramatically different formative experiences than those who served under them. As one former senior official remarked, "There's a huge gap between the general officers and the rank and file." Few served in combat; those who had done so served in conflicts like Panama, Grenada, the Cold War, and the Persian Gulf War. They became general and flag officers around the September 11 attacks, so they spent their entire time as senior leaders in a wartime military, but because of their seniority, many were not necessarily in harm's way. Like nearly all of his contemporaries, for example, Army General George Casey had never been in combat before he was put in charge of the Iraq War. Likewise, Army General David Petraeus did not command troops in combat until he was a major general in Najaf, Iraq.[15]

The formative experiences for their troops, however, included repeated and seemingly endless early-career deployments to war zones. This generational chasm in experience manifested itself in one disheartening remark made by a mid-grade officer during an interview: "Every now and then you get a general who wants to sit with us while we do route clearance so they can get a combat ribbon . . . that was painful . . . they said they couldn't go home without that ribbon."

The imprints made by the post-9/11 conflicts will remain on the military's leaders for decades. The CJCS in 2024 will have experienced a smidge of the Cold War, seen immaculate victory in the Persian Gulf War, and spent much of the rest of his or her career during the messiness of the post-9/11 wars, becoming a general officer as those wars waned. The CJCS in 2034 will represent the last generation with some memory of the U.S. military before the September 11 attacks. The vast majority of his or her career will have been spent in a wartime force. One scholar suspects that the United States will, thus, have "a generation of senior officers who sensibilities were formed in an ambiguous conflict that did not go according to plan, soldiers whose youthful idealism and certainty have been tempered by reality and disappointment at the beginning of their military careers."[16] Given their experiences, these future military leaders may be skeptical of what force can achieve, be operationally risk averse, and be particularly sensitive to how the experiences of their junior officers differ from their own.

SELECTING MILITARY LEADERS

The selection of senior general and flag officers often is a mysterious process that involves balancing the organizational interests of many diverse players with heavy doses of rumor, gossip, personal ambition, and politics. However, many of the post-9/11 wars' senior military leaders were selected through a process set up during Secretary of Defense Rumsfeld's tenure. Perturbed that the military services were the "dominant voices" in choosing the military's leaders, and concerned about prioritizing service needs over the broader needs of the joint force, Rumsfeld decided to take a more hands-on approach.[17] That decision would expand throughout his tenure to include promotions below the four-star general officer level. Rumsfeld specifically cited the example of Lieutenant General Ricardo Sanchez replacing General David McKiernan in Iraq as motivation for his decision to become more personally involved.

Rumsfeld explains that he had not been told about the leadership transition and decided that a different approach was needed as the security situation worsened in Iraq under Sanchez—who, at the time, was understaffed by more than 60 percent—and yet "no senior official in the Army, CENTCOM, or the Joint Staff recommended a change."[18] However, Rumsfeld's account has been disputed, including by General Sanchez, who reports that he told the then Secretary of Defense that "all of the senior leadership in the Pentagon knew what was happening" and that senior military leaders like CENTCOM Commander General Abizaid had tried—unsuccessfully—to fix it.[19]

Prior to Rumsfeld's second tenure in office, the role of the secretary of defense in selecting general and flag officers was usually limited and ad hoc. Rumsfeld exaggerates only slightly when he says that secretaries of defense were expected "to give pro forma approval to the candidates presented by the services and to duly forward their recommendations to the President . . . [whose] approval was expected to be a similar formality."[20] He introduced a more active approach, making the selection of senior military leaders a secretarial priority rather than relying overwhelmingly on the recommendations of CJCS or the military service leadership.[21] He downgraded input by military services in selection, and prioritized the views of "his immediate civilian and military advisers."[22]

His process sought to look holistically across positions that were vacant or would soon be vacant and to consider grooming opportunities that would prepare senior leaders for future assignments.[23] It included drafting a list of specific attributes for senior roles and incentivizing the military services to put forward their most talented leaders rather than to expect they would automatically have a "turn" at a certain senior role.[24] Over time, these attributes included "change agent," "ethics," "candor," "ability to lead," and "intellect."[25]

In practice, the Rumsfeld approach to choosing senior military leaders, especially with respect to joint billets, was difficult and time-consuming. It also generated little enthusiasm among certain senior military leaders, although some were more generous. "Rumsfeld wanted to know who these people are, what skill sets they had . . . that's hard work," argued one retired senior general officer. Others criticized the approach for lacking transparency.[26] In his memoirs, General Norton Schwartz recalls interviewing for the Joint Staff J3 (operations) role: the process involved seven separate interviews with different people, including Rumsfeld, and writing a quick memo responding to pretend intelligence about Osama bin Laden's location and recommending a course of action.[27]

The military services themselves adapted to the Rumsfeld approach in different ways. For example, "the Navy was well organized, conducted 360 reviews on all its senior officers, and would come into meetings with Secretary Rumsfeld and do a thorough job in discussing why a certain officer was suited for a particular position . . . other services did not have that kind of data," explained a retired senior general officer who was intimately familiar with the process. Still others thought it was exactly the right approach. One retired senior general officer was an adamant supporter: "The secretary is the one that signs the nomination letter to the President of the United States, recommending people for senior positions and more responsibility. Should he just do that blindly? Is that serving the president well? No, in my opinion . . . That was a responsibility he [Rumsfeld] took very seriously. It was the essence of civilian control of the military, the way it should be done."

Analyzing the extent to which Rumsfeld's process changed the composition of the most senior military leadership is tricky given how little detail exists about the other candidates he considered. It is clear, however, that Rumsfeld prioritized joint experience and also reconceptualized the deputy combatant commander position, making these "developmental assignments." He also sought to shake up service-dominated promotion patterns in the combatant commands. An Army general officer nearly always led Southern Command, for example, but Rumsfeld put Admiral James Stavridis in charge. Rumsfeld similarly tried to break the Navy's dominance of Pacific Command by nominating Air Force General Greg Martin as commander, although Martin, ultimately, withdrew his nomination following congressional displeasure.

Finally, the service chiefs noted his willingness to push back against senior military leaders by "considering candidates other than those they had identified."[28] This did not endear him to many high-ranking officers. Indeed, one senior military leader who worked closely with Rumsfeld underscored that "Rumsfeld pushed diversity in the general officer ranks, to the point of sometimes irritating the services . . . [he] wanted to be bolder, [and] take more risk" than the services by selecting leaders with different backgrounds. However, this interviewee then noted two examples where Rumsfeld was unsuccessful in doing so, including in pushing a female general officer to lead a military service academy and in pushing for Lieutenant General Sanchez to receive a fourth star.

After Rumsfeld's departure, subsequent secretaries of defense have taken a more hands-off approach.[29] As former Secretary of Defense Robert Gates explains in his memoir, he was interested in the same qualities as Rumsfeld and "would be checking the services' homework" as he reviewed selections, but he was generally satisfied with "returning the process to the services and the Joint Staff."[30] In contrast, Secretary of Defense Ashton Carter selected General Mark Milley as chief of staff of the Army and Lieutenant General Robert Neller as the Marine Corps commandant, candidates who did not appear on lists of possible candidates provided by the military services themselves. He does not, however, appear to have adopted Rumsfeld's systematic approach to senior military leader selection.[31] Secretaries Panetta, Hagel, and Mattis have not publicly addressed the issue of senior military personnel selection, but there is no evidence that they adopted Rumsfeld's hands-on approach, either.

To the extent that senior civilian leaders can shape senior military leadership positions, they can profoundly influence the force and its future. They can fundamentally inform whether and how the military's leadership looks and acts differently from its predecessors—and because military leaders serve as models, changing the senior leadership can influence the broader force, as well. If Rumsfeld's heavy involvement in the most critical military personnel decisions represents how the secretary of defense can shape the force's leadership, however, then the way he operated also soured many who perceived his activism as counterproductive civilian meddling. How senior civilian leaders utilize their authority, in other words, is just as important as whether they do so.

HOW DID THEY LEAD?

A number of senior military leaders distinguished themselves in combat and as policymakers on no shortage of wrenchingly difficult issues throughout the post-9/11 wars. Nevertheless, three key worrisome characteristics are reflected in the post-9/11 wars: a dearth of accountability; a widespread personalization of those killed in combat; and a culture facing serious challenges in terms of micromanagement, politicization, and ethics.

Accountability Soup

The first attribute—the dearth of accountability—is best encapsulated by scholar and retired general officer Paula Thornhill's term "accountability soup," which refers to the difficulty of knowing who to blame for which actions.[32] There are two types of accountability: individual and collective. Individual accountability focuses on one's actions, such as deliberately engaging in an illegal use of force or poorly leading one's troops. Collective accountability, which lies at the operational or strategic level, involves responsibility for broader aspects of the conflicts.

Given the character of the post-9/11 wars, it is neither fair nor right to conceptualize it as a singular conflict in which one can easily pinpoint the individuals who won or lost it on the whole; however, the dearth of collective accountability, in particular, merits serious exploration.

This phenomenon of accountability soup has flourished in the post-9/11 wars, likely as a result of the United States's diffuse threats and the sprawling organizations it built and used to fight them. The most infamous, and probably the most important, example is the scandal at Abu Ghraib prison, where U.S. soldiers committed horrific abuses of detainees. Where responsibility lay in the chain of command, however, was not immediately clear, because of the involvement of CENTCOM, the Army itself, and military contractors; by the time the events had been publicized and investigated, many of those responsible had already departed their roles.[33] Another example can be found in General John Abizaid's dilemmas over how, when, and under what circumstances to offer dissent from, or different perspectives on, how to fight in Iraq. In his first press conference as the commander of Central Command, Abizaid frankly shared his views. He even publicly contradicted Secretary Rumsfeld regarding the character of the war.[34] Yet that frankness may not always have governed his more private conduct. For example, Abizaid recounts hearing positive endorsements from his division commanders about the weakening state of the Iraqi insurgency and being skeptical about their validity. He, nevertheless, conveyed that misplaced optimism to Secretary of Defense Rumsfeld.[35]

Perhaps the best description of the accountability soup problem came from a former officer who focused on the lack of collective accountability in the post-9/11 wars. As he explained:

Everyone can look at [the failures of the post-9/11 wars] and it's a Rorschach test. The Army can say we won the operational piece, but we were let down by policymakers . . . the Marines, too. The Air Force can say we delivered precision airpower and tore apart our force. Civilians can say we tried. The Administrations can say we've been eating different types of shit sandwiches and every time we try to pull out, the military says no. It's like a weird and

bad Thanksgiving dinner happens in a family and everyone in
that family has a different perspective about what was the original sin . . . Everyone's got their own different opinion about where
it started and who is to blame. Those things are lost in the fog of
history. We may never really know.

One must be cautious, of course, of assuming that any set of actors
in these conflicts, whether civilian leaders or senior military leaders,
represented a collective *deus ex machina,* immaculate and free from accountability. But across nearly 100 interviews, it was dismaying to see so
many lost in the accountability soup. While most interviewees quickly
acknowledged a wide variety of failures in conceptualizing, planning,
and operationalizing the post-9/11 wars, very rarely did any of them
name the senior military leadership or a specific senior military leader
as culpable for any of them. One retired senior general officer referenced
the "self-delusion" in these wars, but blamed only civilian leaders for
mistakes; another explained that senior military leaders "don't look at it
more broadly" and, instead, argue that "I was asked to do this and I did
a good job." Such dynamics shape, and are shaped by, the crisis of meaningful civilian control.

The saga of General George Casey provides a good example of accountability soup in action. Casey was promoted to lead the Iraq War
during its nadir despite clear evidence that he and his superior, CENT-
COM Commander General Abizaid, were pursuing a failed strategy. He
was then both relieved of command and promoted to chief of staff of
the Army—a trajectory similar to General William Westmoreland, who
flubbed the U.S. military's approach in the Vietnam War but was promoted to chief of staff of the Army during one of the darkest periods
of that conflict.[36] Casey was the only senior military leader tagged with
any blame during my interviews. Yet the few interviewees who assigned
Casey any culpability for missteps in the Iraq War effort also felt the
need either to explain his conduct or to convey their empathy for his
decisionmaking. Casey had "stayed too long [in Iraq] and was too tired
to even see the changes in the situation he got himself in in the fall of
2006, winter of 2007," according to one retired general officer. Similarly,

General Stanley McChrystal recounted giving General Casey a farewell gift as he departed Iraq: "We both knew that in the years ahead he'd receive less credit and more blame than he deserved . . . he had been rock solid—the epitome of a professional throughout his time in command."[37] These generous words came despite Casey's failure to recognize that the U.S. military was losing a war he led. Indeed, he even failed to recognize it as President Bush removed him, after which Casey remarked that, "I left not really understanding what the hell had happened."[38]

When he was going through his confirmation hearing to serve as chief of staff of the Army, then Secretary of Defense Robert Gates's biggest concern was Casey's morale, as he feared that the relief from command would be "discouraging to George after all his service."[39] Similarly, President Bush did not want him to be blamed, declaring, "I am not going to make him the fall guy for my strategy."[40] However, one must wonder who does appropriately deserve blame, if not Casey, the commander in the field. Bush's answer meant that he accepted total responsibility, but this approach risks forming a presidential aegis that protects senior military leaders from reasonable criticism and, thus, thickens the accountability soup.

To the extent that current military personnel are willing to identify mistakes made by the senior military leadership over the length of the post-9/11 wars, they normally focus on just a small number of officers. In particular, interviewees expressed frustration with General Franks, General Casey, and Admiral William Fallon, CENTCOM's commander from 2007 to 2008. In informal discussions with cadets at one of the military academies, moreover, I was struck by their descriptions of who deserved blame for the post-9/11 wars. They listed a wide range of civilian policymakers—some very reasonably—but were flummoxed when I asked them if any military leaders might have made mistakes as well.[41] Given that they were toddlers during the early years of the post-9/11 wars, their internalization of a narrative that assigns blame solely to specific civilian Defense Department leaders in the Bush administration is revealing, both about the status of the national debate on this issue and as the contours of their military socialization.

They are also not alone. Another scholar, for example, has argued that "blaming the generals is wrong . . . U.S. military leaders have done exactly what they should have," whereas civilians and political elites deserve responsibility for inconclusive outcomes.[42] This calls into question what appropriate expectations should be for military leaders in wartime. A more nuanced warning comes from Peter Feaver, who warns about the risk of "McMasterism," a bastardized version of H. R. McMaster's arguments in *Dereliction of Duty*, in which military leaders are blamed "for going along with civilian preferences rather than blocking those preferences."[43]

There has, however, been some internal criticism of the military leadership. Most famously, then Lieutenant Colonel Paul Yingling wrote a scathing article that basically ended his career. "A Failure in Generalship" was published as Iraq was ravaged by its worst violence to date. Comparing the impending defeat of the U.S. military in Iraq to the Vietnam War, he argues that "America's generals have failed to prepare our armed forces for war and advise civilian authorities on the application of force to achieve the aims of policy," and highlights their failure to accurately assess partners and adversaries while failing to convey crucial assessments to civilian leaders.[44]

After his article was published, one major general convened officers at Fort Hood to dispute it. They were not convinced, according to journalists Greg Jaffe and David Cloud, because "they wanted someone to take accountability for what had gone wrong."[45] General Casey, who was serving as chief of staff of the Army when the essay was published, was so insulted by the article that he refused to reach out to Yingling, despite his speechwriter urging him to do so in the hope that it would encourage a more open and honest command climate.[46]

To take a very different leadership example, General Peter Chiarelli, who went on to become vice chief of staff of the Army under Casey one year after the essay was published, reflected that he saw his younger self in Yingling's writings. Chiarelli made it a point to close his briefings to the Army's new general officers by quoting it.[47]

More recently, retired Lieutenant General Daniel Bolger asserted, "I am a United States Army general, and I lost the Global War on Terrorism" in his book. He argues that "our primary failing in the war involved generalship," and he specifically underscores the failures of senior military leaders to accurately assess the U.S. military's capabilities, its partners, and its assumptions—failures he blames on "a distinct lack of humility."[48] Bolger calls out a number of senior general officers for misreading political leaders' goals and intentions throughout the post-9/11 wars and rues that "all too often, the military offered advice hardly worth hearing."[49]

Willingness to criticize military leadership also materialized in interviews for this book. One former officer complained over the lack of accountability and wondered "how many truly incompetent officers did we promote or allow to retire with honor?" Another criticized leaders for their willingness to "dial the rheostat to just under the level by which the public will be outraged . . . we've kept it just at the level where, ok, so long as we're only wasting $50B per year and lose only 15 American lives, we can continue this indefinitely."

Relief from command should not be the only recourse, of course, but it is the most public and forceful means of reasserting accountability. And one cannot help but be dismayed at how rarely military leaders have been fired for reasons related to the post-9/11 wars. Journalist Tom Ricks put it best: "In World War II, the firing of a general was seen as a sign that the system was working as planned. Yet now, in the rare instances when it does occur, relief tends to be seen, especially inside the Army, as a sign that the system has somehow failed."[50] When senior military leaders have been relieved over the course of the post-9/11 wars, moreover, it has rarely been because of mistakes related to the war effort, and—much like during the Vietnam War—those firings were the result of interventions by senior civilian leaders.[51] Two four-star general officers resigned from their jobs because of misspeaking to the press. Admiral William Fallon gave a journalist from *Esquire* magazine the impression that he was the only thing stopping the Bush administration from going to war with Iran. General Stanley McChrystal's staff mocked Vice President Biden in front of an embedded *Rolling Stone* reporter.

"I just couldn't understand the lack of political awareness by senior officers of the impact at the White House of their remarks to the press," explained a dismayed former Secretary of Defense Robert Gates in his memoirs—interestingly, he was referring to then CJCS Admiral Michael Mullen, who was discussing a possible war with Iran.[52] Explaining these missteps, one former senior official underscored that having embedded journalists meant the media had a "ubiquitous presence," which "led a lot of military guys to think they are media wizards," meaning that they believed they knew how to safely manipulate the press.

Engaging the media from the battlefield in a 24/7 communications environment was critical for the military leadership, of course, even though the stakes were invariably high. Recounting his time leading the U.S. war in Afghanistan, Lieutenant General David Barno referenced the complaints he received—likely from civilian leaders or on their behalf—underscoring that the "only negative phone calls I ever got in each case were media things. In over nineteen months, that was it— nothing on a military operation, nothing on a political operation, nothing on anything going on with the interagency process, nothing on dealing with the embassy, nothing with dealing with allies—the media, yes. That's out of whack."[53]

Three other senior general officers were pushed out of, or severely weakened in, their roles, but none represent satisfying examples of proper accountability because they were due to bureaucratic politics and mandatory congressional oversight functions rather than their operational handling of the wars. CJCS General Peter Pace served only one term as the nation's senior officer because Gates feared a grueling and potentially negative confirmation hearing if Pace was renominated. "In my heart, I knew I had, for all practical purposes, sacrificed Pete Pace to save the surge. I was not proud of that," explained Gates in his memoirs.[54] General Eric Shinseki, who infamously suggested to Congress that the Army would need many more troops for the Iraq War than Rumsfeld approved, found his successor publicly named while he still had a year left as chief of staff of the Army. Lieutenant General Ricardo Sanchez retired rather than accept a promotion to SOUTHCOM commander due to concerns that he would not get confirmed because of his "leadership" during the Abu Ghraib prison scandal.[55]

The only example of a four-star general officer being fired due to failures in the post-9/11 wars is General David McKiernan, who com-

manded the war in Afghanistan. Even this decision lacked clear explanation. Gates announced that McKiernan was leaving as a result of a
new U.S. approach to the war: "We have a new strategy, a new mission,
and a new ambassador. I believe that a new military leadership is also
needed."[56] Gates did not point to McKiernan's specific failures but, instead, explained that it simply was not working out.[57] It seems Gates
felt that McKiernan was less suited for the role than General Stanley
McChrystal. McChrystal had racked up successes early in the Afghanistan War and then in the Iraq War, including commanding the troops
who captured Iraqi president Saddam Hussein and killed key al Qaeda
leader Abu Musab al-Zarqawi. McKiernan's firing represented, to Gates's
utter surprise, "the first time a wartime commander had been relieved
since Truman fired Douglas MacArthur in 1951."[58]

In only a slight exaggeration, one senior general expressed his perturbation that "nobody was ever fired or held accountable at the leader level
for battlefield incompetence or for failing in the fight." Otherwise, those
relieved during this period worked on issues unrelated to the wars or
were more junior. Chief of Staff of the Air Force General Michael Mose-
ley was fired following various nuclear mishaps and his focus on future
wars, as discussed earlier; a Marine major general was fired for problems
with the F-35 program.[59] Two Marine major generals were fired for failing to adequately protect a base in Afghanistan, and one Army major
general was fired due to awful conditions at Walter Reed Army Medical
Center.[60] Indeed, as Paul Yingling lamented, "A private who loses a rifle
suffers far greater consequences than a general who loses a war."[61]

Both a worrisome pattern and a concerning implication emerge from
this analysis. No senior military leader was relieved for strategic-level
reasons in Iraq, and only one was in Afghanistan. Civilians were more
sensitive to military accountability than the military leadership itself,
but typically focused on political-bureaucratic issues rather than the operational handling of the wars. This suggests that who is, or who is not,
doing the disciplining has contributed to the murkiness of accountability soup. It also, perhaps, fomented the rise of the celebrity general officer. While the celebrity general officer is not uncommon in wartime—an
illustrative list would include General Norman Schwarzkopf in the 1991

Persian Gulf War, General Douglas MacArthur in the Korean War and World War II, and General George McClellan in the U.S. Civil War—the length of the post-9/11 wars meant that these leaders remained in the military, and in the public's eye, for a sustained stretch of time. Yet the post-9/11 celebrity military leaders generally fell, not because of operational missteps or substantive reasons but, rather, media and personal issues.

The best example of the recent celebrity general officer is General David Petraeus, who was seen as the solution to many of the challenges that emerged throughout the first decade of the post-9/11 wars.[62] Nicknamed "King David" by some in Iraq and in the press, he repeatedly took senior positions as a replacement for previous military leaders, including for General Casey in Iraq, Admiral Fallon at CENTCOM, and General McChrystal in Afghanistan. Stories about his intellectual and physical prowess dominated the headlines.[63] Toward the end of his second administration, President Bush relied on him so much that valid concerns emerged about a civil-military imbalance.[64]

Like MacArthur in the 1940s and 1950s, Petraeus's future career in national politics was bandied about—indeed, often by him. In Iraq, he once described his role as "a combination of being the president and the pope." He also would extemporaneously tell people that he was not interested in being president or in entering politics.[65] Perhaps unsurprisingly, his swift rise was exceeded only by his even faster fall. Petraeus was caught leaking classified information to his biographer, with whom he was also having an affair.[66] His legacy remains complicated. Some look past these indiscretions to focus on his undeniable achievements. Others have seen them as a reason to toss aside his often-resented celebrity status.[67]

A few other general officers also took on a celebrity aura, including General McChrystal and Lieutenant General H. R. McMaster. McChrystal's ascetic lifestyle was written about glowingly and he was the runner-up for *Time* magazine's "person of the year."[68] His downfall was rapid following the bizarre *Rolling Stone* incident already described.

McMaster's tale is similarly littered with extremes: he distinguished himself in the 1991 Persian Gulf War by leading an armored cavalry troop in the Battle of 73 Easting that destroyed an Iraqi formation with six times as many vehicles. In the next Gulf war, he was vaunted as one of the key officers who promoted a counterinsurgency approach rather than a traditional firepower-centric conventional one.[69] His book *Dereliction of Duty,* moreover, became required reading across the military leadership in the 1990s and throughout the post-9/11 wars for its indictment of the senior military leadership's failures to appropriately advise civilian leaders during the Vietnam War, although it is best described by scholar Kori Schake, who argues that it "tries to leach the politics out of policy" and is "written from the perspective of someone inexperienced judging the compromises of their elders."[70] McMaster was twice passed over for promotion to general officer, until senior civilian officials intervened to ensure that General Petraeus would chair his selection board. He further politicized himself while still in uniform by serving as President Trump's national security adviser. Although debate continues over how much blame he personally deserves for the dynamics within the Trump administration, it appears he may have fallen into the same trap as those elders he castigates in his book; one cannot help but wonder how he would grade his own performance.[71] A senior official perhaps put it best: "We created the rock star general, who was accustomed to *getting* anything they wanted, [and] the adversary was not that sophisticated, so they could *do* whatever they wanted—except get a sustainable outcome." It's been hard to see victory, let alone swim to it, through the post-9/11 wars' accountability soup.

Personal Loss amid Exhaustion

During the post-9/11 wars, senior military leaders—those who make the most fundamental decisions on the use of violence—were profoundly affected by losses among their troops. This occurred in part because of changes in battlefield medicine that enabled the deep personalization of casualties. Scholar Tanisha Fazal finds that 200 years ago the ratio of killed to wounded among U.S. combatants was 1 to 1.4, but by the year 2000 it had become 1 to 10, largely because of improved preventative medicine, evacuation times and logistics, and protective equipment.[72]

Particularly relevant for the post-9/11 wars, she also demonstrates that wounded troops resonate differently with the public than do fatalities. Simply put, the public pays much less attention when troops are wounded than when they are killed.[73] So, while the post-9/11 wars have produced proportionally more disabling injuries than other U.S. conflicts, that these are injuries rather than deaths has had the perverse impact of muting the legacy of the wars and their political impact at home. Moreover, the heavy reliance on military contractors in the post-9/11 wars—more contractors died in Afghanistan than U.S. military personnel, a trend that quite possibly applies to the wars in other countries, as well—makes it difficult for the public and the national security apparatus alike to recognize the full human cost of these conflicts.[74]

The remarkable change in the U.S. killed-to-wounded ratio is consonant with dynamics inherent in the AVF, including the rise of the "family business" and shifts in deployment procedures. Unlike in the Vietnam War, as one retired senior general officer underscored, "When someone was shot and medevac'd out, no one heard from them. No one went to their funeral. It was an individual. There was no unit basis like today. All these soldiers are a part of a family. When they deploy and there's a death, it's like a death in the family . . . none of this was like that in Vietnam." And, the relative dearth of big battles—which would have been commemorated like in other wars—meant that memorialization in the post-9/11 wars has invariably focused more on individual sacrifice than collective achievement or loss.

While the retired senior general officer's remark may be somewhat of an exaggeration, much evidence exists to support the notion that the ways in which senior military leadership internalized the loss of those killed in combat were different from their predecessors in previous American wars. Reflecting on this phenomenon, a former senior general officer remarked that the military's leadership "felt these casualties far more dramatically even though the numbers were infinitesimally smaller than Vietnam." Over the course of the post-9/11 wars, for example, general officers were known for carrying laminated pictures of those they lost in their breast pocket.

During his tours at CENTCOM, TRADOC (training and doctrine

command), as chief of staff of the Army, and as CJCS, General Martin Dempsey had a box filled with cards of every soldier who had died under his command and would put a few in his pocket every single day.[75] During Dempsey's retirement ceremony, President Obama remarked that the box was inscribed "Make It Matter," and that, for Dempsey, "every meeting, every trip, every decision, every troop review—every moment of every day some of those fallen heroes are with him."[76]

General John Campbell also carried cards of those who died under his command while he led the war in Eastern Afghanistan. As journalist Greg Jaffe masterfully chronicles, once, while Campbell fumbled in front of his troops to put the cards away, he explained, "I carry these because I don't want to forget that there is a human cost."[77]

Other senior military officers had experiences similar to those of General Stanley McChrystal, who states in his memoir that he spent most of his evenings in Afghanistan sending letters to the families of those who had died under his command.[78] During a fifteen-month deployment to Iraq at the height of the violence, a division commander—a general officer who commanded 12,000 servicemembers—made an effort to seek out every casualty that occurred among his troops in an effort to find meaning in the conflict. Those around him observed that "putting his hand on the body bag or head of each one and praying . . . nearly broke him."[79] In a more recent example, when asked about "whether American lives had been given in vain" in the Afghanistan War, CJCS General Mark Milley responded darkly: "Absolutely not, [otherwise] I couldn't answer myself at 2 or 3 in the morning when my eyes pop open and I see the dead roll in front of my eyes."[80]

The senior political leadership also felt these losses personally and directly. President Obama recounted how "clear-eyed" he was after visiting wounded servicemembers, including "about the true costs of war, and who bore those costs."[81] He reflected on Lincoln's experience doing the exact same thing during the Civil War and "wondered how Lincoln had managed it, what prayers he said afterward."[82] Both former Secretaries of Defense Robert Gates and Leon Panetta have discussed the intense emotions they felt about the human costs of the war. The emotional impact of sending troops into harm's way echoes throughout Gates's memoir.

He recounts learning all about those killed in combat and signing letters to their families, that he soon began writing the letters himself—at
times, more than 100 per month—and that "virtually every night for
four and a half years, writing condolence letters and reading about these
mostly young men and women, I wept."[83] He also describes the intense
emotions he felt while meeting troops, and how he once awkwardly told
some of them, "I love you."[84] Like his predecessor, Panetta spent hours
each week signing letters to families, as well.[85]

There is, of course, a historical precedent for the feelings that Gates
and Panetta describe. While Secretary of Defense McNamara's memoirs
do not reflect on how losses in the Vietnam War affected him personally, his more recent reflections illustrate the intensity of his feelings
as the American losses accumulated.[86] In 1967—a low point in the
war during which President Lyndon Johnson wondered if McNamara
could, or should, continue serving as secretary of defense—McNamara
was known for regularly and uncontrollably weeping in meetings as he
learned about the course of the war. He tried to hide this, as one of his
secretaries described, by gazing out of the window and "cry[ing] into the
curtain."[87]

What impact did all these efforts to personalize and memorialize
those killed in combat have on senior political and military decisionmakers? Gates was blunt: "I would do everything I could for us to win
in Iraq and Afghanistan. But I knew the real cost. And that knowledge
changed me."[88] Panetta says he went to Dover, Delaware, to welcome back
the bodies of those killed in combat and, "after I returned from Dover,
I never looked at a deployment order book the same way again."[89] However, neither Gates nor Panetta share more about how they approached
policy decisions on the post-9/11 wars differently given their cognizance
of the costs. And a few months into the post-9/11 wars, Secretary of Defense Rumsfeld told his staff that he wanted to write condolence letters
to all the families of those who died in Afghanistan—although for two
years, until the media uncovered it, he used a mechanical signature machine.[90]

For the military leaders who lived and breathed the losses in a much
more direct way than the civilians, efforts to personalize and memori-

alize them may have taken an even greater emotional toll. It is curious that so many believed that the only way to ensure they thought seriously about the costs of the war was to carry around small personal reminders. Doing so may have affected their ability to make clear-headed decisions on gut-wrenching issues involving danger to their troops. The example of General George McClellan in the Civil War provides an illustrative analogy. As Union losses accumulated, he grew increasingly hesitant about using force—a hesitancy that grew into intransigence. Most notably, he blamed President Lincoln and the secretary of war for the Army for the Potomac's losses. To take one example, McClellan declared to the secretary of war after one ugly battle in the summer of 1862, "I again repeat that I am not responsible for this . . . the Government must not and cannot hold me responsible for the result . . . If I save this army now, I tell you plainly that I owe no thanks to you [Lincoln] or to any other persons in Washington. You have done your best to sacrifice this army."[91]

At a minimum, however, personalizing the losses increased leaders' stress. This always has an impact on decisionmaking, either for good or for ill.[92] One retired senior general officer was deeply concerned that carrying around cards:

Flies in the face of what senior leaders have to do in combat. It's a pernicious idea . . . you get into a major war, take a lot of casualties, you can't have that kind of connection. On one hand, it is praiseworthy and humane and I would want my children [to have a commander who would carry these cards around]. But from a professional standpoint, it worries me that our senior leaders are too close to the casualties.

This notion resonated with other senior military leaders, as well. Perhaps the best description comes from General Stanley McChrystal, who declared that it was "critical to maintain as much discipline over my emotions" as possible.[93] His memoir describes his desire to emulate General Ulysses Grant, who was famously willing to let his army suffer heavy casualties if it meant victory: "I remembered Grant's admission that he rarely visited his wounded in field hospitals because he felt seeing the cost of his decisions so starkly would prevent him from making the difficult decisions he believed were necessary. I found strength in Grant's candor."[94]

Personalizing losses in combat influences decisionmaking by heightening casualty sensitivity. This is largely a good thing for military leaders, as long as it does not, as one scholar warned, slip into a "casualty phobia" that elevates risk as the top concern rather than as one variable among many when making decisions on the use of force.[95] This can empower senior military officers in their relationships with civilian leaders.

As scholar Yagil Levy, for example, has found in his exploration of how civilian control in Israel was affected by the 2006 Israel-Hizballah war and the 2009 Gaza war, casualty sensitivity has two effects. First, the personalization of losses encourages leaders to adopt "policies of casualty aversion" that manifest in more restrained approaches to fighting. But "military and political leaders' efforts to compensate for these restraints [in order to win] ultimately give the military even more latitude. These efforts involve military doctrines that allow rapid decision making, contingency plans that weaken civilian control, and the military's control over the cost-informed discourse."[96] Interestingly, when military leaders personalize losses in combat, their influence is, therefore, often strengthened, to the detriment of civilian control.

The personalization of losses contributed to another easy-to-overlook but important factor in the practice of leadership during the post-9/11 wars: exhaustion. Secretary of Defense Gates describes the Pentagon as "weary" when he left in 2011 after his five draining years in office.[97] General Stanley McChrystal shows the exhaustion bred by obsessive focus on the wars—a focus exemplified by the fact that he was apart from his family for nearly half a decade—in his description of visiting troops in the stifling Iraqi heat: "I had told the men that day what I believed and what had come to be my life: *It's the fight. It's the fight. It's the fight.*"[98] After more than a decade of fighting, the American public had not, in general, personalized U.S. losses or felt the depths of wartime exhaustion, but its leadership had to wrestle with their grief and their exhaustion for years on end. Doing so invariably exacerbated the difficulties of military leaders' repeated deployments to war zones, in particular, as they sought to lead under strained circumstances throughout the post-9/11 wars.

The legacy of personalizing losses in the post-9/11 wars is best described through the concept of the "sunk cost fallacy." This occurs when individuals or institutions continue behaviors because of previously committed resources, such as time, treasure, or blood, even when it is irrational to do so. The status quo is maintained or even deepened. To what extent did the personalization of sacrifice shape the advice that military leaders provided to civilians on how best to conclude the post-9/11 wars? General Milley's description of how he justified losses, and the "Make it Matter" box on General Dempsey's desk, suggest that the pull to stay the course for the sake of honoring the dead may have been strong. Like Robert McNamara, we cannot help but weep over spilled blood.

COMMAND CLIMATE CHALLENGES

Throughout the post-9/11 wars, the senior military leadership also faced three command climate challenges in particular: micromanagement; increased politicization; and ethics problems. These dynamics are far from unique to the post-9/11 wars, but there is worrisome evidence that they have intensified in the past two decades. They were exacerbated by a number of factors, none more significant than modern communications technologies. Military leaders may have tolerated and even fomented them, however, because of their commitment to the mission. Lesser issues with command climate were ignored out of military leaders' desires to solve problems and to convince their troops that they had good cause to fight.

Micromanagement

While micromanagement is a charge often levied at civilian leaders, it plagued the military leadership, as well. Two Army issues exemplify how micromanagement surged: the proliferation of PowerPoint concept of operations (CONOP) requirements and the subsequent weakening of mission command. These issues bled into one another, as the ability to see on the battlefield and into the battlefield increased dramatically.

The first issue, the PowerPoint CONOP process, involved the preparation of slide deck descriptions of mission plans and became popular early in the post-9/11 wars, when the Army employed them as a way of conveying information to senior military leaders. The process quickly became ubiquitous across different levels of command, and was employed to convey a level of detail about proposed battlefield engagements to which senior military leaders had not previously had easy access. And once the engagement was approved and executed, participants then had to build a PowerPoint slide deck known as a "storyboard" to describe what had occurred. As one senior officer explained, "Every contact with the enemy required" it. He then went on to clarify that the requirement became so onerous and frustrating that "people did not report enemy contact because they knew the storyboard was useless and they didn't want to go through the hassle" of making one.[99] The result was that senior military leaders had much more information about operations at the microlevel than in previous conflicts.

The second issue, mission command, is the Army's concept for conveying guidance in a manner such that the commander's intent can be appropriately interpreted and executed by soldiers.[100] It was described by one senior general officer as "you give me your left and right, tell me your end state, and I've got freedom of action to accomplish that . . . I've got freedom of action to get it done." As then Chief of Staff of the Army General Mark Milley described, it is "disciplined disobedience to achieve a higher purpose."[101]

Taken together, the CONOP process constrained junior leader decisionmaking across the Army. The level of required detail and the length of the approval process was destructive to the notion of "disciplined disobedience." Counterinsurgency-related restrictions on the application of firepower and the subsequently senior level of approval required for employing it further weakened mission command. Criticizing this process, one senior general officer argued that the CONOP process had "done more to hamper and inhibit mission command than anything else . . . everything was 'ask permission.'" Concurring, a different senior general officer explained that "today we have leaders who don't believe [in mission command] because they have had to ask 'mother may I' for ten years . . . May I go? May I shoot? May I drop a bomb?" He described it as an "inadvertent and unforeseen second and third order effect" of the military's implementation of counterinsurgency doctrine. Having to constantly seek permission for and report on so many engagements may imbue those junior officers with a skewed and more reluctant approach toward mission command as they grow more senior. Indeed, a more junior officer argued, "Young leaders are absolutely capable and ready to make decisions and take initiative but are often hindered by chains of command that are risk averse and overly focused on continuous information." He said that the focus for fixing the situation should be on senior military leaders rather than on younger ones. The "real issue that needs treatment is how senior leaders are trained to lead and manage organizations."

Going forward, senior military leaders will need to focus on how to maintain control and common direction while facilitating the environment of trust upon which mission command depends. Failure to do so will inhibit their troops. A mid-grade officer underscored the problem as that of the "12 o'clock general," a senior leader who is interested in hearing advice at 11:00 or at 1:00; that is, advice that is almost wholly in line with his original thinking. A junior officer, in contrast, feared becoming the "tactical general who micromanages and doesn't enable mission command." If the United States is in the position of waging a high-end conventional conflict in the future, of course, this kind of micromanagement will likely be impossible. Concepts like General Stanley McChrystal's "team of teams" approach, which prioritize collaboration between and among cohorts rather than the stiffly hierarchical approach that can encourage micromanagement, will be particularly critical going forward.[102]

Politicization

The senior U.S. military leadership has been an unavoidably politicized body throughout its history. Major General Leonard Wood campaigned for president while in uniform during the 1920 election cycle.[103] General Douglas MacArthur plotted a run for president while leading the war in Korea. More recently, General Colin Powell, while serving as CJCS, published an op-ed titled "Why Generals Get Nervous" a few weeks before the 1992 presidential election. In it, he praised President George H. W. Bush, who, "more than any other recent President, understands the proper use of military force."[104] Nevertheless, the character of this politicization shifted during the post-9/11 wars, in part because of the growing partisanship of society itself.[105]

One of the challenges in even discussing the issue of politicization of the military is that it can ignore the inherently political nature of military force. Carl von Clausewitz's often-quoted maxim that "war is the continuation of politics by other means" is a reminder that no discussion of the military can be safely detached from politics. The apolitical norm that populates the military would be better conceptualized, as James Golby and I have written, as: (1) a recognition that the military is fundamentally a political creature; and, (2) the development of tangible and practical rules for how best to engage in this complex political landscape. Specifically, the military would benefit from leaders who urge its members to avoid partisanship, institutional endorsements, and electoral influence.[106]

Over the course of the post-9/11 wars, the United States has grown increasingly polarized along partisan lines, which—when coupled with widespread support of the military, which is more trusted than any other public institution—puts the military in an exceedingly awkward position.[107] Such dynamics amplify the crisis of caring and the crisis of meaningful civilian control. This polarization has heightened pressures on the military and perniciously seeped into its internal dynamics. Some recent examples include President Trump signing a temporary travel ban on Muslim-majority countries inside the Pentagon's Hall of Heroes; regaling troops at Central Command and Special Operations Command about how much political support he commanded in the election because of them; urging sailors to lobby members of Congress on the defense budget; and granting clemency to convicted war criminals and then bringing them onstage during a political fundraiser.[108] Civilian leaders' failure to insulate the military from partisan domestic politics has resulted in dismaying events like servicemembers covering up the name of the USS *John McCain* out of fear that the president would be upset to see a ship named after a political opponent, and troops bringing red "Make America Great Again" hats and a Trump campaign banner for him to sign on his visit at Ramstein Air Base.[109]

No event, however, challenged the military's hard-earned reputation for nonpartisanship like the June 1, 2020, decision by CJCS General Mark Milley, in uniform, to join President Trump for a photo op on his walk across Lafayette Square to Saint John's Church in the middle of the ongoing Black Lives Matter protests. In a powerful commencement speech to the National Defense University faculty and students the following week, Milley apologized for participating and stated, "I should not have been there."[110] Not long after, Air Force Chief of Staff General David Goldfein warned about how politicization can affect public support of the military. He feared that if the military became involved in politics, this support would be shattered since it is "a Fabergé egg that can be broken if we're not careful."[111]

Two key issues demonstrate the shifting character of military politicization: voting by senior military leaders—or, rather, not voting—and their public alliances with political parties following retirement.

During the post-9/11 wars, a growing number of senior military leaders publicly proclaimed that they did not vote.[112] Examples include General Petraeus, who bragged about not voting, as well as Admiral Mullen. There is some data on this issue of voting—or, rather, the lack thereof. According to a 2018 survey of servicemembers, voting registration was 12 percent lower among military personnel than among their civilian counterparts, and turnout was more than 25 percent lower.[113] While data on those who chose not to vote due to perceptions of partisanship is unavailable, anecdotally, it seems to have gotten increasingly popular. When discussing this issue of voting with a mix of typically mid-career military and civilian graduate students, I have repeatedly found in recent years that the overwhelming majority of students in the military are proud of their decision not to vote. They chose not to do so out of deep-seated concern that they would be perceived as political. Civilian students are usually floored by this revelation, and view it as an abdication of their responsibility as citizens. These views are shared by some senior military leaders, as well. Before the 2016 election, CJCS General Joseph Dunford made a point to emphasize that he votes, declaring that "I didn't spend 39 years in uniform not to exercise my responsibility and right as a citizen."[114]

Public alliances with political parties by retired senior military leaders also have gained steam throughout the post-9/11 wars. Perhaps this should be unsurprising because, as scholar Jason Dempsey pointedly argues, "The more members of the military build a reputation for apolitical service to the country the greater a political prize the military becomes."[115] Research by Zachary Griffiths and Olivia Simon finds that endorsements are occasionally for financial reasons, more often for ideological reasons, and, overwhelmingly, to support colleagues.[116]

Although this issue of political endorsements often came up in interviews, many senior military leaders inaccurately saw it as a recent phenomenon associated primarily with the 2016 presidential cycle, during which retired Generals Mike Flynn and John Allen endorsed candidates at their respective national conventions. That is "not the way our country operated," argued one senior general officer, who explained that he is "afraid the political activities, the politicization of our retired general and flag officers, is going to bleed over to our active duty officers." He feared that military leaders would someday be asked, "What's your party? How do you vote?" His fixation on the 2016 election—shared with many others—ignores that this has been an issue for decades. At the 2004 Republican and Democratic national conventions, just-retired General Tommy Franks and former CJCS John Shalikashvili endorsed candidates. At the 1996 Republican national convention, recently retired CJCS General Colin Powell enthusiastically endorsed Bob Dole. Even further back, in 1988, the former commandant of the Marine Corps endorsed President George H. W. Bush. As scholars James Golby, Heidi Urben, Kyle

Dropp, and Peter Feaver fear, such endorsements may "damage . . . the trust the American people place in a nonpartisan military."[117] Moreover, surveys show that the public is unable to tell the difference between retired and current military leaders, which makes it more likely that these scholars' fears will come to fruition.[118]

As these practices grow more ubiquitous, they risk harming the military both internally and externally. The military's increasing partisanship, and the American peoples' perceptions of it, are worrisome trends.[119] Scholar and active-duty Army officer Colonel Heidi Urben found evidence of increasing politicization in a survey of 4,000 active-duty Army officers, but that the officer corps does not recognize it as such. She notes, for example, that "the fact that a quarter of respondents feel it is appropriate for active duty military to publicly criticize elected officials and a third feel there should be no limits on their public, political expression is startling."[120] Social media makes this dynamic even more troubling.[121]

The military's leadership is aware of these challenges, and is trying to balance between enabling former military personnel to be active in the national security discourse and ensuring that their partisanship does not harm the military itself. For example, two former CJCSs, Admiral Michael Mullen and General Martin Dempsey, discouraged their fellow retired general and flag officers from wading too deeply into politics.[122] In the run-up to the 2016 election, CJCS General Joseph Dunford also spoke out against politicization and partisanship, warning those in uniform to determinedly avoid both.[123] These efforts may have informed the decrease in former and retired military endorsements for presidential candidates during and after the 2016 election. Yet there is a need for these voices to be heard on issues in which they have unique expertise, particularly regarding issues associated with the force itself.

It also is incumbent on civilians, particularly political appointees, to help protect the military from the dangers posed by politicization. Practically speaking, however, civilians will not always live up to that responsibility, even though they should. Going forward, the military's leaders must, therefore, grow comfortable encouraging dialogue regarding the force's politicization. They can ensure that General Milley's June

1, 2020, walk across Lafayette Square is a case study debated in professional military education classrooms. As they continue to learn from that walk, they also can remind incoming and retiring general and flag officers to not take their own politically partisan steps, whether in or out of uniform.[124]

Ethics

Expectations for ethical conduct among senior military leaders are high—indeed, often higher than for their civilian counterparts because of the military's special responsibility to wage violence on behalf of the state. As then CJCS General Martin Dempsey underscored in the midst of a flurry of ethics concerns across the force, the "overwhelming majority of our military leaders are tremendous professionals and citizens who show up to serve, to bring their best, and often sacrifice greatly."[125] He was exactly right. Nevertheless, the growth of ethics violations among senior military leadership, particularly in the second decade of the post-9/11 wars, merits exploration.

These violations, and the often-lacking official treatments for them, differ by military service. The Defense Department Inspector General's tally of misconduct shows a massive uptick in complaints and violations since 2008, which more than doubled throughout this period, with a particular spike in 2012.[126] Then Secretary of Defense Leon Panetta asked CJCS General Dempsey to review the ethics of general and flag officers. His findings, which were briefed to President Obama, underscored the importance of briefing officers on ethical dilemmas more regularly and earlier in their careers, as well as regularly assessing the roles of aides in supporting senior military leaders.[127] "The Bathsheba Syndrome: The Ethical Failures of Successful Leaders," a piece that discusses poor leadership decisions through a biblical lens, was assigned as required reading at the Secretary of Defense's quarterly gathering of senior political and military leaders in 2012. Its assignment followed the publication of a scathing New York Times piece reporting a wide range of ethical violations by general and flag officers, including "poor judgment, malfeasance and sexual improprieties or sexual violence."[128]

The rate of violations remains worryingly high. From 2013 to 2017, hundreds of senior officials participated in a wide range of misconduct, even though fewer investigations were conducted throughout this period by all of the military services except the Navy.[129] Over fiscal years 2013 to 2017, 963 general and flag officers were accused of misconduct, and these allegations were substantiated at a startling rate: 124 from the Air Force, 181 from the Army, thirty-six from the Navy, and fifteen from the Marines. The associated punishments, however, appear to have been light: only two were reduced in rank, six were retired, and six were removed from their assignments.[130] This disjuncture between cause and consequence did not go publicly unnoticed. *Duffel Blog*, for example, satirically noted what appeared to be a pattern of weak punishments for senior leaders and more severe treatment of the lower ranks. As one piece joked, the military apparently aimed "to promote good leadership, which is exemplified by actions such as destroying morale within your organization by levying draconian punishments for minor infractions for the sake of political expediency."[131]

In a devastating study, "Lying to Ourselves: Dishonesty in the Army Profession," scholars Leonard Wong and Stephen Gerras argue that the Army leadership is "ethically numb."[132] Their work is filled with disturbing anecdotes in which Army officers declare their stringent ethics while simultaneously offering example after example of those officers lying or acting dishonestly, including falsifying reports about the Army's readiness and capabilities, the completion of training requirements, the status of partner military capabilities, and engagements with enemy forces.[133] There was no shortage of excuses offered by the Army officers for doing so, including the perceived silliness of certain rules, the impossibility of actually fulfilling the spirit of those rules, and the existence of higher priorities.[134] Perhaps the most alarming quote comes from a major who feared that the officer corps was "creating an environment where everything is too rosy because everyone is afraid to paint the true picture."[135] Gerras and Wong urge the Army "to introspectively examine how it might be inadvertently abetting the very behavior it deems unacceptable."[136] When paired with other concerning analysis—such as Mark Cancian's compilation of senior military leaders' quotes about Afghanistan from 2001 to 2018, which brimmed with overoptimism about the likelihood of victory—it is hard not to be moved by their scathing indictment of the Army leadership.[137]

For the Navy, the Fat Leonard scandal discussed in chapter 6 represented the most spectacular example of widespread ethics violations. That it brought down numerous senior Navy officers, however, tells only part of the story of Navy leadership's wider ethical issues, particularly over the last decade. In one of his final interviews as chief of naval operations, Admiral Richardson addressed the repeated problems with fragging, sexual assaults, and spying on journalists that plagued the Navy throughout his tenure, as well as the Navy's hollow and occasionally egregiously trivial attempts to address misconduct.[138] His successor, Admiral Gilday, sent a message to the Navy after three months on the job that underscored the criticality of being "men and women of integrity . . . [and] honorable . . . standard-bearers . . . above reproach."[139] He did not, however, directly address the ethics failures engulfing the Navy or offer any guidance about his willingness to punish violators.

Although these three dynamics are not a direct indictment of the military leadership, they should inspire concern. Perhaps what looks like a rise in unethical behavior actually reflects something more healthy—a more stringent redefinition of what is acceptable and an increased willingness to confront issues like toxic leadership. Whether they are due to exhaustion, frustration, inconclusive outcomes, or other reasons, the senior military leadership would do well to study the implications of its issues with command climate to ensure their successors are not captured by them.

The legacies of the post-9/11 wars will shape who leads the U.S. military in the future. There will be those in the military who praise the wartime military leadership and do not blame them for the mistakes that occurred. They may be skeptical of meaningful civilian control and hesitant to employ force absent overwhelming resources and clear end-states. There also will be those in the military who feel the wars were mishandled, who are perturbed about how they transpired, and who attribute responsibility for them and the casualties they caused to previous generations of military leaders. They also may seek, like Powell before them, to offload responsibilities and risk by seeking overwhelming resources and clear end-states from civilians while assiduously avoiding gray situations and unconventional enemies. Both groups are likely to feel a sense of loss, unclear accountability, and muddied outcomes, which will invariably intertwine with the crisis of confidence and the crisis of meaningful civilian control. These two different groups will, undoubtedly, grow very different leaders, and while the implications for future civil-military relations and command climate are unclear, they are worthy of further exploration.

And that, of course, will make all the difference for the future U.S. military.

9

The Military's Preparedness
for Future Conflicts

"We can't decide which theory of war is right."

Over nearly two decades of war, a number of different approaches to waging war flitted in and out of popularity with the U.S. military as it sought to deal with the consequences of the 9/11 attacks. Unsurprisingly, senior political and military leaders hoped to find an approach that would yield victory. Four examples are worth exploring, as they interacted with each other to shape the military's approach to fighting: technology as a singular solution; counterinsurgency doctrine; by, with, and through partnerships; and, whole-of-government solutions. Each of these four approaches for how the U.S. military should fight and win rose and fell—and sometimes fell and rose—throughout the wars.

"We can't decide which theory of war is right, which makes it hard to hold leaders accountable and hard to figure out which lessons to carry forward," one former officer told me. These four approaches were theoretical emperors regarding how to win the post-9/11 wars, but each wore less clothing than expected, magnifying the crisis of confidence and shaping the crisis of meaningful civilian control. As a result, the military finds itself in a situation somewhat similar to the post-Vietnam War period, when it was not sure how to fight and embarked on years in the theoretical wilderness, hunting for a new approach. Uncertainty over which approach is right and, thus, what conclusions to draw from the post-9/11 wars themselves, is among their key legacies, as that uncertainty will continue to refract through the military's looking glass as it contemplates the future of war.

THE REVOLUTION IN MILITARY AFFAIRS WILL NOT BE TELEVISED

The most popular approach to war in the United States in the decade before the 9/11 attacks was the "revolution in military affairs," or RMA. Following the U.S. military's spectacular and speedy victory against Iraq in the 1991 Persian Gulf War, the notion that technological change could play an outsized role in military effectiveness surged within the defense community. Best described by Michael Vickers and Robert Martinage, the revolution in military affairs approach held that "periods of discontinuous change . . . render obsolete or subordinate existing means for continuing war."[1]

While there was profound anxiety before the 1991 Persian Gulf War about the potential costs of fighting the Iraqi military, battle-hardened after its eight years of war with Iran, U.S. losses, ultimately, proved minimal.[2] An enormous air campaign enabled a four-day ground war. Profound technological asymmetries between U.S. and Iraqi militaries shaped combat in both domains.[3] The rapid victory was quickly mythologized as manifesting a revolution in military affairs, which the military had achieved through its late-Cold War investments in advanced technologies.[4] Certainly, the war had demonstrated the value of combining a sophisticated command and control architecture, stealth aircraft, and conventional precision strike capabilities to facilitate a new quality of power projection against legacy military forces.

As one senior general officer described it, "The Gulf War was a big eye opener for everybody . . . [it] brought the mindset of 'what's possible,'" inspiring the imaginations of defense analysts and practitioners of warfare about how to maximize and utilize the revolution to its fullest. Another former senior official exhorted, "We surprised ourselves at how good we were; we were so dominant on that battlefield . . . [and] demonstrated with a mix of capabilities military dominance in conventional warfare that was totally unprecedented [and] made us feel good."

Nevertheless, the specific details of the RMA remained vague, even as key Defense Department leaders such as Secretary of Defense William Perry and Office of Net Assessment Director Andrew Marshall propagated the approach. Indeed, the 1997 defense strategy contained an entire section on the transformation of U.S. military power, but with little attendant detail.[5] Maintaining a decisive advantage in key technological areas was the prerequisite for victory in the wars of the future.

Prior to September 2001, this faith in technology deepened, particularly once Donald Rumsfeld returned as the Defense Department's chief. As one former senior military officer explained, "He came into the Pentagon with his RMA and this attitude of you guys have really screwed up." The defense strategy published just after the September 11, 2001, attacks underscored the significance of the RMA, which, it hastened to add, was premised "not only [on] technological innovation but also development of operational concepts, undertaking organizational adaptations, and training and experimentation."[6] Rumsfeld viewed the RMA as the impetus for overhauling defense strategy, military organization, and acquisition priorities.[7] He also, notoriously, emphasized the utility of high-end technology during the first part of the post-9/11 wars, most notably in his unwillingness to deploy a larger ground force to Iraq, which he feared would result in nation-building—a mission he desperately sought to avoid.

Rumsfeld and the RMA theorists were partially right: technological progress did play a meaningful role in the U.S. military's operations over the post-9/11 wars. To take just one example, the U.S. military used ten times as many munitions, the vast majority of which were unguided, in the 1991 Persian Gulf War than it did in the 2003 Iraq War's initial air campaign.[8] That suggests that, over about a decade, the military had developed a much more operationally effective arsenal. Powerful conventional precision strike capabilities enabled the United States to project power. In combination with a sophisticated command and control architecture, it also gave the United States a unique ability to find, fix, and finish targets nearly anywhere on earth.[9] But this ability did not translate into strategic success in the case of counterinsurgency in Afghanistan or Iraq.

Some parts of the military entered the post-9/11 wars as "technophiles," but the parts that fought it on the ground left more "technophobic," skeptical of revolutionary technologies as the decisive factor in war.[10] The Marine Corps is traditionally in the latter category, not least due to its limited resources, and the Army may be shifting in that direction, as well. Over the last decade, senior Army general officers were known to quip that "quantity has a quality of its own" to justify prioritizing investments in personnel rather than technology—probably without recognizing they were paraphrasing Marxist ideology.[11] The Army's colossal study on the Iraq War declares one of its primary findings to be that "technology does not always offset numbers."[12] When Obama administration Deputy Secretary of Defense Robert Work and his staff developed the Third Offset concept—an effort to regain the U.S. military's comparative operational advantages vis-à-vis the Chinese and Russian militaries—it received heavy pushback from many corners of the Pentagon.[13] While Work emphasized that it involved "technology, operational concepts, and organizational constructs," the technological thrust was often front and center in discussions about its components, including artificial intelligence and autonomy.[14] Resistance to the Third Offset may be traced, in part, to the heightened sensitivity regarding technology's limits that some military leaders acquired in Iraq and Afghanistan. Views of technology reflect both the crisis of confidence and the crisis of meaningful civilian control as Army leaders, in particular, were much less confident in the scale of the "offset" provided by technology, from General Shinseki's troop number recommendation to skepticism of the Third Offset—whereas civilian leaders have met resistance in efforts to shape force structures that assume more advantages from technology.

The military, undoubtedly, will need to find a new balance between technology's prospects and its limits. It would do well to heed Paula

Thornhill's observation about how the currency of the military is changing. In her masterful exploration of the United States's evolving military, she imagines a fictional colonel who struggles to write his retirement speech. He laments his lack of clarity, manifesting the crisis of confidence in his exclamation, "There is so much about today's military, my military, that doesn't make sense: how it's organized, its tenuous relationship to organized violence, what the nation really wants it to do."[15] The expansion of modern conflict into new domains will surely shift the fundamental contours of what makes a superior military—from who counts as warfighters to what counts as a weapon.[16]

"SOME THINK YOU CAN DO COIN NOW; SOME SAY IT'S TOO MESSY"

While the war in Afghanistan started as an unconventional fight in every sense—the memorable images of the conflict early on were U.S. military personnel on horseback riding next to Afghans while directing strikes by sophisticated aircraft firing precision guided munitions on al Qaeda and Taliban targets—the Iraq War began much more conventionally. Indeed, this conventional approach was deliberately pushed by Secretary of Defense Rumsfeld, and it achieved some notable early successes, including the capture of Baghdad after approximately three weeks of fighting. However, that success turned out to be fleeting as a powerful insurgency grew and turned America's strengths into weaknesses.

As the security situation in Iraq and Afghanistan became increasingly bumpy from 2004 to 2005, there was slow acknowledgement that the wars were morphing into insurgencies. Recognition that insurgencies had rooted in both countries, however, did not come until 2006. In Iraq, the Samarra mosque bombing that year helped convince optimistic skeptics that the country was embroiled in a horrific sectarian conflict that could no longer be waged conventionally. In Afghanistan, an insurgency had already exploded across the country, and Afghan President Hamid Karzai was denouncing civilian casualties caused by the American military before reality imprinted itself on military decisionmakers, not least because Afghanistan had been a lower priority in the run-up to, and the early years of, the Iraq War.

Across the military, there was a desperate effort to figure out how best to deal with the changing character of the wars. Lieutenant General David Barno, the commander of U.S. troops in Afghanistan, recalled asking troops in Afghanistan how they were adapting to the rise of the insurgency in Afghanistan. He proudly recounted the response from one commander, who told him that the answer was, "Easy, sir: booksamillion.com," and then went on to explain that "he had actually ordered books on the internet from Afghanistan on counterinsurgency warfare, had them shipped into his units, and had his people read them as they were in the middle of this fight."[17] At a much more junior level, one officer recounted, "We were using World War I tactics to defeat an insurgency; that's when I knew we were losing" and needed a different approach.

Two authors in particular became very popular in defense circles in the Pentagon from 2004 to 2006: David Galula and T. E. Lawrence. Galula's books, *Pacification in Algeria: 1956–1958* and *Counterinsurgency Warfare*, focus on the French war in Algeria. Lawrence's *Seven Pillars of Wisdom* describes his experience advising Arab insurgents against the Ottomans in the First World War.[18] It is perhaps ironic that, rather than studying U.S. experiences with insurgency and revolutions, such as when it fought against insurgents in the Vietnam War or waged an insurgency during the American Revolutionary War, the military's preference was to turn to the lessons of others—specifically French and British colonial-era thinkers like Galula and Lawrence. While some contemporary thinkers became popular over the years, like American John Nagl and Australian David Kilcullen, the earlier texts remained foundational.[19]

This is problematic because Galula and Lawrence's works, although highly readable, are riddled with flaws. Lawrence's book brims with fictionalized accounts of his experience, which means it is especially readable and alluring, particularly for desperate readers searching for answers amid brewing and confusing violence. Galula's work suffers from even more severe problems. First, the military should have been intrinsically cautious of over-learning lessons from a spectacularly failed French approach that employed extreme methods like brutal torture and was, ultimately, focused on colonial "pacification" to maintain control.[20] Moreover, as scholar Douglas Porch argues, Galula largely ignores theorist Carl von Clausewitz's emphasis on politics. Instead, "tactics became the end-all, a formula that, if properly applied, would win such contests, irrespective of the strategic environment, just so long as governments have the stamina to see the enterprise through to a successful conclusion."[21] This tactical emphasis risks absolving the military from its mistakes and, instead, pinning the blame on other government actors—civilians, in other words—for failing to do their part.

The civil-military implications are clear and problematic. Galula also largely dismisses the potentially corrosive impact of counterinsurgency on the military that wages it, particularly concerning its relationships with civilian leaders.[22] Other problems with his work include, as scholar Joshua Rovner underscores, insinuations that "the civilian population is basically homogenous and that civilians have only three options: support the insurgents, support the government, or remain neutral."[23]

Galula and Lawrence's work permeates the Army and Marine Corps counterinsurgency (COIN) manual published in 2006.[24] The manual, FM 3-24, was an instant hit. It was downloaded more than a million times in the first month after its release, a record for military doctrine, and subsequently published by a respected university press.[25] Its lead developer, General David Petraeus, was a well-known celebrity and had actively engaged with—and courted—the media and the think tank community, in part to proselytize the manual's contents. Within weeks of the manual's publication, Petraeus was placed in charge of the U.S. war in Iraq. He was seen as "a world class explainer," as journalist Mark Bowden nicknamed him, given his role as the public face of the Iraq war.[26] Petraeus's assumption of command in Iraq signaled the rise of the "COINdinistas," well-known military leaders and civilian defense thinkers who supported counterinsurgency doctrine, many of whom had been involved in writing the manual, and who, one scholar argues, "played an important role in the domestic re-legitimization of failing missions in Iraq and Afghanistan between 2006 and 2010."[27]

The manual proved so popular for two reasons in particular. First, General Petraeus's effort to include prominent thinkers in its development, combined with his subsequent masterful strategic communications effort, meant that it was both well-known and welcome in many parts of the defense community even before its release. Second, and probably more importantly, the military leadership and defense policy-makers were desperate and distressed as the post-9/11 wars spiraled into sustained violence. Fire extinguishers that spout military solutions—like FM 3-24—are popular when war efforts appear to be on fire.

But FM 3-24 was riddled with paradoxes, Zen-like koans, ephemeral advice, and almost Sun Tzu-like aphorisms. These helped mask its four fundamental flaws beneath a primer on insurgency and counterinsurgency: an overemphasis on tactical adaptation at the expense of the importance of strategic adaptation; a skewed assumption that the partner state and the counterinsurgent hold the same views on both threats and how best to counter them; an approach that largely discounts the role of politics; and a misapplication of case studies. Nonetheless, it represented the military's first senior-level recognition that the post-9/11 wars had changed and that doctrinal adaptation was desperately needed. As retired Brigadier General Martin Schweitzer observed, the most important "impact of FM 3-24 was that it helped a lot of young leaders who had no context understand COIN. Prior to that, there was no key to the Rosetta Stone."[28]

Much of the criticism of the counterinsurgency approach, moreover, is misplaced. Its adoption should never have been seen as a panacea for victory, and its subsequent failure to generate enduring victory is, thus, insufficient grounds to dismiss its contributions to the U.S. way of war. Support for counterinsurgency, nonetheless, cooled after a few years as the wars in Iraq and Afghanistan continued to rage.[29] And, of course, waging counterinsurgency remained frustrating for those on the ground. "We were told you can't shoot back," described one enlisted servicemember.

Nevertheless, the U.S. military did become better at waging counterinsurgencies, but the COINdinistas and their fellow travelers "didn't—they couldn't—make this war acceptable either to the American public or to the people in the lands where it was fought," Fred Kaplan compellingly argues.[30] More importantly, the military, ultimately, could not win the counterinsurgency fight because the need for a political solution in both Iraq and Afghanistan was neglected.

The approach and practice of counterinsurgency as applied by the

U.S. military in the post-9/11 wars has resulted in extreme—often strawman—arguments for and against the approach. As one former senior civilian official explained, the military remains divided on it: "Some think you can do COIN now; some say it's too messy" to ever sufficiently succeed. Scholar Stephen Biddle offers a particularly nuanced set of judgments. He finds that the U.S. experience in Iraq and Afghanistan demonstrates that counterinsurgency is, as he puts it with characteristic understatement, "not impossible." It *can* work, but not cheaply or quickly."[31] He rebukes the military for its insufficient willingness to train and equip its own forces for counterinsurgencies, which he argues had made waging them more challenging.[32] While some in the military leadership might question whether or not the military should conduct counterinsurgencies in the future, the real dilemma it faces is how best to prepare should the political leadership tell it to do so again.

PROBLEMATIC PARTNERS

Since before its formal establishment, thanks to France's crucial assistance during the Revolutionary War, the U.S. military has worked with a wide range of foreign partners. Over the last seventy-five years, and particularly throughout the post-9/11 wars, this pattern of behavior expanded as the U.S. military worked with partner militaries to stabilize fragile states. It is, thus, unsurprising that the third approach, which surged and then plummeted in popularity only to rise up again but with more sobriety, regards the utility of partnerships.[33]

The logic for focusing on partner military and security forces was clear. There are many fragile states that cannot secure a monopoly on violence, the sine qua non of statehood.[34] This fragility increasingly affects the United States, especially in the wake of the September 11, 2001, terrorist attacks. Yet the United States often does not want to send its military to fix these problems for many reasons, including its other security priorities as well as its sensitivity to casualties. Therefore, the United States needs to stabilize fragile states without expending large amounts of its own blood, treasure, or time. It does so by delegating authority and working "by, with, and through" foreign partners.

As large-scale interventions like the wars in Iraq and Afghanistan grew less appealing, demand among U.S. officials for a cheaper and quicker model of stabilization grew. Secretary of Defense Robert Gates called weak states "the main security challenge of our time" and made the case for dealing with them by "helping other countries defend themselves or, if necessary, fight alongside U.S. forces by providing them with equipment, training, or other forms of security assistance."[35] In response, "champions of the by, with, and through model argued that it would provide a better (and cheaper) means of fighting wars and winning the peace than sending U.S. troops into harm's way," as Frances Brown and I have argued.[36] This approach gained enthusiasm among U.S. officials who hoped that a capable Iraqi or Afghan military would quickly enable the U.S. military to focus elsewhere.

The execution of this approach, however, represented an overcorrection from the Vietnam War, during which the U.S. military sought to build its partner South Vietnamese military in its image.[37] Instead, in the post-9/11 wars, it typically prioritized deference to partners at the expense of thoughtful nudging and a willingness to productively exercise leverage. For example, the Army's study of the Iraq War describes a disturbing scene in which General Casey offers "apparent deference" to Iraqi Prime Minister Maliki. Despite Secretary of Defense Rumsfeld's request that Casey push Maliki to maintain military checkpoints in the hopes of facilitating security and accountability for a missing U.S. soldier, Maliki was unwilling to do so. Although Rumsfeld reminded Casey that you "don't work for the PM [prime minister]. You report through us—Abizaid and SECDEF—then to POTUS [President of the United States]. We decide. He's not your political leader," Casey explained that Maliki was "my partner."[38]

More broadly, in her deep exploration of U.S. military strategies employed to influence the Iraqi military from 2004 through 2011, scholar Rachel Tecott finds a dismaying emphasis on relationship building for its own sake: from "the general officers commanding coalition force in Iraq down to the majors embedded within Iraqi battalions, U.S. personnel relied almost exclusively on persuasion to influence Iraqi military organizational practices." Indeed, this emphasis on persuasion was so

deep that "advisors were taught *not* to exercise carrots and sticks to in-
centivize Iraqi compliance . . . [they] were taught that their mission was
to develop relationships with their Iraqi counterparts, and that these
relationships would serve as their primary—indeed their only—tool of
influence."[39]

Yet attempts to build those militaries, as well as other militaries in
fragile states throughout the post-9/11 wars, stumbled and suffered.
Chunks of the Iraqi army disappeared as ISIS took over large swathes
of Iraq. The Afghan military faced no shortage of challenges over more
than a decade and a half, including "ghost soldiers," desertions (particularly during training excursions in the United States), and heavy casualties.[40] The Yemeni military has been unable to effectively tackle Houthis
and al Qaeda affiliates despite substantial assistance from the United
States. The Lebanese military has countered al Qaeda affiliates and ISIS,
but largely and deliberately ignored non-Sunni domestic threats.

Nevertheless, the by, with, and through approach has a lot of support across the military and assumed a new centrality as the Trump administration sought to reduce U.S. military commitments abroad. From
2017 to 2018, for example, combatant commanders from CENTCOM,
AFRICOM, and SOCOM all hailed the partnership approach as critical
for their mission, as did Secretary of Defense Mattis on a visit to the
Asia-Pacific.[41]

However, the U.S. military's leadership appears to have grown more
sober about how, and in what ways, to expect meaningful collaboration
from partners. In my previous book, I argue that building militaries in
weak states is not the panacea for security challenges the U.S. defense
community often imagines it, and history shows that American efforts
to build up local security forces are an oversold half-measure that is
rarely as cheap or as effective as promised.[42] This argument has proven
to be much less provocative than I expected. To its credit, the Defense
Department has increasingly assessed, monitored, and evaluated its approaches to security cooperation—due to heavy congressional pressure
and also because of recognition that both the people who implement it
and the policy itself need to be closely aligned with broader U.S. national
security goals.[43]

It is of some concern that such increased sobriety apparently does not extend to U.S. relationships with violent non-state partner forces.[44] In Syria, for example, the Obama and Trump administrations have collaborated with the Syrian Democratic Forces (SDF) to severely weaken ISIS. Although the military objectives they achieved with U.S. support are significant, the SDF suffers from serious flaws, such as a lack of inclusivity, and, given its relationship with the Kurdish terrorist organization PKK, also forms a thorn in the U.S.-Turkish alliance.[45] Despite U.S. government pledges to maintain a transactional relationship with the SDF, many in the U.S. military have romanticized it and the long-term gains of maintaining a close partnership, as well, something that has grown more complicated as the U.S. approach to Syria fluctuates dramatically.

Going forward, the United States can increase the effectiveness of its partnerships by being a more constant, disciplined, and deeply engaged sponsor.[46] It must both support and push its partners—it must be willing to raise sensitive issues like mission, organization, and operational conduct, to regularly assess the impact and implications of partnering and to acknowledge that these relationships are, ultimately, political endeavors. Above all, the United States should recognize that partnering still holds great promise—even as the post-9/11 wars remind us that it poses real peril as well.[47]

"THE H-O-L-E OF GOVERNMENT"

Another approach that grew popular across the national security community early in the post-9/11 wars, but then became ridiculed across the military, is known as "whole of government." It is the idea that the interagency—the various departments and agencies across the U.S. government—should approach difficult problems together rather than independently or, in the case of the armed forces, through a military-centric lens. Whole of government became an increasingly appealing concept, particularly given the focus on fragile states in the 2006 National Security Strategy and following the emphasis on interagency cooperation within the 2006 Quadrennial Defense Review Report.[48] Its spirit is clear in earlier government and think tank work, including the

1997 Presidential Decision Directive "Managing Complex Contingency Operations" and the 2004–2005 "Beyond Goldwater-Nichols" projects conducted by the Center for Strategic and International Studies.[49]

However, the actual phrase "whole of government" does not appear to have gained ground until scholars Stewart Patrick and Kaysie Brown published an article titled "Greater than the Sum of Its Parts? Assessing 'Whole of Government' Approaches to Fragile States."[50] It was then repeated ad infinitum throughout the post-9/11 wars in government and across the wider national security community. Its popularity reflected not just its intuitive appeal but also bureaucratic politics, as military and civilian agencies and departments alike saw it as a conceptual means to relevance, resources, and responsibility.

Exposure to, and forced collaboration with, other agencies during the wars paid some positive dividends within the armed forces. "It introduced to our military what it means to be on a team with other individuals from across the U.S. government," explained one former senior general officer. The depth and sustained length of this interaction was different from the shallower interagency cooperation of the 1980s and 1990s in particular. As a result, another former senior general officer argued that the wars "introduced into our interagency more of a mutual respect for what everybody brings to the equation of our national security."

But whole of government efforts faced severe challenges due to differences in bureaucratic participants' resourcing and culture, particularly between the Department of State, the Department of Defense, and the U.S. Agency for International Development. As journalist Ronan Farrow underscores, for example, "On September 11, 2001, the State Department was 20 percent short of staff, and those who remained were undertrained and under-resourced."[51] These asymmetries were exacerbated by bureaucratic turf fights. Even before the attacks, the military had begun filling the State Department's foreign policy role, with the enthusiasm—or at least acceptance of—much of the rest of the U.S. government. "The military simply filled a vacuum left by an indecisive White House, an atrophied State Department, and a distracted Congress," explained journalist Dana Priest.[52]

Lacking personnel and resources, the State Department, which still has far fewer foreign service officers than the military has troops assigned to music bands, couldn't keep up with the Pentagon as the post-9/11 wars gained steam. Also, many within the State Department questioned their role in the Department of Defense's war efforts. A representative example is provided by William Burns, who served as a deputy assistant secretary of state in the Bureau of Near Eastern Affairs at the beginning of the post-9/11 wars and went on to serve as deputy secretary of state in the Obama administration. He criticized the character of the State Department's participation in the wars, lamenting that "it seemed as if we were trying to replicate the role of the nineteenth-century British Colonial Service."[53]

The balance of power across the national security apparatus never meaningfully shifted away from the Department of Defense. Instead, "the trend [of dependence on the military] accelerated dramatically," explains Priest.[54] Wartime does, of course, naturally privilege the military. However, this trend flourished despite calls for larger State Department budgets and responsibilities among senior defense leaders. Most famously, then Secretary of Defense Robert Gates regularly urged Congress to better fund his Foggy Bottom counterparts.[55] More pointedly, before he retired as the CENTCOM commander, General James Mattis testified before Congress that "if you don't fund the State Department fully then I need to buy more ammunition ultimately."[56] Nevertheless, these calls have been largely ignored.

As a result, the interagency often lacked the resources to support the military in the ways uniformed leaders expected. Frustrations about the civilians not "showing up" have grown across the military as a result, fueled by perturbation that the U.S. government was touting its whole of government approach while actually relying overwhelmingly on the military "easy button."[57] These frustrations erupted in a few interviews. The most diplomatic response was from a senior general officer who sighed and then said, "The hard part for people who served in Afghanistan is that we didn't—the general feeling is—we probably could have done much more, but we didn't have the full will and support of our 'whole of government.'" A retired flag officer was blunter. After complaining that the State Department was not effective and, expressing his exasperation with the interagency, he exhorted, "Let's stop teaching 'whole of government': it's 1-800-DoD [Department of Defense]."

Some of the military's frustration with the whole of government approach is almost surely embedded in the politics of military affairs. "Find me the guy with the sign on his door, 'I'm the guy working the political solution,'" one exasperated former general officer told me. In his experience, he consistently heard "the macro talking point that we can't pull back militarily because it's the only way to have influence," but reflected that such an argument "discounts the interagency argument that we need State and USAID . . . it says that the military solution is the only one." This dynamic is best captured in a quote by retired Lieutenant General David Barno who, years after running the U.S. war in Afghanistan, described, "The military has somehow gotten off on what I call fragmentism, where we've boxed our little part of the war into a nice, neat container, and we're working to get all green block checks in our part while everyone else goes down the tubes and gets red checks in theirs. Then we blame it on them."[58]

Another retired general officer explained the disagreements he has with his fellow senior military leaders when they tell him they are just staying in the "military's lane." In line with Barno's comment, he would retort, "Your lane has impact on their lane; you must make sure it's subordinated."

Others warn that the military's frustration with the whole of government concept allows it to avoid serious introspection. One general officer said it was a way to ignore internal challenges. As he explained:

> The military wants to rationalize . . . we want to point fingers at politicians, the State Department, other folks who perhaps haven't provided the appropriate guidance or resourcing, but in the context of doing that we haven't taken a look [at ourselves] . . . we've been willing to take on more expansive roles in these conflicts absent some other parts of the government and the expectation is that we'll continue to do that.

Dishearteningly, one senior official who worked closely with senior military officers recalled them mock the whole of government concept: "I'd hear four stars [general officers] talk about the h-o-l-e of government."[59] Such perturbation reflected a crisis of caring in which many in the military felt alone, unsupported even by the rest of the U.S. government.

When the State Department could not keep up—or was unwilling to do so, such as by mandating foreign service officer assignments to Iraq or Afghanistan—the military increasingly tried to conduct diplomacy itself. As a result, the military running U.S. foreign policy through imperial viceroys became increasingly normalized. Military leaders did not always thrive in these roles. As Priest explained, "The language of diplomacy and politics was like a second language for them—learned, not natural. But they accepted it and tried their best to become fluent."[60] Given these developments, the military developed "an out-of-proportion sense of its role in national security," explained one civilian official with substantial interagency experience, which, arguably, is maintained to this day.

Indeed, the impact may be even deeper than Priest describes, because the military may have seeped into interagency roles and missions not as temporary interlopers but as permanent residents. There is now "a generation of generals who don't think their job is strategy," warned one respected journalist on military affairs. He found that in the post-9/11 wars, "We have generals who try to do other people's jobs rather than their own." One senior civilian official worried that "when the military doesn't know what to do or doesn't want to do it, it becomes 'whole of government.'" A former officer lamented that the public now believes "all officers are gods on earth who can become mayors and fighters and diplomats." Perhaps the most compelling description of this dynamic comes from a joke that a former senior civilian official shared in an interview. In it, the PACOM commander and a foreign service officer are chatting about their futures with a congressional delegation. The foreign service officer asks the PACOM commander what he is thinking about doing after retirement, and the commander responds, "I'm thinking about becoming an ambassador." He then asks the foreign service officer the same question, who flippantly responds, "I'm thinking about becoming an admiral." The joke underscores the shortsighted but often-accepted assumption that a senior military officer can easily fill other roles across the foreign policy and national security space even in the absence of direct experience.[61]

Poor interagency decisionmaking processes also left a sour taste among senior defense leaders in the post-9/11 wars and represented a continued source of civil-military tension. The growth of the National Security Council (NSC) staff throughout the Bush and Obama administrations almost surely contributed to this.[62] Secretary of Defense Rumsfeld complains heartily in his memoirs about National Security Advisor Condoleezza Rice mucking around in Pentagon affairs: Rice "and her staff did not seem to understand that they were not in the chain of command and therefore could not issue orders, provide guidance, or give tasks to combatant commanders."[63] His successor, Secretary of Defense Robert Gates, also was deeply frustrated with NSC staff—especially when he found out they had set up a direct phone line to Bagram Air Base in Afghanistan. He complained that the Obama administration's NSC staff would call four-star generals, and at one point he even gave CENTCOM Commander James Mattis candid guidance to "tell [the NSC staff] to go to hell."[64]

In part because of these issues with process, flawed interagency communications exacerbated mistrust between the military and senior civilian leaders. The Obama administration's 2009 review of U.S. strategy toward Afghanistan and Pakistan provides a particularly salient example. President Obama expressed his frustration with how the review proceeded: he felt boxed in and rushed by the military. Obama recounted an unpleasant exchange with Chairman of the Joint Chiefs of Staff Admiral Michael Mullen: "Just so I understand, after almost five years where we managed with twenty thousand or fewer U.S. troops, and after adding another ten thousand over the past twenty months or so, it's the Pentagon's assessment that we can't wait another two months before deciding to *double* our troop commitment," he inquired with an undercurrent of perturbation.[65] After General Stanley McChrystal's assessment leaked, Obama had a difficult discussion with Gates and Mullen about how he felt like the Department of Defense didn't respect him, didn't think it needed to advise him on the troop numbers decision, and didn't support the process.[66]

The lack of trust between the White House and the Pentagon continued throughout the review and informed its conclusion, as well. Gates expressed annoyance with President Obama and Vice President Biden in an Oval Office meeting to finalize the president's decision to surge tens of thousands of troops to Afghanistan. During that meeting, Obama and Biden wanted to confirm that CJCS Admiral Michael Mullen and General Petraeus supported the new strategy. Biden referred to a statement by Obama as an "order" and Obama concurred, which in Gates's mind "demonstrated . . . the complete unfamiliarity of both men with the American military culture. That order was unnecessary and insulting, proof positive of the depth of the Obama White House's distrust of the nation's military leadership."[67] Picking favorite general officers played into this dynamic, as well. President Obama had privately sought the views of Vice Chairman of the Joint Chiefs of Staff James "Hoss" Cartwright during the Afghanistan review, undermining CJCS Mullen—just when Cartwright was being considered as Mullen's replacement.[68] The most generous description of the review's disconnect comes from General McChrystal, who said, "I saw good people all trying to reach a positive outcome, but approaching the problem from different cultures and perspectives, often speaking with different vocabularies."[69]

Inside the Pentagon, senior leaders took crucial steps to deal with these communication challenges. Secretary Gates pulled together a memorandum of understanding in response to the NSC staff's predilection for "bypassing the chain of command and reaching down and talking to commanders in the field, COCOMs, and Joint Staff directly, bypassing the Secretary and his staff," as one former senior official explained. The memorandum of understanding had two purposes: (1) to ensure that the senior Department of Defense leadership was looped into interagency dialogues; and, (2) to provide "quality control" over materials given to the White House. Yet, when the individuals who created this improved system left the Pentagon and White House, so, too, did the collaboration they had codified.

Although frustration may color the views of many in the military about whole of government approaches, and much energy and attention has been devoted to an idea whose execution was, ultimately, underwhelming, leveraging the unique capabilities and expertise distributed across government in unison remains vital. Failure to do so surely contributed to the United States's struggles in the post-9/11 wars. The last two decades suggest that whole of government approaches are important, but the right words are no replacement for process. In the future, the government must focus on improving communications and better distributing resources across the government. That might come at the expense of some military funding—but it also might mean that the military needs to buy fewer bullets. This may prove essential, as fighting is increasingly in the gray zone beneath the traditional frontiers that delineate war.[70]

THE CONTOURS OF FUTURE WARFARE

Alice: Would you tell me, please, which way I ought to go from here?
The Cheshire Cat: That depends a good deal on where you want to get to.
Alice: I don't much care where.
The Cheshire Cat: Then it doesn't much matter which way you go.[71]

Throughout the post-9/11 wars, the U.S. military adopted and subsequently tossed aside various theories of victory in its attempts to win. This has, inevitably, shaped its views on the contours of war in the future. Throughout the interviews for this book, there was surprisingly wide agreement across the senior military establishment on what future wars will look like—but, like so often in the past, there almost surely will be a yawning chasm between these military expectations and wartime reality.

Many current and former senior military leaders argued that the post-9/11 wars have been anomalous. They view them as an aside from the "proper" wars they trained for and expected as junior officers, to be waged against high-end conventional adversaries. Their almost universal belief that future wars will not look like the post-9/11 wars—that they will not focus on fighting terrorists and insurgents across the Middle East and South Asia, among other places—is, therefore, unsurprising. For them, the last two decades were an interlude between the late Cold War and the "real" wars of the future, which will involve countering great power competitors like China and Russia in conventional conflicts. The military is facing threats that, according to one senior general officer, are "back to the future." Lamenting that "a generation of people growing up . . . haven't had a lot of focus on a Korea [conflict] or on a near-peer competitor," one former senior officer said future wars would be much more global, like in the Cold War. Similarly, another former senior general officer warned about "the future war in a big conflict." Overall, one former senior civilian official put it clearly, "We always knew it would be China; it just now *is*."

As a result, these officers believe the post-9/11 wars have carried with them enormous opportunity costs. One officer described them as a "pre-game warmup" and expressed his concern that the military has been "running wind sprints," working too hard and losing crucial capabilities it needs for the real fight ahead. Other senior general officers discussed how the military "mortgaged the future" by focusing on fights that were a lower priority, and argued that the post-9/11 wars have "been a drag on our ability to turn to the future."

Interestingly, today's senior leaders also worry that an appropriate focus on conventional war will be abandoned by future officers. One senior general officer bluntly declared that "we were so busy training for the COIN fight that we forgot how to fight major conflicts." Another senior general officer feared that those who have served in the post-9/11 wars are familiar only with "a small, distributed battlefield," which has made it "hard to think about competition" with peer adversaries. "Artillery did not know how to fire; armor did not know how to maneuver," explained another, arguing that both will be crucial in a major conventional conflict. Agreeing with him, a senior retired general officer warned that the force has no experience fighting without "air superiority like these wars have."

In a similar vein, a senior general officer believed the battlefield of the future will be "a very austere environment" in comparison to the experience of many current U.S. military personnel. Another senior officer warned that for the last two decades, the U.S. military could assume that "my average guy is smarter, more technically competent with billions of dollars of American taxpayer-funded R&D behind us [compared to] the guy who blows himself up . . . [but] that asymmetry will be much closer in future wars."

Summing up these arguments, a final general officer warned that those who fought in the post-9/11 wars at junior levels are "now imprinted with the wrong way of warfare . . . they don't know what right looks like." This Manichean conceptualization—which emphasizes "right" and "wrong" types of warfare—makes it exceedingly difficult to appreciate and learn from the last two decades of combat and, thus, to predict the future of war. And learning from wars is always hard, even when a military is committed to doing it. The 1991 Persian Gulf War, for example, "gave us a false sense of how potent we were, but that was not representative of the threats we were going to face in the future," recalled one former senior flag officer.

The 2014 Russian invasion of Crimea—the archetypal "gray zone," sub-conventional conflict—represents one potential example of the future of war, and the difficulty of learning from it. A general officer underscored that it was the "sobering wake-up call that we needed to turn away from counterinsurgency." The Army studied this invasion as deeply as it had examined the 1973 Arab-Israeli War, which it viewed as a precursor to the 1991 Persian Gulf War, according to one general officer.[72] After a study tour to Crimea, the Army team returned and declared, "We're screwed," according to a senior general officer familiar with the study. Although studies of this conflict are unlikely to be terribly illuminating for those who fear the potential of major combat between great powers, they are more compelling for those who are concerned about China and Russia "tak[ing] us on indirectly in the gray zone," as one former senior official described, or facing conflicts that are "sepia-toned," per another. The Army has since made key changes to its training based on its examination of Russia's invasion of Crimea. Underscoring that the Army was "lucky" about the timing of Russia's aggression, one senior general officer predicted that "we were [still] 4–5 years from not having a key leader" who could refocus the service on high-end conventional warfare. While it may sound dramatic, and perhaps even gratuitous, one senior general officer outlined the updated training as follows:

> We've taken the worst of all ends of the spectrum and put them all together. It's based on a near peer adversary that has the capacity to challenge us in all domains. But just to make sure we don't lose all we've learned, it also has criminal gangs on the battlefield, terrorists, guerrillas, enemies, chemical agents . . . all those things are in that decisive action training environment. That's our sparring partner.

Future wars, according to these senior military leaders, would be characterized by heavy American casualties. Thanks in part to the AVF and the character of the Persian Gulf War as well as the post-9/11 wars, however, the American public and military, have "inherited an expectation of deathless American wars . . . an irresponsible expectation of impossibly low casualties," feared one senior officer. He was particularly concerned that the public "will feel betrayed" when the losses start to add up.

Similarly, a former senior general officer warned, "We're ill prepared for the type of losses we could incur" in a war against a conventionally powerful adversary. He, too, wondered how the public and the military could be conditioned for conflict at such a large scale. Such views also may exacerbate the generational tension between senior and junior military officers. One retired general officer said that many of those who have been fighting in the post-9/11 wars are militarily naïve: they "haven't seen the ugly part of war . . . most junior officers think we're still great [and] we're really capable."

Another senior officer disagreed. Reflecting on discussions within his cohort, this officer expressed frustration that what senior military leaders describe as low intensity conflict (LIC) "probably doesn't feel like LIC to the guys sitting in Syria," and it is "what we do 90% of the time."

Experiencing violence firsthand and up close is ugly, in other words, regardless of whether it is the result of a counterterrorism fight in Syria today or a conventional war in World War II France.

Many senior military officers also argued that future wars would be long. The most colorful statement in this vein came from a former officer who quipped that the U.S. military "doesn't want to lose quickly . . . we like to take our time doing so!" In the wake of America's longest wars, one of the Army's findings in its Iraq study is that "U.S leaders and planners operated under the constant assumption that the war would be short," which carried high costs as the insurgency grew.[73] That observation is a reminder of the incessant yet misplaced expectation of short conflicts that has colored U.S. war planning since World War II. Yet, expecting future wars to inevitably be long also may be misguided, because the character of the conflict and U.S. national security interests will inform its length.

There are, of course, some iconoclasts who believe that the past two decades are prologue. CJCS General Joseph Dunford, for example, warned those who focus solely on gray zone or high-end conventional conflicts that violent extremism will not go away, and predicted that fighting terrorists and insurgents will remain a mission for the U.S. military. However, he underscored that executing this mission requires a "sustainable solution . . . And when I say sustainable it's got to be politically sustainable, it's got to be fiscally sustainable, it's got to be militarily sustainable."[74] He is pinpointing a core tension in force design and development.

Going forward, colossal confidence in predictions about the character of future conflicts must be challenged. It is worth recalling former Secretary of Defense Robert Gates's infamous quip about how the U.S. record of predicting the next war is perfect—it is always wrong—just as it is critical to recognize that sage military preparations also prevented or deterred other conflicts.[75] Nevertheless, as one former senior civilian official reminded me, "Whatever guess is being made right now is probably going to be the wrong one." Indeed, another declared that it is especially difficult to predict the future because "it's almost like [the U.S.

military is at] the dawn of the Cold War . . . [straddling] two different national security eras." And, it has been a very long time since there was a major conventional conflict between military powers, making prediction even harder.

Whatever the permutations of future wars may be, the U.S. military will, undoubtedly, face difficulties in prioritizing between them. One former senior general officer explained that "the U.S. military has to be like the guy in the circus keeping many plates spinning at the same time while ensuring that some plates get much more focus than others." In his view, the U.S. military will have to simultaneously operate globally, across domains, and in dramatically different types of conflict. Bringing intellectual or theoretical clarity to this complex strategic order will surely be taxing and may be impossible.

Two former senior civilian officials could offer only vague suggestions regarding the implications therein: "It's going to be incredibly dynamic in 20 years," and "look for the things that people aren't looking at; that's where trouble comes." While this lack of clarity is understandable, it also is profoundly unhelpful in shaping the future military. Indeed, perhaps the very best advice comes from one former senior general officer who compared the diversity and constancy of threats to another military experience: that of the British Empire. As he put it, the post-9/11 wars may reflect future conflicts. "Is this part of serving in a modern military?" he asked. "Like the British military, we're always [going to be] doing campaigns?"

This lack of clarity about future war should caution future U.S. military leaders not to read too deeply into their personal experiences, particularly if they are disenchanted by the various approaches tried in Iraq, Afghanistan, and beyond. "The higher up you get, the more likely you are to see every fight as one you have done before," warned one former senior civilian official. They will have experienced a dizzying number of approaches to fighting and winning the post-9/11 wars, frustrating experiences that are reflected in the crisis of confidence. While takeaways will be diverse, the unsatisfying outcomes and lack of theoretical clarity around the right approach may foment skepticism around the utility of force. Nevertheless, these experiences should inform, but not entirely shape, how they see the future, just as it should inform, but not entirely shape, the future military force. Future wars may rhyme with those of the past, but military leaders would do well to recognize the danger of fighting the previous fight again.

10

Now What?

"If you want a happy ending, that depends, of
course, on where you stop your story."

Being at war for two decades has fundamentally shaped the U.S. military of today and, as this book argues, also will shape the U.S. military of tomorrow. The fundamental legacies of the post-9/11 wars for the U.S. armed forces are the three interrelated civil-military crises discussed earlier: the crisis of confidence, the crisis of caring, and the crisis of meaningful civilian control. These influence, and are influenced by, lessons learned from the wars, including about how the United States goes to war, how it fights, who serves, who leads, and which theories of war it adopts and rejects. And, the military has maintained its ballast over these two decades, which is notable and worth celebrating.

But the post-9/11 wars continue. Their ending remains uncertain, both on the battlefield and in our collective memory. This presents an opportunity to take a hard look at what has occurred over the last two decades of conflict. Conducting an autopsy presents no shortage of struggles, but it is essential to honor those who have sacrificed in these wars by considering how the military can learn from its experiences at war—by identifying the key questions for the U.S. military going forward and engaging in serious dialogue and assessment of their potential answers. Moving forward responsibly requires remembering Orson Welles's adage: "If you want a happy ending, that depends, of course, on where you stop your story."[1]

HOW DO THE "LOSERS" LEARN?

Refocusing the military's energies such that there is meaningful learning from the post-9/11 wars is a critical step going forward. Meaningful learning will not focus merely on tactical and operational improvements but on the strategic level as well. This will be challenging, especially because the military history literature suggests that "losers" in conflicts typically have greater incentives to learn than victors.[2] Two good examples are found in the German military after World War I and the Israeli military after the 2006 war with Hizballah. However, these analogies are imperfect—the U.S. military has not "lost" the post-9/11 wars but, rather, faces a much fuzzier situation in which the wars have faded into inconclusiveness rather than culminated in clear failure.

In Germany after World War I, there was a deep and textured effort to learn the war's lessons.[3] Although the Treaty of Versailles made it tougher to do so, the military, nevertheless, managed to establish at least fifty-seven military committees to probe what went wrong.[4] Across the German military and from a variety of perspectives, leaders explored the strategic-level course of the conflict; unlike many German civilians, "few General Staff officers or higher commanders actually believed" stab-in-the-back narratives, like the loss being due to the mistakes of civilian leaders rather than their own errors.[5] Just as importantly, Germany's military, ultimately, acted upon these learning processes. Over the interwar period, it implemented massive technological and organizational innovations, vastly increasing its militarily effectiveness in the early years of World War II.

In Israel, the government established an official committee to investigate its 2006 war with Hizballah—the Winograd Commission—and the military's chief of staff set up "at least 70" internal committees to examine lessons learned.[6] On the basis of its painful wartime experience, Israel's military made dramatic changes in how it fights, including in training, doctrine, organization, and investments. Its willingness to probe what had transpired in the war with Hizballah meant that, within two years, the military "had undergone an almost complete transformation."[7] Given how differently these states waged their next major conflicts—World War II in the case of Germany and the 2009 Gaza War in the case of Israel—their efforts to meaningfully interrogate their military failures bore fruit.

Over the last fifty years, however, the U.S. military has made more serious efforts to learn from its wins than its losses. It has intensively studied wars in which it has prevailed, like the 1991 Persian Gulf War, and in which others have done so, like the 1973 Arab-Israeli War and the 2014 Russian War in Crimea.[8] In contrast, the military has proved unwilling to deliberately learn from its defeat in the Vietnam War. Of course, studying conflicts or events in which one has won is invariably less painful. As one officer explained, examining "a Desert Storm is more pleasant than a Desert One [the failed attempt to rescue American hostages in Iran], but a Desert One makes you have to learn all the lessons you might not have."

Failing to learn from defeat is dangerous. Militaries are naturally resistant to change.[9] Under high stakes, like in combat—or even perceived higher stakes, like after suffering an earlier loss or an inconclusive conflict—they will be even more cautious. At worst, such resistance and caution can produce a tendency toward "disinnovation." Rather than making meaningful adaptation to the evolving character of warfare and the changing security environment, such disinnovation could result in reverting back to previous ways of waging war in line with the pre-defeat status quo. This could manifest as intentional failure to make meaningful innovations due to philosophical or bureaucratic disagreements—or simply disinterest in disentangling why defeat occurred. That would, of course, be profoundly unhelpful in facilitating military victories and safeguarding U.S. national security in the future. The U.S. military needs to make important changes, and while the 2018 National Defense

Strategy may have started to shift the trajectory, implementation to date has been sporadic and significant questions remain. Absent rigor and focus on learning, such progress may, ultimately, be asymptotic.

TACKLING THE INHERITANCE: QUESTIONS TO CONSIDER

Three crucial questions emerge from the United States's two decades at war.

First, how and in what ways should the United States assess the balance sheet of the post-9/11 wars? This book attempted to answer that question by identifying the war's key legacies for the military and the civilian managers of violence. But some other important elements on that balance sheet are worth additional consideration. For example, there have not been other spectacular attacks on American soil; how should it value that nonevent? There were other complex sociopolitical outcomes associated with the wars; how much have they cost? The United States, for example, has adopted a zero-risk tolerance on security and militarized police forces across the country, with pernicious consequences for its civil liberties, race relations, and immigration policies.[10]

Second, what is the United States willing to fight for? There is a danger of overreacting to threats and attacks, as the United States did in response to the September 11, 2001, attacks—an overreaction that manifested over two decades, across many regions, and at massive cost. There is also a danger of under-responding, as the United States has done in its persistent inability to recognize and act on the growing security threats posed by China and Russia to the U.S.-led global order over the last decade or so. Just before the Peloponnesian War started, Pericles told the assembled citizens, "I hope that none of you think that we shall be going to war for a trifle."[11] Athens had a superior navy, better alliances, and deeper coffers than its adversaries—advantages that may sound eerily familiar to U.S. defense experts—but it managed to squander its strengths on expeditions that were not worth the price. In looking to the future, one can only hope the United States, and its military in particular, does not make the same mistakes.[12]

Defining what the United States is willing to fight for should not, however, be unrealizable—as the Powell Doctrine's resurgence may be interpreted. If Washington's threshold for intervention is not clear to Washington, then it cannot be clear to its competitors or adversaries. This will increase the danger of profound miscalculation, both domestically and abroad. That going to war has cost so little to the average American over the last two decades has enabled the United States to entertain sustained interventions; if those costs increase, it could make it harder for the United States to go to war in the future.

Third, how have the post-9/11 wars changed Americans' understanding of what it means to win and lose in war? Despite—and perhaps because of—the U.S. government's overreliance on the military relative to other instruments of national power, the search for ersatz victories has shaped expectations among many U.S. military leaders about what is achievable through the use of force. The bitter lessons of the last two decades, however, could be forgotten in a mixture of accountability soup and inconclusiveness. A key lesson, however, is coming into view: the lack of disciplined prioritization of interests and objectives resulted in overambitious approaches overflowing with resources contributing little to a lasting political victory.

DIALOGUE AND ASSESSMENT: IN THE MILITARY, ACROSS THE GOVERNMENT, AND WITH THE PUBLIC

As the United States approaches the third decade of its post-9/11 wars, it is time to engage in broader dialogue in the military, across the government, and with the American people about what military force can and cannot be expected to achieve in the future. As one former senior civilian official explained, the crux of the matter should be: "How do we learn and do better next time?"

This dialogue should serve three purposes. First, it should help those involved in waging the post-9/11 wars—including both the military and civilians—process what happened, consider their roles in it, and build resiliency. Second, given that the wars are ongoing, dialogue should involve regular and systematic attempts led by civilian leaders to baseline how and in what ways the wars are proceeding, and to diagnose what is and is not working. Third, dialogue should facilitate an understanding inside the military of how and in what ways the post-9/11 wars have shaped its conception of warfare, including both its permutations and the roles and responsibilities of those who wage it.

Within the Department of Defense itself, civilians need to drive this dialogue. It will help imbue a sense of teamwork and greater belief across the defense community that genuine collaboration is the best way to solve national security problems. It is also the best way for senior civilian leaders, in particular, to reckon with what the force has become and how it should evolve.

This dialogue, moreover, should be driven by regular, rigorous, and meaningful strategic assessments. Although the executive branch conducted at least half a dozen strategy and policy review on parts of the post-9/11 wars between 2004 and 2009, these rarely resulted in radical change to the status quo.[13] One possible way of making strategic assessments affect strategy more consistently would be to use the regular review process to prompt dialogue, particularly regarding how to better focus on future conflicts. Additionally, the national security apparatus would benefit from regular internal dialogues to build a common baseline of how the post-9/11 wars are progressing. As one model, these convenings could be titled "State of the Wars" and bring together key interagency stakeholders as well as outside experts and critical foreign allies and partners as useful.[14]

Congress can have an important role in these assessment processes. For example, Congress recently instituted a requirement for the secretary of defense to submit an annual assessment of the National Defense Strategy.[15] This assessment must examine the current strategy, its implementation, and the extent to which it needs adjustment.[16] Congress could require a similar assessment of various aspects of the post-9/11 wars, including lessons learned and alternative futures. To be most effective, such assessments will need to look across the community of bureaucratic actors within the Department of Defense and to engage national security thinkers outside of it, as well.[17]

Congress also will need to reassess its largely open-ended approach to the authorization of force in the post-9/11 wars. This authorization has, in many ways, been overly generous and deferential toward the executive branch. Meaningful legislative oversight is necessary to monitor strategy and resource allocation. Without such mechanisms, the national security apparatus can easily—and inadvertently—slip into situations in which "decision-making often has more to do with our desires than it does with reality," as one scholar found in his study of policymaking dynamics surrounding the Vietnam War.[18]

The broader national security community would benefit from assessment of its performance in the post-9/11 wars, as well. One potential way to facilitate such assessment involves an approach developed by psychologist Michael Castellana to help wounded Marines elucidate responsibility for events that occurred in war. He has Marines discuss their experiences and tries to get them to see how these were part of a broader venture. In doing so, the Marines would "list and assign a percentage of responsibility to every person or factor that played a role in the injuring incident . . . The idea is to help the patient see, even while acknowledging his own role, that he doesn't have to bear 100 percent of the responsibility."[19] This approach is obviously imperfect, both because of the special responsibilities associated with civilian control of the military and because of the complexity of the post-9/11 conflict on and off the battlefield. Nevertheless, helping those involved in wars reckon with and learn from their experiences may facilitate meaningful assessments of a thorny topic.

The national security community also must inculcate a culture of strategic skepticism. It must avoid hubris by stress-testing its objectives and interrogating its theories of victory. It must ensure that it is not simply going through the motions or uncritically parroting its own talking points. It must be careful of what James Thompson describes in his autopsy of the Vietnam War as "the domestication of dissenters," in which those who disagree with the policy path are swallowed by a bureaucracy that ignores their views.[20] Above all, in the words of one former senior civilian official, "We constantly have to question what we're doing and if it's worth it." As the Washington Post's "Afghanistan Papers" demonstrated, there have been too few moments in which first-order questions about crucial aspects of the post-9/11 wars were raised in national security debates over the last two decades.[21]

A lack of dialogue also has harmed the relationship between America's military and American society. Its absence is best felt in its rare performance—like those offered by Theater of War. In a Theater of War production, actors perform scenes from ancient Greek tragedies. Creator Bryan Doerries then facilitates a conversation between the audience, the actors, and, usually, a few hand-selected participants who have expressed a willingness to discuss how those plays reflect their own experiences with conflict. They had performed to military audiences and mixed military and civilian audiences nearly 500 times as of early 2020.[22] During the first Theater of War performance, in front of a group of Marines, actors performed Sophocles's *Ajax*, a heartrending tragedy in which a war hero commits suicide. After the performance, hundreds of Marines sat for three hours discussing how it resonated with them. To Doerries, it "was as if these ancient plays had found their intended audience, almost twenty-five hundred years after they had first been performed."[23]

I have hosted Theater of War performances at the Johns Hopkins University's School of Advanced International Studies and have been awed by the dialogues they catalyze. For civilians, in particular, uncomfortable and thorny topics are addressed in an accessible manner. For servicemembers or veterans, "it doesn't feel judgmental," as Doerries notes, because it focuses on a play written thousands of years ago.[24] By facilitating conversations between those who serve and those whom they serve, Theater of War plays a critical role in bridging the military-society gap. Its impact—and the ultimate goal of such dialogue—is best described by Brigadier General Sutton, the Army's senior mental health professional. After one Theater of War performance, Sutton turned to the crowd and declared, "Sophocles wrote these plays to comfort the afflicted and afflict the comfortable."[25]

Finding forums to facilitate these dialogues requires planning because, although the American public and the American military may inhabit the same country, they often live in very different worlds. In 2017, while sailing around the world as a professor on Semester at Sea, a study abroad program, I lived on a ship with 600 college students for whom the post-9/11 wars were mainly ambient noise.[26] They knew only an

America at war, but, as chapter 3 discussed, most did not know anyone who had gone *to* war. The military, even to some of the other professors, was a baffling and bewildering institution. The handful of veterans on our ship were not at all surprised to hear this and were understandably hesitant to begin an unstructured dialogue that, in the experience of many, might start with extremely personal questions.

Nevertheless, the veterans wanted to have a conversation in a comfortable intellectual space where the community could learn about their service. Together, we organized a dialogue featuring six veterans, who spanned three generations, and for two hours, hundreds of people listened to their descriptions of life in the military. The veterans shared stories of combat photography in the Vietnam War, and of leaving the Marine Corps in late 2016 after multiple tours overseas. They explained different reasons for joining the military, different descriptions of being in the military, and different transitions to civilian life. Three generations of veterans gave firsthand accounts of experiences as varied as fighting in Iraq and watching friends die to processing tedious paperwork to training ad infinitum for a war they would never fight.

The audience listened because the people on stage were not "veterans" but, rather, friends. They sat next to one another in class, shared meals, and traveled together. More healthy relations between the military and the public, in other words, can be built only on the micro-foundations of more numerous civilian-military relationships.

For its part, the public should expect more transparent discussions regarding warfare with its political leaders. Rather than fawning over the military, or expecting it to fulfill responsibilities for which it is not well suited, public leaders should engage the public more soberly about the limits and costs of using force. One in four Americans have never known a country at peace, but public engagement with the wars remains limited.[27] At the same time, one scholar's survey research has found that, although future military leaders vehemently believe they should be "civically literate," fewer than half think they actually are.[28] That makes it disturbingly easy to imagine, as Max Brooks has, a future three decades from now in which the public decides to privatize the U.S. military and the mercenary force then strikes for higher pay.[29] This scenario remains far away, but it is not as far-fetched as one would like given the United States's increasing reliance on contractors in warzones, the rising personnel costs of its all-volunteer force, and the growing crisis of caring.

The United States must begin to fix the concerning pattern of American civil-military relations established during the post-9/11 wars. The military has been thrust into a new and unfamiliar position in American politics. It garners tremendous respect across American society, especially relative to other institutions, despite the public's superficial knowledge of it. Yet, it is more insular than it has been in generations and, as this book has argued, is deeply harmed by its growing distance from the American people. Embracing dialogue with the public and fundamentally widening the aperture of public service while encouraging an American "*culture* of service"—as the congressionally-mandated National Commission on Military, National, and Public Service has sought—will be important remedies.[30]

MEMORIALIZING

A new war memorial in Washington, DC, is currently being built—but it is for the 1991 Persian Gulf War. Its design and placement, like all memorials, reflects the war's inheritances. Designed to imitate the spectacular left hook U.S. ground forces took through the Saudi Arabian desert to cut off Iraqi troops, it will stand near the Vietnam War memorial.[31] The symbolism of that placement is overt. As described by the commander of the air campaign during the Persian Gulf War, Air Force General Chuck Horner, with a vitriol that testifies to the military's deep-rooted neuralgia about its experience in Vietnam, it is appropriate to have the memorials close to one another because the wars "are inexorably linked together." The new memorial, he argued, should be visited by everyone in the military so "they learn to stand up when they have to, to avoid the stupidness that led to that [Vietnam War] disaster."[32]

How should we memorialize the post-9/11 wars? Of course, there are already temporary memorials, such as a display at Fort Bragg with more than 7,500 combat boots marked with photos and dates of death to represent the wars' fallen servicemembers,[33] and Arlington National Cemetery's Section 60—where thousands of servicemembers who died in Iraq and Afghanistan, among other places, are buried. These in many ways served as de facto memorials to the post-9/11 wars.[34] But none are permanent.

Planning remains nascent for the official memorial to the post-9/11 wars under development in Washington, DC, which is slated for completion in 2024.[35] Indeed, President Trump waived the ten-year postwar waiting period, so this memorial will be the first ever built for a war that has not ended. This, in itself, is symbolic of the wars themselves. If the memorial also takes much longer and costs much more to build than expected, it will serve as a true microcosm of the war it represents. Such an outcome is eminently possible, because its design faces the challenge of memorializing a convoluted web of wars whose varied participants fought across a fluid geography, from Afghanistan and Iraq and across the breadth of Africa and Asia. Perhaps an appropriate design would, therefore, itself be convoluted and jarring. The memorial to the Lebanese civil war (1975–1990), which stands near the Lebanese Ministry of Defense in Yarze, seems fitting—a giant, jumbled stack of weapons and tanks encased in concrete that reaches toward the sky.

But the most powerful memorial, in my view, might be a clock without hands. This would symbolize the wars' unfinished mandate, their interminable fighting, their inconclusive endings, and most importantly, that it is time to honor their sacrifices and talk about their legacies.

FINAL THOUGHTS ON UNFINISHED WARS

We inherit from two decades of war a set of interlinked crises that will require a lot of work to fix. They stand in the way of implementing the 2018 National Defense Strategy and subsequent strategies, as well. Relying on a future conflict to provide military catharsis—expecting a neo-Persian Gulf War to exorcise the ghosts of our latest interminable interventions abroad—is a dangerous gamble. Although the recent refocus on great power threats is rational, the U.S. military may well fight other wars in the future that—like those of the last two decades—end in unsatisfying inconclusiveness.

If that is the case, it will be incumbent on all of us to recognize such conflicts for what they are. The civilian overseers of violence will need to provide the best guidance possible, encourage frank assessment, and insist on accountability. And it means that, above all, we must recognize those who heed the call to serve the nation in all of its wars. The best way to do so is to mend the broken dialogue: to heal the crises of confidence, of caring, and of meaningful civilian control so the military can restore its sense of purpose, repair its connections to the society it serves, and regain the trust in civilian leadership essential to the safety and security of democracy in the United States. Unless and until the broken dialogue is mended, the "happy ending" will remain elusive.

Brief Chronology of the Post-9/11 Wars

Date	Location	Event
September 11, 2001	United States	Terrorist attacks on the United States
September 26, 2001	United States	President George W. Bush signs into law the Joint Resolution for the Authorization of the Use of Military Force (AUMF) against those responsible for the 9/11 attacks
September 25, 2001	United States, Afghanistan	U.S. Secretary of Defense Donald Rumsfeld announces Operation Enduring Freedom
October 7, 2001	Afghanistan	United States and UK airstrikes launched at Taliban and Al Qaeda
October 19, 2001	Afghanistan	Special forces teams insert into Afghanistan, beginning the ground war
November 13, 2001	Afghanistan	Kabul falls to the United States and the Afghan Northern Alliance
December 6–17, 2001	Afghanistan	Battle of Tora Bora
December 7, 2001	Afghanistan	Kandahar falls
March 19, 2003	Iraq	U.S. and coalition forces launch Operation Iraqi Freedom

Date	Location	Event
May 1, 2003	USS *Abraham Lincoln*, Iraq	U.S. President George W. Bush delivers a speech declaring "mission accomplished" in Iraq
December 13, 2003	Iraq	U.S. soldiers capture Saddam Hussein
June 19, 2004	Pakistan	United States launches first known drone strike in Pakistan
April 4–May 1, 2004	Iraq	United States launches Operation Valiant Resolve, also called First Battle of Fallujah
November 7–December 13, 2004	Iraq	Joint U.S., UK, and Iraqi forces launch Operation Al-Fajr ("Dawn") and Operation Phantom Fury, also called the Second Battle of Fallujah
June 7, 2006	Iraq	U.S. airstrike kills Abu Musab al-Zarqawi, leader of al-Qaeda in Iraq
February 22, 2006	Iraq	Al-Qaeda in Iraq bombs the al-Askari Mosque in Samarra, accelerating the sectarian civil war between Iraqi Shia and Sunnis
December 6, 2006	Iraq	Saddam Hussein executed
January 7, 2007	United States, Iraq	U.S. President George W. Bush announces an increase of 20,000 troops in Iraq, also known as the "surge"
December 1, 2009	United States	President Barack Obama announces a surge of an additional 30,000 U.S. troops to Afghanistan, along with a timeline for their withdrawal
August 30, 2010	United States, Iraq	U.S. President Barack Obama ends U.S. combat operations in Iraq
September 1, 2010	United States	Operation Iraqi Freedom is renamed Operation New Dawn by the United States to reflect the reduced role of U.S. troops
May 2, 2011	Pakistan	U.S. special operations forces kill Osama bin Laden
June 22, 2011	United States, Afghanistan	U.S. President Barack Obama announces withdrawal of U.S. troops from Afghanistan by 2014

Date	Location	Event
October 2014	Cameroon, Nigeria, Niger, Chad	President Obama sends 300 troops to Cameroon; begins assistance to Lake Chad Basin countries fighting Boko Haram
June 2014	Iraq, Syria	ISIS forces capture Mosul and declare the establishment of a "caliphate"
October 17, 2014	United States, Iraq, Syria	U.S. Department of Defense formally establishes Combined Joint Task Force – Operation Inherent Resolve to formalize ongoing military efforts against ISIS in Iraq and Syria
December 28, 2014	United States, Afghanistan	U.S. President Barack Obama announces end to Operation Enduring Freedom, though troops remain
January 1, 2015	Afghanistan	U.S. mission to Afghanistan begins assisting Afghan security forces in Operation Freedom's Sentinel
October 30, 2015	Syria	U.S. establishes first sustained military presence inside Syria to fight ISIS
December 2016	Libya	Assisted by U.S. and UK SOF, Libyan militias capture Sirte from ISIS
March 2017	Somalia, Yemen	President Trump declares portions of Yemen and Somalia "Areas of Active Hostilities," increasing the pace and frequency of airstrikes
October 4, 2017	Niger	U.S. special forces team ambushed near Malian border, killing four and sparking domestic debate about "endless war"
October 17, 2017	Syria	Raqqa, the de-facto ISIS capital, captured by coalition-backed forces
October 26, 2019	Syria	U.S. SOF kill Abu-Baghdadi, the leader of ISIS, in raid near Idlib, Syria
February 29, 2020	Qatar	The United States and the Taliban sign an agreement for bringing peace to Afghanistan

Notes

Preface

1. David Halberstam, *War in a Time of Peace: Bush, Clinton, and the Generals* (New York: Scribner, 2001), p. 509.

Chapter 1

1. Viet Thanh Nguyen, *Nothing Ever Dies* (Harvard University Press, 2016), p. 4.

2. See, for example, Robert D. Hormats, *The Price of Liberty—Paying for America's Wars* (New York: Times Books, 2007); and Sarah E. Kreps, *Taxing Wars* (Oxford University Press, 2018).

3. Carl Von Clausewitz, *On War,* edited and translated by Michael Howard and Peter Paret (Princeton University Press, 1976), p. 89. Relatedly, Peter Feaver argues that societies that have these three distinct groups thus manifest the concept of civil-military relations. Peter Feaver, "The Civil-Military Problematique: Huntington, Janowitz, and the Question of Civilian Control," *Armed Forces & Society,* 23, no. 2 (Winter 1996), pp. 149–78.

4. For example, a large majority of veterans, including those who fought in the post-9/11 wars, believe the wars in Iraq and Afghanistan were not worth fighting. Ruth Igielnik and Kim Parker, "Majority of U.S. Veterans, Public Say the Wars in Iraq and Afghanistan Were Not Worth Fighting," Pew Research Center, July 10, 2019, www.pewresearch.org/fact-tank/2019/07/10/majorities

-of-u-s-veterans-public-say-the-wars-in-iraq-and-afghanistan-were-not-worth
-fighting/.

5. I am grateful to Chris Dougherty for this conceptualization.

6. See, for example, Mira Rapp-Hooper, *Shields of the Republic: The Triumph and Peril of America's Alliances* (Harvard University Press, 2020); and Christian Brose, *The Kill Chain: Defending America in the Future of High-Tech Warfare* (Hachette Books, 2020).

7. Alan Cowell, "Monument to '73 War: An Egyptian Alamo?" *New York Times*, February 15, 1990, www.nytimes.com/1990/02/15/world/monument-to -73-war-an-egyptian-alamo.html.

8. I am grateful to Scott Cooper for crystallizing this idea. The Met Collection, "The Veteran in a New Field, Winslow Homer," 1865, www.metmuseum .org/art/collection/search/11145.

9. American Battlefield Trust, "Civil War Casualties," Battlefields.org, www .battlefields.org/learn/articles/civil-war-casualties; and Mark E. Neely, *The Abraham Lincoln Encyclopedia* (New York: Da Capo Press, 1982).

10. While President Truman signed Executive Order 9981 in 1948 to desegregate the military, actually accomplishing that was, nevertheless, an uphill battle. "Executive Order 9981: Establishing the President's Committee on Equal Treatment and Opportunity in the Armed Services," Harry S. Truman Library, July 26, 1948, www.trumanlibrary.gov/library/executive-orders/9981/executive -order-9981.

11. Jimmy Byrn and Gabe Royal, "What Should West Point Do about Its Robert E. Lee Problem?" *Modern War Institute*, June 22, 2020, https://mwi.usma .edu/west-point-robert-e-lee-problem/; and James Barber, "10 Army Bases Named after Confederate Officers," *Military.Com Off the Radar* (blog), May, 2020, www.military.com/undertheradar/2018/10/03/ten-army-bases-named-after -confederate-officers.html. Many of these bases were named in 1940. See, also, Mike Pietrucha, "Of Course the U.S. Military has a White Supremacy Problem. It's Baked In," *War on the Rocks*, May 7, 2020, https://warontherocks.com/2020 /05/of-course-the-u-s-military-has-a-white-supremacy-problem-its-baked-in.

12. Jay Winter, *The Legacy of the Great War: Ninety Years On* (University of Missouri Press, 2009); and Othon Anastasakis and others, *Balkan Legacies of the Great War* (London: Palgrave Macmillan, 2016).

13. G. Kurt Piehler, *Remembering War the American Way* (Washington: Smithsonian Institution Press, 1995), pp. 92–97

14. Ibid., p. 7.

15. Mark A. Lawrence, "Policymaking and the Uses of the Vietnam War," in *The Power of the Past: History and Statecraft*, edited by Hal Brands and Jeremi Suri (Brookings, 2016), p. 51.

16. "Remarks on the 50th Anniversary of D-Day at the United States Cemetery in Colleville-sur-Mer, France," *Weekly Compilation of Presidential Documents*, 30, no. 23 (June 13, 1994), p. 1240, www.govinfo.gov/content/pkg/WCPD -1994-06-13/pdf/WCPD-1994-06-13.pdf.

17. Quoted in Dave Phillips, "To Stand Out, the Army Picks a New Uniform with a World War Two Look," *New York Times*, May 4, 2019, www.nytimes.com/ 2019/05/05/us/new-army-greens-uniform.html.

18. Piehler, *Remembering War the American Way*, pp. 155–57.

19. Lawrence, "Policymaking and the Uses of the Vietnam War," p. 52; Robert D. Schulzinger, editor, *A Time for Peace: The Legacy of the Vietnam War* (Oxford University Press, 2006); Anthony Lake, editor, *The Vietnam Legacy: The War, American Society, and the Future of American Foreign Policy* (New York University Press, 1976); Gil Dorland, editor, *Legacy of Discord: Voices of the Vietnam War Era* (New York: Potomac Books, 2002); Charles E. Neu, editor, *After Vietnam: Legacies of a Lost War* (Johns Hopkins University Press, 2000); and Ronald Spector, "What McMaster Gets Wrong about Vietnam," *Politico Magazine*, October 3, 2017, www.politico.com/magazine/story/2017/10/03/hr-mcmaster-book -vietnam-war-215673.

20. Dorland, *Legacy of Discord*, pp. 159–63.

21. Neu, *After Vietnam*, p. xiii.

22. George C. Herring, *America's Longest War: The United States and Vietnam, 1950–1975*, 2nd ed. (New York: McGraw-Hill, 1986), p. 256.

23. I'm grateful to Scott Cooper for this point, as well. In the film, Sylvester Stallone plays John Rambo, a retired Green Beret sent to recover American prisoners of war in Vietnam. George P. Cosmatos, *Rambo: First Blood Part II* (Santa Monica, Calif.: Artisan Home Entertainment, 1985).

24. Patrick Hagopian, *The Vietnam War in American Memory* (University of Massachusetts Press, 2009), p. 31.

25. Those interested in learning more about the history of this transition should read *Bernard Foster, I Want You! The Evolution of the All-Volunteer Force* (RAND, 2006), www.rand.org/content/dam/rand/pubs/monographs/2007/ RAND_MG265.pdf.

26. John Bodnar, *The "Good War" in American Memory* (Johns Hopkins University Press, 2010), p. 241.

27. H. R. McMaster, *Dereliction of Duty: Lyndon Johnson, Robert McNamara, the Joint Chiefs of Staff, and the Lies that Led to Vietnam* (New York: Harper Collins, 1997).

28. Fred Kaplan, "Annual General Meeting: Finally the Army is Promoting the Right Officers," *Slate*, August 4, 2008, https://slate.com/news-and-politics/ 2008/08/finally-the-army-is-promoting-the-right-officers.html.

29. Neu, *After Vietnam*, pp. 83–84.

30. Andrew Krepinevich, *The Army and Vietnam* (Baltimore: Johns Hopkins University Press, 1986); and Conrad Crane, "Avoiding Vietnam: The U.S. Army's Response to Defeat in Southeast Asia," Strategic Studies Institute Monograph, September 2002, www.files.ethz.ch/isn/47370/Avoiding_Vietnam_US.pdf. While Krepinevich's book was vaunted by the *New York Times*, he was shunned by the Army, the superintendent at West Point banned him from speaking on campus, and his military career was derailed. David Cloud and Greg Jaffe, *The Fourth Star* (New York: Three Rivers Press, 2009), p. 60.

31. Neu, *After Vietnam*, pp. 21, 31.

32. James Mann, *The Great Rift: Dick Cheney, Colin Powell, and the Broken Friendship that Defined an Era* (New York: Henry Holt and Co., 2020), p. 135.

33. Lawrence, "Policymaking and the Uses of the Vietnam War," pp. 60–61.

34. Ibid., p. 56.

35. George Packer, "What Obama and the Generals are Reading," *New Yorker*, October 8, 2009, www.newyorker.com/news/george-packer/what-obama-and -the -generals-are-reading.

36. Neu, *After Vietnam*, pp. 75–77.

37. Caspar W. Weinberger, "The Uses of Military Power," National Press Club, Washington, D.C., November 28, 1984. Note: the final element was de-livered differently in his speech than in the prepared text, according to con-temporary reporting from the *New York Times*. See Richard Halloran, "U.S. Will Not Drift into a Latin War, Weinberger Says," *New York Times*, November 29, 1984, www.nytimes.com/1984/11/29/us/us-will-not-drift-into-a-latin-war -weinberger-says.html, p. A1.

38. John T. Correll, "The Weinberger Doctrine," *Air Force Magazine*, March 2014, www.airforcemag.com/PDF/MagazineArchive/Documents/2014/March %202014/0314weinberger.pdf, pp. 62–67.

39. Colin Powell with Joseph E. Persico, *My American Journey* (New York: Ballantine Books, 1995), pp. 420–21. More background on Powell's thinking can be found in Colin Powell, *It Worked For Me: In Life and Leadership*, Leadership (New York: HarperCollins, 2012), pp. 202–07.

40. Powell, *It Worked For Me*, pp. 202–03.

41. To be sure, civilian leaders involved in the Persian Gulf War also were heavily shaped by its legacy. In one telling example, before 9/11, Deputy Secre-tary of Defense Paul Wolfowitz whined to his boss, Secretary of Defense Donald Rumsfeld, that Secretary of State Colin Powell was obsessed with the Gulf War, to which Rumsfeld retorted that his deputy was as well. Tom Ricks, *Fiasco: The American Military Adventure in Iraq* (New York: Penguin Books, 2007), p. 231.

42. David Barno and Nora Bensahel, *Adaptation under Fire: How Militaries Change in Wartime* (Oxford University Press, 2020), p. 107.

43. Antoine Prost, "The Algerian War in French Collective Memory," in *War and Remembrance in the Twentieth Century*, edited by Jay Winter and Emmanuel Sivan (Cambridge University Press, 1999), p. 161.

44. Julian Jackson, *France: The Dark Years* (Oxford University Press, 2003); and Ronald C. Rosbottom, *When Paris Went Dark: The City of Light under German Occupation, 1940–1944* (New York: Bay Back Books, 2015).

45. Nataliya Danilova, *The Politics of War Commemoration in the UK and Russia* (New York: Palgrave Macmillan, 2015), pp. 121, 125.

46. Lawrence, "Policymaking and the Uses of the Vietnam War," p. 51.

47. Ian Hacking, *Rewriting the Soul: Multiple Personality and the Sciences of Memory* (Princeton University Press, 1998); and Jan-Werner Muller, editor, *Memory and Power in Post-War Europe* (Cambridge University Press, 2002), p. 1–35.

48. Eliot Cohen, "The Historical Mind and Military Strategy," *Orbis*, no. 49 (Fall 2005), p. 578.

49. Richard Neustadt and Ernest May, *Thinking in Time: The Uses of History for Decision Makers* (New York: Free Press, 1986), pp. 34–75.

50. Neustadt and May, *Thinking in Time*, p. 161.

51. Matt Gallagher, *Youngblood* (New York: Atria Books, 2016), pp. 53–54.

52. Daniel Kahneman, Dan Locallo, and Olivier Sibony, "Before You Make That Big Decision," *Harvard Business Review* (June 2011), pp. 50–60.

53. John F. Kennedy, "Yale University Commencement Address," June 11, 1962, www.americanrhetoric.com/speeches/jfkyalecommencement.htm.

54. James C. Humes, *The Wit and Wisdom of Winston Churchill* (New York: Harper Perennial, 1995), p. 77.

55. George Packer, "Home Fires," *New Yorker*, April 7, 2014.

56. Joel Rayburn, Frank Sobchak, Jeanne Godfroy, Matthew Morton, James Powell, Matthew Zais, *The U.S Army in the Iraq War* (U.S. Government Printing Office, 2019), https://publications.armywarcollege.edu/publication-detail.cfm?publicationID=3667.

57. Richard D. Hooker and Joseph J. Collins, *Lessons Encountered: Learning from the Long War* (National Defense University Press, 2015), https://ndupress.ndu.edu/Publications/Books/Lessons-Encountered/.

58. Joint and Coalition Operational Analysis (JCOA), *Decade of War, Vol. 1: Enduring Lessons from the Past Decade of Operations*, June 15, 2012. There were lower-level assessments of various aspects of the wars, as well, such as by the Center for Army Lessons Learned.

59. An illustrative but not exhaustive list includes: Rajiv Chandrasekaran, *Imperial Life in the Emerald City: Inside Iraq's Green Zone* (New York: Random House, Inc., 2007); Rajiv Chandrasekaran, *Little America: The War within the War for Afghanistan* (New York: Vintage Books, Inc., 2012); Dexter Filkins, *The Forever War* (New York: Alfred A. Knopf, 2008); Michael R. Gordon, *Cobra II: The Inside Story of the Invasion and Occupation of Iraq* (New York: Random House, Inc, 2006); Michael Gordon and Bernard Trainor, *The Endgame: The Inside Story of the Struggle for Iraq, from George W. Bush to Barack Obama* (New York: Random House, Inc, 2012); Brian Michael Jenkins and John Paul Godges, *The Long Shadow of 9/11: America's Response to Terrorism* (RAND, 2011); Seth G. Jones, *In the Graveyard of Empires: America's War in Afghanistan* (New York: W. W. Norton & Company, 2009); George Packer, *The Assassins' Gate: America in Iraq.* (New York: Farrar, Straus, and Giroux, 2006); Thomas E. Ricks, *Fiasco: The American Military Adventure in Iraq* (New York: Penguin Press, 2007); Thomas E. Ricks, *The Gamble: General Petraeus and the American Military Adventure in Iraq* (New York: Penguin Group, 2009); Joby Warrick, *Black Flags: The Rise of ISIS* (New York: First Anchor Books Edition, 2015); and Michael E. O'Hanlon and Hassina Sherjan, *Toughing it Out in Afghanistan* (Brookings, 2010).

60. An illustrative but not exhaustive list includes: Richard Betts, Michael Desch, and Peter Feaver, "Civilians, Soldiers, and the Iraq Surge Decision," *International Security*, 36, no. 3 (Winter 2011/2012); Peter Feaver, "The Right to Be Right: Civil-Military Relations and the Iraq Surge Decision," *International Security*, 35, no. 4 (Spring 2011); and Francis G. Hoffman, "Strategic Assessment and Adaptation: Reassessing the Afghanistan Surge Decision," *Naval War College Review*, 69, no. 3 (2016), pp. 45–64.

61. Stanley McChrystal, *My Share of the Task—A Memoir* (New York: Portfolio, 2013), p. 287.

62. As full disclosure, the author has participated in both types of strategy reviews: she was a key policymaker for the 2014 Quadrennial Defense Review and a staff member of the 2018 National Defense Strategy Commission. "2014 Quadrennial Defense Review," Department of Defense, March 4, 2014, https://archive.defense.gov/pubs/2014_Quadrennial_Defense_Review.pdf. Eric Edelman, Gary Roughead, and others, "Providing for the Common Defense: Assessment and Recommendations of the National Defense Strategy Commission," November 13, 2018, www.usip.org/sites/default/files/2018-11/providing-for-the-common-defense.pdf.

63. Edelman, Roughead, and others, "Providing for the Common Defense."

64. An illustrative but not exhaustive list includes: David Abrams, *Fobbit* (New York: Black Cat, 2012); David Bellavia, *House to House: An Epic Memoir of War* (London: Simon & Schuster UK Ltd., 2007); Eric Blehm, *Fearless: The Un-*

daunted Courage and Ultimate Sacrifice of Navy SEAL Team SIX Operator Adam Brown (Colorado Springs, Colo.: WaterBrook Press, 2012); Rusty Bradley, *Lions of Kandahar: The Story of a Fight against All Odds* (New York: Bantam Books, 2011); Colby Buzzell, *My War: Killing Time in Iraq* (New York: Putnam's Sons, 2005); Brian Castner, *The Long Walk: A Story of War and the Life that Follows* (New York: Anchor Books, 2012); Nathaniel Fick, *One Bullet Away: The Making of a Marine Officer* (New York: Houghton Mifflin Harcourt Trade & Reference Publishers, 2005); Matt Gallagher, *Kaboom: Embracing the Suck in a Savage Little War* (Cambridge: Da Capo Publishing, 2011); Michael Golembesky and John R. Bruning, *Level Zero Heroes: The Story of U.S. Marine Special Operations in Bala Murghab, Afghanistan* (New York: St. Martin's Press, 2014); Jess Goodell and John Hearn, *Shade it Black: Death and After in Iraq* (Philadelphia: Casemate Publishers, 2011); Bryers J. Pepper, *American Warfighter: Brotherhood, Survival, and Uncommon Valor in Iraq, 2003–2011* (Barnhill House, 2016); Phil Klay, *Redeployment* (New York: Penguin Press, 2014); Chris Kyle, *American Sniper* (New York: HarperCollins Publisher, 2012); Kevin Lacz, Lindsey Lacz, and Ethan E. Rocke, *The Last Punisher: A SEAL Team Three Sniper's True Account of the Battle of Ramadi* (New York: Threshold Editions, 2016); Marcus Luttrell and James D. Hornfischer, *Service: A Navy SEAL at War* (New York: Little, Brown and Co., 2012); Malcolm MacPherson, *Roberts Ridge: A Story of Courage and Sacrifice on Takur Ghar Mountain, Afghanistan* (New York: Bantam Dell, 2005); Dakota Meyer and Bing West, *Into the Fire: A Firsthand Account of the Most Extraordinary Battle in the Afghan War* (New York: Random House, 2012); Robert O'Neill, *The Operator: Firing the Shots that Killed Osama Bin Laden and My Years as a SEAL Team Warrior* (New York: Scribner, 2017); Mark Owen and Kevin Maurer, *No Easy Day: The Firsthand Account of the Mission that Killed Osama Bin Laden* (New York: Penguin Books Ltd., 2012); Sean Parnell and John R. Bruning, *Outlaw Platoon: Heroes, Renegades, Infidels, and the Brotherhood of War in Afghanistan* (New York: HarperCollins Publishers, 2012); Michael Pitre, *Fives and Twenty-Fives* (New York: Bloomsbury Publishing, 2014); Piers Platt, *Combat and Other Shenanigans: Tales of the Absurd from a Deployment to Iraq* (CreateSpace Independent Publishing Platform, 2014); Kevin Powers, *The Yellow Birds* (Boston: Little Brown & Company, 2012); Jason Redman and John Bruning, *Trident: The Forging and Reforging of a Navy SEAL Leader* (New York: HarperCollins Publishers, 2013); John Renehan, *The Valley* (New York: Penguin Random House, 2015); Ross Ritchell, *The Knife* (New York: Penguin Random House, 2015); Christopher Robinson and Gavin Ford Kovite, *War of the Encyclopaedists* (New York: Scribner, 2015); Clinton Romesha, *Red Platoon: A True Story of American Valor* (New York: Penguin Random House, 2016); Roy Scranton, *Fire and Forget* (Boston: Da Capo Press, 2013); Brian Turner, *My Life as a Foreign Country: A Memoir* (New York: Norton, 2014); Howard Wasdin,

SEAL Team Six: Memoirs of an Elite Navy SEAL Sniper (New York: St. Martin's Press, 2011); Kayla Williams and Michael E. Staub, *Love My Rifle More than You* (New York: Norton, 2005); and Evan Wright, *Generation Kill: Devil Dogs, Ice Man, Captain America, and the New Face of American War* (New York: The Berkley Publishing Group, 2004).

65. For an overview of the report's key points, see "Chilcot Report: Key Points from the Iraq Inquiry," *The Guardian*, July 6, 2016, www.theguardian.com/uk-news/2016/jul/06/iraq-inquiry-key-points-from-the-chilcot-report; and David Sanger and Steven Erlanger, "Chilcot Report on Iraq War Offers Devastating Critique of Tony Blair," *New York Times*, July 6, 2016, www.nytimes.com/2016/07/07/world/europe/chilcot-report.html. For the full report, see "The Iraq Inquiry," *National Archives* (UK), https://webarchive.nationalarchives.gov.uk/20171123123237/http://www.iraqinquiry.org.uk/.

66. David Wroe, "The Secret Iraq Dossier: Inside Australia's Flawed War," *Sidney Morning Herald*, www.smh.com.au/interactive/2017/iraq-dossier/; and Dr. Albert Palazzo, "The Australian Army and the War in Iraq, 2002–2010, Directorate of Army Research and Analysis (AUS), March, 2011, Declassified December, 2017, www.defence.gov.au/FOI/Docs/Disclosures/049_1617_Documents.pdf, pp. 34, 527.

67. See, among others, Nora Bensahel and others, *After Saddam: Prewar Planning and the Occupation of Iraq* (RAND, 2008), www.rand.org/content/dam/rand/pubs/monographs/2008/RAND_MG642.pdf; and Ricks, *Fiasco*.

68. Claire Bond Potter and Renee C. Romano, *Doing Recent History* (University of Georgia Press, 2012), p. 5.

69. Scholar Lee Ann Fujii urges researchers to reflect on "silences," not just statements, when conducting interviews. Lee Ann Fujii, *Interviewing in Social Science Research: A Relational Approach* (New York: Routledge, 2018), pp. 76–78.

70. Arthur M. Schlesinger Jr., *The Crisis of the Old Order, 1919–1933* (New York: Houghton Mifflin Company, 1957), p. xi.

71. Mara Karlin and John E. McLaughlin, "How to Name this Era in US Foreign Policy," *Global Brief*, July 3, 2019, https://globalbrief.ca/2019/07/how-to-name-this-era-in-us-foreign-policy/.

72. Stephanie Savell and 5W Infographics, "This Map Shows Where in the World the U.S. Military is Combatting Terrorism," *Smithsonian Magazine*, January 2019, www.smithsonianmag.com/history/map-shows-places-world-where-us-military-operates-180970997/.

73. Readers interested in learning more about positionality and research should read Romain Malejacq and Dipali Mukhopadhyay, "The 'Tribal Politics' of Field Research: A Reflection on Power and Partiality in 21st-Century Warzones," *Perspectives on Politics*, 14, no. 4 (December 2016), pp. 1011–28.

Chapter 2

1. Samuel Huntington describes a profession as having three characteristics: "expertise, responsibility, and corporateness." Samuel Huntington, *The Soldier and the State: The Theory and Politics of Civil-Military Relations* (Harvard University Press, 1957), pp. 8–18.

2. "Strengthening Our Military, Supporting Our Veterans," White House Press Office, August 2004, https://georgewbush-whitehouse.archives.gov/in focus/achievement/chap2.html.

3. "President Obama's Farewell Address to the Armed Forces," *Time*, January 4, 2017, https://time.com/4622417/president-obama-armed-forces-speech-tran script/.

4. "Remarks by President Trump in Briefing with Military Leaders," White House Press Office, October 7, 2019, www.whitehouse.gov/briefings-statements /remarks-president-trump-briefing-military-leaders/.

5. Brad Roberts, "On the Need for a Blue Theory of Victory," *War on the Rocks*, September, 2020, https://warontherocks.com/2020/09/on-the-need-for -a-blue-theory-of-victory/.

6. Colon-Lopez had just been named the new senior enlisted adviser to the chairman of the joint chiefs of staff when he made this remark. Meghann Myers, "Senior Enlisted Leaders React to Afghanistan Papers: 'I've Never Been Lied To,'" *Military Times*, December 9, 2019, www.militarytimes.com/news/ your-military/2019/12/09/senior-enlisted-leaders-react-to-afghanistan-papers -ive-never-been-lied-to/. The "Afghanistan Papers" were a set of declassified memos and interviews with former senior civilian and military officials about lessons learned from the Afghanistan conflict. They were published in December 2019 and can be accessed at Craig Whitlock, "At War with the Truth," *Washington Post*, December 9, 2019, www.washingtonpost.com/graphics/2019/ investigations/afghanistan-papers/afghanistan-war-confidential-documents/.

7. Barack Obama, *A Promised Land* (New York: Crown, 2020), pp. 319–20.

8. Colonel Harry Summers began his book *On Strategy: The Vietnam War in Context* by sharing a conversation with a former North Vietnamese Army colonel. Summer commented that "you know you never defeated us on the battlefield." In response, the NVA colonel said, "That may be so, but it is also irrelevant." Harry Summers, *On Strategy: A Critical Analysis of the Vietnam War* (Toronto: Presidio Press, 1995), p. 1.

9. This piece discussed a staff ride sponsored by the Strategic Studies Department at Johns Hopkins University's Paul H. Nitze School of Advanced International Studies (SAIS) that I directed and was organized by two thoughtful graduate student quartermasters, Keel Dietz and Claire Harrison. See David Barno and Nora Bensahel, "Revisiting the Vietnam War at Home—and What it

Means for Today," *War on the Rocks*, November 12, 2019, https://warontherocks .com/2019/11/revisiting-the-vietnam-war-at-home-and-what-it-means-for -today/.

10. Quoted in Elliot Ackerman, *Places and Names—On War, Revolution, and Returning* (New York: Penguin Press, 2019), p. 32.

11. Stanley McChrystal, *My Share of the Task: A Memoir* (New York: Portfolio, 2013), p. 380. Italics in original.

12. Matt Gallagher, *Youngblood* (New York: Atria Books, 2016), p. 135.

13. Carl Von Clausewitz, edited and translated by Michael Howard and Peter Peret, *On War* (Princeton University Press, 1976), pp. 523–66.

14. Clausewitz, *On War*, p. 80.

15. As exemplified by the *Washington Post*'s series on the Afghanistan Papers, which argued that the frame for understanding senior decisionmaking on Afghanistan is best understood as "lying." Craig Whitlock, "At War with the Truth," *Washington Post*, December 9, 2019, www.washingtonpost.com/graphics/2019/ investigations/afghanistan-papers/afghanistan-war-confidential-documents/.

16. Pauline Kaurin, *The Warrior, Military Ethics, and Contemporary Warfare: Achilles Goes Asymmetrical* (New York: Routledge, 2016), p. 19. See, also, Christopher Coker, *Humane War* (New York: Routledge, 2001), and Rob Thorton, *Asymmetric Warfare: Threat and Response in the 21st Century* (Malden: Polity Press, 2007).

17. Kaurin, *The Warrior, Military Ethics, and Contemporary Warfare*, p. 20.

18. David Wood, *What Have We Done: The Moral Injury of Our Longest Wars* (New York: Brown Spark, 2016), pp. 16–17. Moral injury is the "distressing psychological, behavioral, social, and sometimes spiritual aftermath of exposure" to upsetting events which can occur when one "feel[s] like a transgression occurred and that they or someone else crossed a line with respect to their moral beliefs." Examples of upsetting events in wartime that may trigger moral injury include making decisions about who to kill and who to save given unclear information and finite resources. Sonya B. Norman and Shira Maguen, "Moral Injury," *U.S. Department of Veterans Affairs*, www.ptsd.va.gov/professional/treat/ cooccurring/moral_injury.asp.

19. Brett T. Litz, Nathan Stein, Eileen Delaney, Leslie Lebowitz, William P. Nash, Caroline Silva, and Shira Maguen, "Moral Injury and Moral Repair in War Veterans: A Preliminary Model and Intervention Strategy," *Clinical Psychology Review*, 29, no. 8 (2009), p. 695.

20. Quoted in Wood, *What Have We Done*, p. 241.

21. Sean Kimmons, "New Chief of Staff: 'Taking Care of People Key to Winning the Fight,'" *Army News Service*, October 8, 2019, www.army.mil/article/

225377/new_chief_of_staff_taking_care_of_people_key_to_winning_the_ fight.

22. Kimmons, "New Chief of Staff."

23. Jonathan Shay, *Achilles in Vietnam: Combat Trauma and the Undoing of Character* (New York: Atheneum, 1994), p. 6.

24. Wood, *What Have We Done*, p. 254.

25. Dirk Diggler, "War in Afghanistan Turns 16, Earns Driver's License," *Duffel Blog*, October, 2017, www.duffelblog.com/2017/10/war-in-afghanistan -turns-16-earns-drivers-license/.

26. Paul Sharpe, "Wow! This Man Was Born on 9/11 and Gets to Fight in the Same War It Inspired," *Duffel Blog*, September 2018, www.duffelblog.com/2018 /09/inspiring-this-man-was-born-on-9-11-and-gets-to-fight-in-the-same-war -it-inspired/.

27. "Meet the Teenager Born after 9/11 Who Will One Day Command All Forces in Afghanistan," *Duffel Blog*, May, 2018 www.duffelblog.com/2018/05/ meet-the-teenager-born-after-9-11-who-will-one-day-command-all-forces-in -afghanistan/.

28. *War Machine*, directed by David Michod (Netflix Studios, 2017).

29. Quoted in Steven Matthew Leonard, "The Elusive Silver Bullet: What's it Like to Win a War," *Clearance Jobs*, September 17, 2019, https://news.clearance jobs.com/2019/09/17/the-elusive-silver-bullet-whats-it-like-to-win-a-war/amp/.

30. Elizabeth Samet, *Soldier's Heart—Reading Literature through Peace and War at West Point* (New York: Farrar, Straus, and Giroux, 2007) pp. 18–19.

31. Samet, *Soldier's Heart*, p. 157.

32. Thomas Gibbons-Neff, "A Marine Looks Back at his Battle's in Afghani-stan," *New York Times*, September 16, 2019, www.nytimes.com/2019/09/16/ world/middleeast/marja-trump-taliban-afghanistan-peace.html#click=https:/ /t.co/LH7XmRbuFM.

Chapter 3

1. Andrew Tilghman, "Retired Gen. James Mattis Says Civilians Know Little about the Military," *Military Times*, September 7, 2016, www.militarytimes.com /2016/09/07/retired-gen-james-mattis-says-civilians-know-little-about-the -military/.

2. As quoted in Tilghman, "Retired Gen. James Mattis Says Civilians Know Little about the Military."

3. Mara Karlin and Alice Hunt Friend, "Military Worship Hurts U.S. De-mocracy," *Foreign Policy*, September 21, 2018, https://foreignpolicy.com/2018/09/ 21/military-worship-hurts-us-democracy-civilian-trump/.

4. Yahoo News, "YouGov Poll," Question 1A, June 9–10, 2020, https://docs .cdn.yougov.com/86ijosd7cy/20200611_yahoo_race_police_covid_crosstabs .pdf. This poll questioned 1,570 U.S. adults.

5. Peter Feaver and Jim Golby, "Military Prestige during a Political Crisis: Use It and You'll Lose It," *War on the Rocks*, June 5, 2020, https://warontherocks .com/2020/06/military-prestige-during-a-political-crisis-use-it-and-youll-lose -it/.

6. Those interested in learning more about the homecoming that some troops received when they returned from Vietnam may wish to read the letters found in Bob Greene, *Home-Coming: When Soldiers Returned from Vietnam* (New York: PG Putnam's Sons, 1989).

7. Jonathan Shay, *Achilles in Vietnam: Combat Trauma and the Undoing of Character* (New York: Atheneum, 1994), p. 197. Italics in original.

8. According to NVivo analysis of senior military leader interviews.

9. Phillip Carter, "For Veterans, Is 'Thank You for Your Service' Enough?" *Washington Post*, November 4, 2011, www.washingtonpost.com/opinions/for -veterans-is-thank-you-for-your-service-enough/2011/11/03/glQA67hZmM_ story.html.

10. Nicholas Mercurio, "Beyond 'Thank You': Recommended Modalities for Meaningful Civilian-Military Discourse," *Journal of Veterans Studies* (March 2019), pp. 15–16.

11. Heidi Urben and Jim Golby, "Thank Them for Their Service," *Army Times*, March 29, 2020, www.armytimes.com/opinion/commentary/2020/03/29/thank -them-for-their-service/.

12. "Full Transcript and Video: Kelly Defends Trump's Handling of Soldiers Death and Call to Widow," *New York Times*, October 19, 2017, www.nytimes.com /2017/10/19/us/politics/statement-kelly-gold-star.html.

13. Morris Janowitz, The Professional Soldier: A Social and Political Portrait (New York: The Free Press, 1960).

14. Jim Golby and Peter Feaver, "Biden Inherits a Challenging Civil-Military Legacy," *War on the Rocks*, January 1, 2020, https://warontherocks.com/2021/01/ biden-inherits-a-challenging-civil-military-legacy/.

15. Risa Brooks, Michael Robinson, and Heidi Urben, "Huntington, Janow- itz, or None of the Above? Conceptions of Professional Norms by Future Army Officers," *APSA Preprints*, October 3, 2020.

16. "Opinion: I Would've Joined the Military Too If I Didn't Think It Was Beneath Me," *Duffel Blog*, August, 2019, www.duffelblog.com/2019/08/opinion -i-wouldve-joined-the-military-too-if-i-didnt-think-it-was-beneath-me/?utm_ campaign=coschedule&utm_source=twitter&utm_medium=DuffelBlog&utm

_content=Opinion:%20I%20would%27ve%20joined%20the%20military%20too
%20if%20I%20didn%27t%20think%20it%20was%20beneath%20me.

17. Robert Saxe, *Settling Down: World War II Veterans' Challenge to the Post-war Consensus* (New York: Palgrave, 2007), pp. 12–20.

18. "Casualty Status," Department of Defense, June 29, 2020, www.defense .gov/casualty.pdf.

19. A tremendous summary of the Niger debacle can be found at Rukmini Callimachi, Helene Cooper, Eric Schmitt, Alan Blinder, and Thomas Gibbons-Neff, "An Endless War: Why 4 U.S. Soldiers Died in a Remote African Desert," *New York Times*, February 20, 2018, www.nytimes.com/interactive/2018/02/17/ world/africa/niger-ambush-american-soldiers.html. The Pentagon's unclassi-fied executive summary of its investigation can be found at https://dod.defense .gov/portals/1/features/2018/0418_niger/img/Oct-2017-Niger-Ambush-Sum mary-of-Investigation.pdf.

20. Phil Klay, "Left Behind," *The Atlantic*, May 2018, www.theatlantic.com/ magazine/archive/2018/05/left-behind.

21. Quoted in David Wood, *What Have We Done: The Moral Injury of Our Longest Wars* (New York: Brown Spark, 2016), pp. 267–78.

22. Ibid.

Chapter 4

1. The best primer of theories surrounding civilian control of the military can be found in Eliot Cohen, *Supreme Command* (New York: Simon & Schuster, 2002), p. 241–64.

2. Charlie Dunlap, "Let's Temper the Rhetoric about Civil-Military Rela-tions," *Lawfire*, May 11, 2018, https://sites.duke.edu/lawfire/2018/05/11/lets -temper-the-rhetoric-about-civil-military-relations/.

3. Peter Feaver, Conference on Civil-Military Relations, Johns Hopkins Phil-lip-Merrill Center for Strategic Studies, February 13, 2020, www.merrillcenter .sais-jhu.edu/events.

4. Ibid.; also, Peter Feaver, "Prologue," in *Reconsidering American Civil-Mil-itary Relations: The Military, Society, Politics, and Modern War*, edited by Lionel Beehner, Risa Brooks, Daniel Maurer (Oxford University Press, 2021), p. viii.

5. Risa Brooks, "Paradoxes of Professionalism: Rethinking Civil-Military Relations in the United States," *International Security*, 44, no. 4 (Spring 2020); Lindsey P. Cohn, "The Precarious State of Civil-Military Relations in the Age of Trump," *War on the Rocks*, March 28, 2018, https://warontherocks.com/2018/03/ the-precarious-state-of-civil-military-relations-in-the-age-of-trump/; and Eric Edelman, Gary Roughead, and others, "Providing for the Common Defense:

The Assessment and Recommendations of the National Defense Strategy Commission," (Washington, DC: U.S. Institute of Peace, November 2018).

6. Jim Golby and Peter Feaver, "Biden Inherits a Challenging Civil-Military Legacy," *War on the Rocks*, January 1, 2021, https://warontherocks.com/2021/01/biden-inherits-a-challenging-civil-military-legacy/.

7. Cohen, *Supreme Command*, p. 233.

8. Readers interested in learning more about either of these examples should refer to Gordon Craig, *The Politics of the Prussian Army* (Ohio University Press, 1956); and George C. Herring, "American Strategy in Vietnam: The Postwar Debate," *Military Affairs*, 46 (April 1982).

9. Jeffrey P. Kimball, "The Stab-In-The-Back Legend and the Vietnam War, *Armed Forces and Society*, 14 (1988), pp. 433–34.

10. Ibid., pp. 438.

11. See, for example, chapter 4 in Joel Rayburn, Frank Sobchak, and others, *The U.S. Army in the Iraq War, Volume I: Invasion and Civil War* (U.S. Government Printing Office, 2019).

12. Robert Timberg, "A War within James Webb," *Baltimore Sun*, July 2, 1995, www.baltimoresun.com/news/bs-xpm-1995-07-02-1995183135-story.html; and James Webb, "The Draft: Why the Army Needs It," *The Atlantic*, April 1980, www.theatlantic.com/ideastour/military/webb-excerpt.html. Webb's fiction reflects these themes, as well. See Jim Webb, *Fields of Fire* (New York: Bantam Books, 1978); and James Webb, *A Country Such as This* (New York: Doubleday, 1983). A profile of Webb during his time as secretary of Navy also reflects how Vietnam informed his thinking. See John Cushman, "James Webb's New Fields of Fire," *New York Times*, February 28, 1988, www.nytimes.com/1988/02/28/magazine/james-webb-s-new-fields-of-fire.html.

13. Peter Feaver, *Armed Servants* (Harvard University Press, 2003); and Peter Feaver, "The Right to be Right: Civil-Military Relations and the Iraq Surge Decision," *International Security*, 35, no. 4 (2011), pp. 87–125.

14. The memoirs of senior civilian defense leaders like Donald Rumsfeld and Douglas Feith represent spectacular examples of failures, particularly regarding Iraq, Afghanistan, and the broader "war on terror."

15. Colin Powell with Joseph E. Persico, *My American Journey* (New York: Ballantine Books, 1995), p. 420–21. As chairman of the joint chiefs of staff, General Powell penned a *Foreign Affairs* article outlining his doctrine. It was a warning shot to the incoming Clinton administration. General Colin L. Powell, "U.S. Forces: Challenges Ahead," *Foreign Affairs* (Winter 1992/1993).

16. Powell, *My American Journey*, pp. 207–08.

17. Tony Lombardo, "Q-and-A: Colin Powell on Vietnam Service, Iraq and Afghanistan, and Black History Month," *Military Times*, January 31, 2017.

18. Colin Powell with Tony Koltz, *It Worked For Me: In Life and Leadership* (New York: HarperCollins, 2012), pp. 202–03.

19. According to Michael Desch, in 1999, Shelton told him, "I firmly believe in [former Secretary of Defense Caspar] Weinberger's doctrine, amplified by General Powell, and I think that we followed that" in the Kosovo operation. Echoing Powell, Shelton argued that military force should be the tool of last resort and proposed what he called "the Dover test" for committing U.S. forces to combat: "When bodies are brought back, will we still feel it is in U.S. interests?" Quoted in Michael C. Desch, "Bush and the Generals," *Foreign Affairs* (May/June 2007), www.foreignaffairs.com/articles/united-states/2007-05-01/bush-and-generals. In his memoirs, Myers discussed the lessons that senior military leaders learned from serving in the Vietnam War: "In any conflict, our forces should be committed in appropriate strength with clear objectives, which keep relentless pressure on the enemy to capitulate." Richard Myers, *Eyes on the Horizon—Serving on the Front Lines of National Security* (New York, Simon & Schuster, Inc., 2007), p. 60.

20. Mike Jackson, "Is the Powell Doctrine Dead and Gone?" *Modern War Institute*, February 22, 2016, https://mwi.usma.edu/is-the-powell-doctrine-dead-and-gone/.

21. General Anthony Zinni, "Farewell Remarks at the U.S. Naval Institute," March 2000, https://web.archive.org/web/20060330163243/http://www.rcaca.org/News-Zinni.htm.

22. Powell, *It Worked For Me*, pp. 202–03.

23. Michael R. Gordon, "Powell Delivers a Resounding 'No' on Using Limited Force on Bosnia," *New York Times*, September 28, 1992.

24. Luke Middup, "The Impact of Vietnam on U.S. Strategy in the First Gulf War," *Comparative Strategy*, 29, no. 5 (November, 2010), pp. 400–01.

25. In Powell's words, his "concept of the Powell Doctrine begins with the premise that war is to be avoided. Use all available political, diplomatic, economic, and financial means to try to solve the problem and achieve the political objective the President has established. At the same time, make it understood that military force exists to support diplomacy and take over where diplomacy leaves off. There is no sharp distinction between the two." Powell, *It Worked For Me*, p. 202.

26. Tony Lombardo, "Q-and-A: Colin Powell on Vietnam Service, Iraq, and Afghanistan, and Black History Month," *Military Times*, January 31, 2017.

27. Powell, *It Worked For Me*, p. 202–03.

28. Eliot Cohen, "Playing Powell Politics: The General's Zest for Power," *Foreign Affairs* (November/December, 1995), www.foreignaffairs.com/reviews/review-essay/1995-11-01/playing-powell-politics-generals-zest-power.

29. Lombardo, "Q-and-A."

30. "Brett Scowcroft Oral History Part II," The Miller Center, recorded August 10 2000, www.millercenter.org/the-presidency/presidential-oral-histories/brent-scowcroft-oral-history-part-ii.

31. Major Douglas E. Delaney, "'Us' And 'Them': Colin Powell and American Civil-Military Relations, 1963–1993," *Canadian Military Journal* (Spring 2002), p. 51. Delaney is currently a professor at the Royal Military College of Canada.

32. Quoted in J. Kael Weston, *The Mirror Test: America at War in Iraq and Afghanistan* (New York: Vintage Books, 2017), p. 523.

33. Peter Feaver and Christopher Gelpi, *Choosing Your Battles: American Civil-Military Relations and the Use of Force* (Princeton University Press, 2004), p. 184. The authors define "elites" as mid-career officers.

34. "The Military-Civilian Gap: War and Sacrifice in the Post-9/11 Era," Pew Research Center, October 5, 2011, www.pewresearch.org/wp-content/uploads/sites/3/2011/10/veterans-report.pdf.

35. Specifically, Golby, Cohn, and Feaver tested the following: "a) Military force should be used only in pursuit of the goal of total victory; b) Use of force in foreign interventions should be applied quickly and massively; c) When force is used, military rather than political goals should determine its applications; d) Public will not tolerate large numbers of US casualties in military operations." James Golby, Lindsay Cohn, and Peter Feaver, "Thanks for Your Service: Civilian and Veteran Attitudes After Fifteen Years of War," in *Warriors and Citizens: American Views of Our Military*, edited by Kori Schake and Jim Mattis (Hoover Institution Press, 2016), p. 130.

36. "Another important step to address potential future force constraint challenges would be for senior military leaders to consider increasing the size of the force, especially the Army and Marine Corps, as soon as the United States is committed to a major conflict." Rayburn, Sobchak, and others, *The U.S. Army in the Iraq War*, p. 623.

37. Frank Hoffman, "A Second Look at the Powell Doctrine," *War on the Rocks*, February 20, 2014, https://warontherocks.com/2014/02/a-second-look-at-the-powell-doctrine/.

38. Steven Matthew Leonard, Timeless: The Powell Doctrine in the Era of the Forever Wars," *Clearance Jobs*, April 6, 2019, https://news.clearancejobs.com/2019/04/06/timeless-the-powell-doctrine-in-the-era-of-the-forever-wars/.

39. Greg Jaffe, "Afghanistan Wasn't Destined to Fail. Here's How We Could Have Fought It Better: Why Hasn't the US Learned to Set Achievable Goals," *Washington Post*, December 20, 2019, www.washingtonpost.com/outlook/afghanistan-wasnt-destined-to-fail-heres-how-we-could-have-fought-it-better/2019/12/19/b7d4ef66-21e7-11ea-a153-dce4b94e4249_story.html.

40. Sections excerpted from Mara Karlin, "Civilian Oversight Inside the Pentagon: Who Does It and How?" in *Reconsidering American Civil-Military Relations: The Military, Society, Politics, and Modern War*, edited by Lionel Beehner, Risa Brooks, and Daniel Maurer (Oxford University Press, 2021), chapter 4.

41. Mara Karlin and Christopher Skaluba, "Strategic Guidance for Countering the Proliferation of Strategic Guidance," *War on the Rocks*, July 20, 2017, https://warontherocks.com/2017/07/strategic-guidance-for-countering-the-proliferation-of-strategic-guidance/.

42. Secretary of Defense, U.S. Code 10, § 113, www.law.cornell.edu/uscode/text/10/113.

43. Amy Zegart, *Flawed by Design* (Stanford University Press, 1999), p. 62.

44. Mara Karlin and Loren DeJonge Schulman, "Keeping up Civ-Mil Relations," *War on the Rocks,* April 19, 2017, https://warontherocks.com/2017/04/keeping-up-civ-mil-relations/.

45. With gratitude to Merriam Webster. *Merriam-Webster's Collegiate Dictionary.* 11th edition (Springfield, Mass.: Merriam-Webster, 2003), www.merriam-webster.com/dictionary/oversight.

46. Office of the Secretary of Defense, U.S. Code 10, § 131, www.law.cornell.edu/uscode/text/10/131.

47. Full list available in Title 10. Office of the Secretary of Defense, U.S. Code 10, § 131, www.law.cornell.edu/uscode/text/10/131.

48. Charles Stevenson. *SecDef: The Nearly Impossible Job of Secretary of Defense* (Potomac: Potomac Books, 2006), p. 186.

49. Stevenson, *SecDef.*

50. Graham T. Allison, and Morton H. Halperin, "Bureaucratic Politics: A Paradigm and Some Policy Implications," *World Politics*, 24 (Spring 1972).

51. Deborah D. Avant, "Are the Reluctant Warriors Out of Control? Why the U.S. Military is Averse to Responding to Post-Cold War Low Level Threats," *Security Studies*, 6, no. 2 (Winter 1996/97), p. 56.

52. Under Secretary of Defense, U.S. Code 10, § 134 (2010), www.gpo.gov/fdsys/pkg/USCODE-2010-title10/html/USCODE-2010-title10-subtitleA-part1-chap4-sec134.htm; and U.S. Congress, *John S. McCain National Defense Authorization Act for Fiscal Year 2019*, H.R. 5515, 115th Congress, April 13, 2018, www.congress.gov/bill/115th-congress/house-bill/5515/text?format=txt.

53. Jim Thomas, "Statement before the Senate Armed Services Committee on Defense Reform, Center for Strategic and Budgetary Assessments, November 10, 2015, www.armed-services.senate.gov/imo/media/doc/Thomas_11-10-15.pdf.

54. Quoted in Dana Priest, *The Mission: Waging War and Keeping Peace with America's Military* (New York: W. W. Norton and Company, 2004), p. 24.

55. Ibid.

56. Quoted in Robert M. Gates, *Duty* (New York: Alfred A. Knopf, 2014), pp. 264–65. Italics in original.

57. Gates, *Duty*, pp. 142–44.

58. Peter Feaver, "The Civil-Military Problematique: Huntington, Janowitz, and the Question of Civilian Control," *Armed Forces & Society*, 23, no. 2 (Winter 1996), p. 154.

59. Gates, *Duty*, p. 101. Italics in original.

60. Jim Garamone, "Dempsey Describes Chairman's Job as Being 'The Dash,'" *DOD News*, July 17, 2015, www.defense.gov/Explore/News/Article/Article/612656/dempsey-describes-chairmans-job-as-being-the-dash/.

61. Mara Karlin and Paula Thornhill, "The Chairman the Pentagon Needs," *War on the Rocks*, January 5, 2018, https://warontherocks.com/2018/01/chairman-pentagon-needs/; "Advance Policy Questions for General Joseph Dunford, USMC, Nominee for Reconfirmation as Chairman of the Joint Chiefs of Staff," Senate Armed Services Committee, www.armed-services.senate.gov/imo/media/doc/Dunford_APQs_09-26-17.pdf; and *National Defense Authorization Act for Fiscal Year 2017*, 114th Congress, Report 114-840, November 30, 2016, www.congress.gov/114/crpt/hrpt840/CRPT-114hrpt840.pdf.

62. "Global Integration—Maintaining a Competitive Advantage," Joint Chiefs of Staff, October 30, 2018, www.jcs.mil/Media/News/News-Display/Article/1681761/global-integrati/.

63. Paul Shinkman, "The Joint Chiefs' Power Surge," *U.S. News*, September 30, 2019, www.usnews.com/news/national-news/articles/2019-09-30/how-joe-dunford-quietly-changed-the-joint-chiefs-role-in-preparing-for-war; and Jim Garamone, "Dunford's Term as Chairman Encompassed Great Changes," *DOD News*, October, 2019, www.jcs.mil/Media/News/News-Display/Article/1973443/dunfords-term-as-chairman-encompassed-great-changes/.

64. Pieces of the rest of this section are excerpted from Mara Karlin, Alice Hunt Friend, and Loren Dejonge Schulman, "Two Cheers for Esper's Plan to Reassert Civilian Control of the Pentagon," *Defense One*, September 9, 2019. See, also, Shinkman, "The Joint Chiefs' Power Surge."

65. The author was a staff member on this congressionally-mandated National Defense Strategy Commission.

66. Edelman, Roughead, and others, "Providing for the Common Defense. The author worked on the commission.

67. Raphael S. Cohen, *The History and Politics of Defense Reviews* (RAND, 2018), pp. 35, 43–45.

68. U.S. Department of Defense, *Management and Review of Campaign and Contingency Plans*, Chairman of the Joint Chiefs of Staff—Instruction 3141.01F,

January 31, 2019, www.jcs.mil/Portals/36/Documents/Library/Instructions/
CJCSI%203141.01F.pdf?ver=2019-03-18-121700-283.

69. For example, the latest Chairman of the Joint Chiefs of Staff's Instruction states that the National Military Strategy is "the central strategic guidance document for the Joint Force," thereby displacing the secretary of defense's national defense strategy. U.S. Department of Defense, *Joint Strategic Planning System*, Chairman of the Joint Chiefs of Staff-Instruction 3100.00.01D, July 20, 2018, www.jcs.mil/Portals/36/Documents/Library/Instructions/CJCSI%203100 .01D.pdf?ver=2018-08-10-143143-823. See, also, Karlin and Thornhill, "The Chairman the Pentagon Needs."

70. Edelman, Roughead, and others, "Providing for the Common Defense," p. 48. Italics in original.

71. In particular, Dunford advocated to Congress for "limited authority for the worldwide reallocation of a limited number of military assets . . . on a short-term basis." See U.S. Department of Defense, *Advance Policy Questions for General Joseph Dunford, USMC Nominee for Reconfirmation as Chairman of the Joint Chiefs of Staff*, Chairman of the Joint Chiefs of Staff, September 26, 2017, www .armed-services.senate.gov/imo/media/doc/Dunford_APQs_09-26-17.pdf.

72. Edelman, Roughead, and others, "Providing for the Common Defense."

73. Mackenzie Eaglen, "Esper is Attempting the Biggest Defense Reform in a Generation," *Defense One*, January 15, 2020, www.defenseone.com/ideas/2020 /01/esper-attempting-biggest-defense-reforms-generation/162457/.

74. Secretary of Defense Mark Esper, "Message to the Force on Accomplishments in Implementation of the National Defense Strategy," U.S. Department of Defense, July 7, 2020, www.defense.gov/Newsroom/Transcripts/Transcript /Article/2266872/secretary-of-defense-mark-t-esper-message-to-the-force-on -accomplishments-in-im/.

75. Kathleen H. Hicks, Andrew Hunter, and others, "Assessing the Third Offset Strategy," Center for Strategic and International Studies, March 2017, https://csis-prod.s3.amazonaws.com/s3fspublic/publication/170302_Ellman _ThirdOffsetStrategySummary_Web.pdf?EXO1GwjFU22_Bkd5A.nx.fJXT KRDKbVR.

76. Notably, the Trump White House—almost surely at some of the Defense Department leadership's urging—objected to these aforementioned Title 10 changes, arguing that they "would also overlap with the Chairman of the Joint Chiefs of Staff's existing responsibilities for strategic and contingency planning [in Title 10]." Office of Management and Budget, *Follow-on to Statement of Administration Policy* (June 26, 2018), www.whitehouse.gov/wp-content/uploads/ 2018/06/saps2987s_20180626.pdf. See, also, Chairman: Functions, U.S. Code 10, § 153, www.law.cornell.edu/uscode/text/10/153.

77. One example can be found in strategic guidance documents. Karlin and Skaluba, "Strategic Guidance."

78. Those who want to better understand the many flaws in Huntington's approach would do well to read Risa Brooks, "Paradoxes of Professionalism: Rethinking Civil-Military Relations in the United States," *International Security,* 44, no. 4 (Spring 2020), pp. 7–44.

79. Sections excerpted from Mara Karlin and James Golby, "Why 'Best Military Advice' is Bad for the Military—and Worse for Civilians," *Orbis,* 62, no. 1 (January 8, 2018), pp. 137–53.

80. Google NGram Viewer shows the increased use of the phrase post-9/11, https://books.google.com/ngrams. Dunford began using it early on as chair. To take one example: Jared Serbu, "Dunford Plans to Trim Joint Staff Workforce after New Year," *Federal News Network,* December 24, 2015, https://federalnewsnetwork.com/defense/2015/12/dunford-plans-trim-joint-staff-workforce-new-year/.

81. To take one example, Joint Staff J7, "Joint Operations: Insights and Best Practices," Department of Defense, November 2017, www.jcs.mil/Portals/36/Documents/Doctrine/fp/joint_ops_fp.pdf?ver=2018-03-29-084007-483; Karlin and Golby, "Why 'Best Military Advice' is Bad for the Military."

82. Joseph Dunford, "Upholding Our Oath," October 25, 2016, https://medium.com/@thejointstaff/upholding-our-oath-b479c572cbd4; Joseph Dunford, "Remarks and Q&A at the Center for Strategic and International Studies," www.jcs.mil/Media/Speeches/Article/707418/gen-dunfords-remarks-and-qa-at-the- center-for-strategic-and-international-studi/; and Taylor McNeil, "Top Brass." Sept. 28, 2015, http://now.tufts.edu/articles/top-brass. Interestingly, one senior general officer asserted that "best military advice" is required by Congress; that is incorrect.

83. Samuel P. Huntington, *The Soldier and the State: The Theory and Politics of Civil-Military Relations* (Harvard University Press, 1957).

84. Michael E. O'Hanlon, "Iraq Without a Plan," *Policy Review,* 128 (December 2004-January 2005).

85. Brooks, "Paradoxes of Professionalism," pp. 26–30.

86. Ibid.," pp. 36–37.

87. Nor, of course do unitary civilian views exist. To take one example, the Iraq surge decision was characterized by varying perspectives by civilians. See Kori Schake, "Civil-Military Relations and the 2006 Iraq Surge," in *The Last Card: Inside George W. Bush's Decision to Surge in Iraq,* edited by Timothy Andrews Sayle and others (Cornell University Press: 2019), chapter 14.

88. *Reconsidering American Civil-Military Relations: The Military, Society, Poli-*

tics, and Modern War, edited by Lionel Beehner, Risa Brooks, Daniel Maurer, introduction, p. 6.

89. Risa Brooks, Michael Robinson, and Heidi Urben, "Huntington, Janowitz, or None of the Above? Conceptions of Professional Norms by Future Army Officers," *APSA Preprints*, October 3, 2020.

90. Ibid.

91. Karlin and Golby, "Why 'Best Military Advice' is Bad for the Military."

92. Luis Martinez, "General Martin Dempsey Lays out U.S. Military Options for Syria," July 22, 2013, http://abcnews.go.com/blogs/politics/2013/07/gen-martin-dempsey-lays-out-us- military-options-for-syria/.

93. Barack Obama, *A Promised Land* (Random House: 2020), p. 159.

94. Martin Dempsey, *No Time for Spectators: The Lessons that Mattered Most from West Point to the West Wing* (New York: Missionday, 2020), p. 103.

95. Richard H. Kohn, "Civil-Military Behaviors that Build Trust," adapted from Kohn, "Building Trust: Civil-Military Behaviors for Effective National Security," *American Civil-Military Relations: The Soldier and the State in a New Era*, edited by Suzanne C. Nielsen and Don M. Snider (Johns Hopkins University Press, 2009), pp. 3–9.

96. "Conference on Civil-Military Relations," Johns Hopkins Phillip-Merrill Center for Strategic Studies, February 13, 2020, www.merrillcenter.sais-jhu.edu/events.

97. Janine Davidson, Ben Fernandes, and Emerson Brooking, "Mending the Broken Dialogue," Council on Foreign Relations, November 2016, www.cfr.org/report/mending-brokendialogue, pp. 41–42.

98. Davidson and others, "Mending the Broken Dialogue," pp. 41–42.

99. Donald Rumsfeld, *Known and Unknown: A Memoir* (New York: Penguin, 2011), pp. 292–93.

100. "Conference on Civil-Military Relations," Johns Hopkins Phillip-Merrill Center for Strategic Studies, February 13, 2020, www.merrillcenter.sais-jhu.edu/events.

101. Major General William Rapp, "Civil-Military Relations: The Role of Military Leaders in Strategy Making," *Parameters*, 43, no. 3 (Fall 2015), p. 19.

102. Brooks, "Paradoxes of Professionalism," p. 11.

103. Of 380 students, approximately 8 choose to take the course. Personal communication from Professor Marybeth Ulrich, General Maxwell D. Taylor Chair of the Profession of Arms and Professor of Government at the U.S. Army War College, January 28, 2019.

104. Karlin and Skaluba, "Strategic Guidance."

105. Readers searching for useful primers on the military services should

turn to one of the following books: Carl H. Builder, *The Masks of War: American Military Styles in Strategy and Analysis* (Johns Hopkins University Press, 1989) or Paula G. Thornhill, *Demystifying the American Military: Institutions, Evolution, and Challenges since 1789* (Naval Institute Press, 2019).

106. Gates, *Duty*, p. 44.

107. John Shy, "Jomini," in *Makers of Modern Strategy: From Machiavelli to the Nuclear Age*, edited by Peter Paret (Princeton University Press, 1971).

108. "Conference on Civil-Military Relations," Johns Hopkins Phillip-Merrill Center for Strategic Studies, February 13, 2020, www.merrillcenter.sais-jhu.edu/events.

109. Brooks, "Paradoxes of Professionalism," p. 39.

110. Richard H. Kohn, "Building Trust: Civil-Military Behaviors for Effective National Security," in *American Civil-Military Relations: The Soldier and the State in a New Era*, edited by Suzanne Nielsen and Don Snider (Johns Hopkins University Press, 2009), pp. 264–89.

111. National Defense Staff, "Exclusive: Q&A with Air Force Chief of Staff Gen. David Goldfein," *National Defense Magazine*, August 4, 2020.

112. Mara Karlin and Alice Hunt Friend, "Towards a Concept of Good Civilian Guidance," *War on the Rocks*, May 29, 2020, https://warontherocks.com/2020/05/towards-a-concept-of-good-civilian-guidance/.

113. "The Good Operation: A Handbook for Those Involved in Operational Policy and Its Implementation," U.K. Ministry of Defense, January 2018, https://assets.publishing.service.gov.uk/government/uploads/system/uploads/attachment_data/file/674545/TheGoodOperation_WEB.PDF, p. 9

114. Peter Feaver, *Armed Servants* (Harvard University Press, 2003), pp. 83–85.

Chapter 5

1. Richard Myers, *Eyes on the Horizon: Serving on the Front Lines of National Security* (New York: Simon & Schuster, 2007), p. 140.

2. The 2001 defense strategy known as the Quadrennial Defense Review was practically finished when the September 11, 2001, attacks occurred. It was published on September 30, 2001. "U.S. Department of Defense: Quadrennial Defense Review Report," September 30, 2001, https://archive.defense.gov/pubs/qdr2001.pdf.

3. Readers seeking additional detail on the process would do well to read Janine Davidson, Emerson Brooking, and Benjamin Fernandes, "Mending the Broken Dialogue: Military Advice and Professional Decision-Making," Council on Foreign Relations, December, 2016, https://cdn.cfr.org/sites/default/files/report_pdf/Discussion_Paper_Davidson_Brooking_Fernandes_Civil_Military_OR.pdf.

4. 10 U.S. Code § 113–Secretary of Defense, Cornell Law School Legal Information Institute, www.law.cornell.edu/uscode/text/10/113.

5. U.S. Constitution, Article I, Section 8, Cornell Law School Legal Information Institute, www.law.cornell.edu/constitution/articlei#section8; U.S. Constitution Article II, Section 2, Cornell Law School Legal Information Institute, www.law.cornell.edu/constitution/articleii#section2.

6. Daniel Ellsberg, *The Doomsday Machine: Confessions of a Nuclear War Planner* (New York: Bloomsbury, 2017), chapters 5 and 6.

7. Charles A. Stevenson, *SECDEF: The Nearly Impossible Job of Secretary of Defense* (New York: Potomac Books, 2007), p. 149.

8. "Interview with Robert M. Gates," Miller Center, George H. W. Bush Oral History Project, July 23, 2000, p. 50.

9. See Tom Ricks, *Fiasco* (New York: Penguin Press, 2006), pp. 32–111, for more detail.

10. Richard Grimmet, "Authorization for Use of Military Force in Response to the 9/11 Attacks (P.L. 107-40): Legislative History," RS22357 (2007), Washington: CRS, https://fas.org/sgp/crs/natsec/RS22357.pdf.

11. Donald Rumsfeld, *Known and Unknown: A Memoir* (New York: Penguin, 2011), p. 370.

12. Ricks, *Fiasco*, pp. 41–43.

13. Readers seeking more detail on this debate should read Ricks, *Fiasco*, pp. 32–39.

14. Lieutenant General Michael DeLong, *A General Speaks Out* (Minneapolis: Zenith Press, 2004), p. 26.

15. Ibid.

16. Ibid., p. 89; and Myers, *Eyes on the Horizon*, p. 225. "Gen. Franks sometimes makes assertions that are wildly inaccurate, but he offers them with great certitude," declared journalist Tom Ricks. See Ricks, *Fiasco*, pp. 38, 33.

17. Robert Draper, *To Start A War: How the Bush Administration Took America into Iraq* (New York: Penguin Press, 2020) p. 234.

18. Nora Bensahel and others, *After Saddam: Prewar Planning and the Occupation of Iraq* (RAND, 2008), www.rand.org/content/dam/rand/pubs/monographs/2008/RAND_MG642.pdf, p. xix.

19. Quoted in Draper, *To Start A War*, p. 233.

20. Joel Rayburn, Frank Sobchak, and others, *The U.S. Army in the Iraq War Volume 1: Invasion—Insurgency—Civil War, 2003-2006* (U.S. Government Printing Office, 2019), p. 37.

21. Ricks, *Fiasco*, p. 75.

22. Ibid., pp. 70–73.

23. Joint Staff-J7 (Joint Operational War Plans Division), "Adaptive Plan-

ning," Department of Defense, http://nsp_intro.golearnportal.org/rawmedia_ repository/af8708f3e749174dc9c3909eeabde988.ppt, slide 4.

24. Joint Staff-J7, "Adaptive Planning"; Anthony Dunkin, "Where Rumsfeld Got it Right: Making a Case for In-Progress Reviews," *Joint Force Quarterly*, 86 (2017), https://ndupress.ndu.edu/Media/News/Article/1220567/where-rumsfeld -got-it-right-making-a-case-for-in-progress-reviews/.

25. Quoted in Myers, *Eyes on the Horizon*, p. 135. Italics in original.

26. Joel Rayburn and others, *The U.S. Army in the Iraq War, Volume I*, p. 37. Note that www.rumsfeld.com, built in support of research conducted for Rumsfeld's memoir *Known and Unknown*, is an extraordinary repository of many of these declassified snowflakes.

27. Rumsfeld, *Known and Unknown*, pp. 453–54.

28. The commandant of the Marine Corps was the only one to mention that he had concerns, but quickly noted those had already been addressed. Draper, *To Start a War*, pp. 313–14; and DeLong, *A General Speaks Out*, p. 96.

29. James Dubik, *Just War Reconsidered—Strategy, Ethics, and Theory* (University of Kentucky Press, 2016), pp. 103–07. Dubik's claims are based on his research, not his personal experience, given that he was commanding general of the 25th Infantry Division at Schofield Barracks, Hawaii, during this immediate period.

30. Stanley McChrystal, *My Share of the Task: A Memoir* (New York: Portfolio, 2013), p. 135.

31. Dubik, *Just War Reconsidered*, pp.107, 119–20.

32. Dov Zakheim, *A Vulcan's Tale—How the Bush Administration Mismanaged the Reconstruction of Afghanistan* (Brookings, 2011), pp. 82–83.

33. Robert D. Hormats, *The Price of Liberty—Paying for America's Wars* (New York: Times Books, 2007), p. xiv. During the War of 1812 and the Civil War, for example, the United States cut entitlements to pay for the ongoing war efforts. The little discussed surge in "black" or classified defense spending focused on research and procurement during the Reagan administration is worth exploring for readers interested in other rapid infusions of resources with minimal oversight.

34. Indeed, two weeks after the September 11 attacks, President Bush urged Americans to travel and to support the economy. "At O'Hare, President Says 'Get On Board,'" President George W. Bush White House Digital Archive, September 27, 2001, https://georgewbush-whitehouse.archives.gov/news/releases/ 2001/09/20010927-1.html.

35. Hormats, *The Price of Liberty*, p. 271–72.

36. Ibid., p. 262.

37. Sarah E. Kreps, *Taxing Wars* (Oxford University Press, 2018), pp. 141–42.

38. Gordon Adams, *The Iron Triangle: The Politics of Defense Contracting* (Council on Economic Priorities, New York, 1981).

39. "Costs of War through 31 March, 2018," Costs of War Project, https://fas .org/man/eprint/cow/fy2018q2.pdf.

40. Neta Crawford, "United States Budgetary Costs of the Post 9/11 Wars through FY2019: $5.9 Trillion Spent and Obligated," Costs of War Project, Brown University, November 14, 2018, https://watson.brown.edu/costsofwar /files/cow/imce/papers/2018/Crawford_Costs%20of%20War%20Estimates% 20Through%20FY2019.pdf.

41. "Caring for US Veterans," Costs of War Project, Brown University, November 14, 2018, https://watson.brown.edu/costsofwar/files/cow/imce/papers/2018/ Crawford_Costs%20of%20War%20Estimates%20Through%20FY2019.pdf.

42. Peter Hale, "Budgetary Turmoil at the Department of Defense from 2010 to 2014: A Personal and Professional Journey," Brookings, August 2014, www .brookings.edu/wp-content/uploads/2016/06/DOD_budgetary_turmoil_final .pdf#page=6, p. 1.

43. Hale, "Budgetary Turmoil," p. 5.

44. Ash Carter, *Inside the Five-Sided Box: Lessons from a Lifetime of Leadership inside the Pentagon* (New York: Dutton: 2019), p. 6. Emphasis in original.

45. Leon Panetta with Jim Newton, *Worthy Fights* (New York: Penguin Press, 2014), pp. 371–76, 440–42.

46. Panetta, *Worthy Fights*, p. 442.

47. Jeff Schogol, "Less than Half of Combat Squadrons Fully Ready for Combat," *Air Force Times*, February 25, 2015, www.airforcetimes.com/news/ your-air-force/2015/02/25/less-than-half-of-combat-squadrons-fully-ready-for -combat/; and Dion Nissenbaum, "Unraveling Navy's Decision on *USS Truman*," *Wall Street Journal*, March 2, 2013, www.wsj.com/articles/SB10001424127887323 29370457833463204101500.

48. G. Had, "Budget Cuts to Bring Military Spending Down to Pre-Civil War Levels," *Duffel Blog*, February, 2014, www.duffelblog.com/2014/02/pentagon -budget/#!xHCkq; and Donnell, "Budget Cuts Force Defense to Downsize Pentagon to a Square," *Duffel Blog*, April, 2016, www.duffelblog.com/2016/04/ downsize-pentagon-to-square/.

49. Kreps, *Taxing Wars*, p. viii.

50. Jonathan D. Caverley, "The Myth of Military Myopia: Democracy, Small Wars, and Vietnam," *International Security*, 34, no. 3 (Winter 2009/2010), p. 120.

51. Nora Bensahel and David Barno, "The Price of Perpetual War," *War on the Rocks*, May 24, 2016, https://warontherocks.com/2016/05/the-price-of -perpetual-war/.

52. This estimate is an extrapolation given the RAND study that U.S. ser-

vicemembers deployed over 5 million times from 2001 to 2015 in support of the 9/11 wars.

53. Leonard Wong and Stephen Gerras, "CU @ the FOB: How the Forward Operating Base is Changing the Life of Combat Soldiers," *U.S. Army Strategic Studies Institute*, March, 2006, https://publications.armywarcollege.edu/pubs/1748.pdf.

54. Nora Bensahel and David Barno, "Mirages of War: Six Illusions from Our Recent Conflicts," *War on the Rocks*, April 11, 2017, https://warontherocks.com/2017/04/mirages-of-war-six-illusions-from-our-recent-conflicts/.

55. Gretel Kovach, "Camp Leatherneck Goodbye," *San Diego Union-Tribune*, November 1, 2014, www.sandiegouniontribune.com/military/sdut-camp-leatherneck-goodbye-afghanistan-helmand-2014nov01-story.html.

56. Wong and Gerras, "CU @ the FOB," p. 6.

57. Ibid., p. 8, 14–17, 20–28.

58. For example, in 2018, special operations forces in Tongo Tongo, Niger—lacking dedicated air support and rapid medical evacuation capabilities like they would have had in Afghanistan—were overrun. See official Department of Defense summary of events, https://dod.defense.gov/portals/1/features/2018/0418_niger/img/Oct-2017-Niger-Ambush-Summary-of-Investigation.pdf.

59. Excerpted from Mara Karlin, "Dilemmas of Debating Military Superiority," *Texas National Security Review*, June 26, 2018, https://tnsr.org/roundtable/policy-roundtable-the-pursuit-of-military-superiority/.

60. David Barno, "Silicon, Iron, and Shadow: Three Wars that Will Define America's Future," *Foreign Policy*, March 19, 2013, https://foreignpolicy.com/2013/03/19/silicon-iron-and-shadow/.

61. Readers seeking a deeper historical understanding of SOF would do well to read Alice Hunt Friend, *Creating Requirements: Emerging Military Capabilities, Civilian Preferences, and Civil-Military Relations*," American University: PhD Dissertation, May 2020, chapter 2.

62. McCrystal, *My Share of the Task*, p. 51. See, also, Charlie Beckwith, *The Army's Elite Counterterrorist Unit* (New York: Avalon Books, 1986); and Mark Bowden, *Guests of the Ayatollah* (New York: Grove Press, 2006).

63. He, like other civilian policymakers, has faced difficulties assessing SOF capabilities, which scholar Alice Friend argues is particularly due to their heavy reliance on that community for information about it and a "lack of access to alternative sources of information." Friend, *Creating Requirements*," chapter 2.

64. Rumsfeld, *Known and Unknown*, p. 650.

65. Thom Shanker and James Risen, "Rumsfeld Weighs New Covert Acts by Military Units," *New York Times*, August 12, 2002, www.nytimes.com/2002

/08/12/world/rumsfeld-weighs-new-covert-acts-by-military-units.html; and Eric Schmitt and Mark Mazzetti, "Secret Order Lets U.S. Raid Al Qaeda," *New York Times*, November 9, 2008, www.nytimes.com/2008/11/10/washington/10military.html.

66. Mark Mazzetti, *The Way of the Knife: The CIA, a Secret Army, and a War at the Ends of the Earth* (New York: Penguin Books, 2014), p. 129.

67. Daniel Byman and Ian A. Merritt, "The New American Way of War: Special Operations Forces in the War on Terrorism," *Washington Quarterly* (Summer 2018), p. 82. According to one senior special operator, special operations forces "meet on the battlefield," so they have "fallen into tribes and sub-specialties."

68. Brian MacQuarrie and Michael Levenson, "For Elite US Troops, a Never-Ending War," *Boston Globe*, December 23, 2018, www.bostonglobe.com/metro/2018/12/22/for-elite-troops-never-ending-war.

69. Dave Phillips, "Special Operations Troops Top Casualty Lists as U.S. Relies More on Elite Forces," *New York Times*, February 4, 2017, www.nytimes.com/2017/02/04/us/navy-seal-william-ryan-owens-dead-yemen.html.

70. "SOF Truths," United States Special Operations Command, www.socom.mil/about/sof-truths. The other truths are: "Humans are more important than hardware. Quality is better than quantity. Competent Special Operations Forces cannot be created after emergencies occur. Most special operations require non-SOF assistance." For more detail on SOF growth in the post-9/11 wars, see Mark Cancian, "US Military Forces in FY 2020: SOF, Civilians, Contractors, and Nukes," CSIS Report, October 24, 2019, www.csis.org/analysis/us-military-forces-fy-2020-sof-civilians-contractors-and-nukes.

71. See, for example, Cancian, "US Military Forces in FY 2020."

72. "United States Special Operations Command Comprehensive Review," United States Special Operations Command, January 23, 2020, https://int.nyt.com/data/documenthelper/6736-special-operations-forces-review/c93cf96d67c341b2d2c3/optimized/full.pdf#page=1, pp. 34–35.

73. Quoted in Susan Katz Keating, "They Want Us to be Choirboys: Special Operations Troops Mock Order to Behave," *Washington Times*, January 31, 2020, www.washingtonexaminer.com/policy/defense-national-security/they-want-us-to-be-choirboys-special-operations-troops-mock-order-to-behave. Also see "Comprehensive Review—Letter to the Force," General Richard Clarke, United States Special Operations Command, January 28, 2020, www.socom.mil/Documents/Multi-star-letter-to-the-force-as-of-27-JAN-20.pdf.

74. Friend, *Creating Requirements*, chapter 2.

75. Norton Schwartz, *Journey: Memoirs of a U.S. Air Force Chief of Staff* (New York: Skyhorse, 2018), p. 296.

76. Loren DeJonge Schulman, "Behind the Magical Thinking: Lessons from Policymaker Relationships with Drones," CNAS, July 2018, www.cnas.org/publications/reports/behind-the-magical-thinking, p. 1.

77. Mazzetti, *The Way of the Knife*, p. 6.

78. According to New America, drone strikes in Pakistan exploded from three in 2005 to 122 in 2010. "Drone Strike: Pakistan," New America, www.newamerica.org/in-depth/americas-counterterrorism-wars/pakistan/.

79. Eyal Press, "The Wounds of the Drone Warrior," *New York Times*, June 13, 2018, www.nytimes.com/2018/06/13/magazine/veterans-ptsd-drone-warrior-wounds.html.

80. While the executive order and fact sheet do not specify whether these were all drone strikes, it is implied that most were. See "The United States Policy on Pre- and Post-Strike Measures to Address Civilian Casualties in U.S. Operations Involving the Use of Force," White House Office of the Press Secretary, July 1, 2016, https://assets.documentcloud.org/documents/2938258/Airstrike-Death-Toll.pdf. For more detail on the Obama administration's efforts to be more transparent about civilian casualties in conflict, see "Fact Sheet: Executive Order on the US Policy on Pre & Post-Strike Measures to Address Civilian Casualties in the US Operations Involving the Use of Force & the DNI Release of Aggregate Data on Strike Outside Area of Active Hostilities," White House Office of the Press Secretary, July 1, 2016, https://obamawhitehouse.archives.gov/the-press-office/2016/07/01/fact-sheet-executive-order-us-policy-pre-post-strike-measures-address.

81. "According to the Bureau of Investigative Journalism, a London-based organization that has been tracking drone killings since 2010, U.S. drone strikes have killed between 7,584 and 10,918 people, including 751 to 1,555 civilians, in Pakistan, Afghanistan, Yemen, and Somalia. The U.S. government's figures are far lower. They claims that between sixty-four and 116 noncombatants outside areas of active hostilities were killed by drones between 2009 and 2016." Press, "The Wounds of the Drone Warrior."

82. Throughout the post-9/11 wars, drone strikes have been carried out by the military under its own authority, by the intelligence community under its own authority, or by the military under the intelligence community community's authority.

83. Schulman, "Behind the Magical Thinking."

84. Quoted in Press, "The Wounds of the Drone Warrior."

85. However, the Army has taken a different approach to drones in terms of both who operates them and how they do so, which demonstrates that at least some elements of the of the Air Force's approach represent self-inflicted wounds rather than inherent challenges posed by drone operations. Phillip Swarts, "Air

Force, Army Need Separate Drones, Generals Tell Congress," *Air Force Times*, March 20, 2016, www.airforcetimes.com/news/pentagon-congress/2016/03/20/air-force-army-need-separate-drones-generals-tellcongress.

86. Schwartz, pp. 295–96.

87. Cancian, "U.S. Military Forces in FY2020," p. 59.

88. Readers interested in learning more about this topic would do well to peruse Paul Scharre, *Army of None: Autonomous Weapons and the Future of War* (New York: W. W. Norton & Company, 2018).

89. Michael C. Horowitz, "Artificial Intelligence, International Competition, and the Balance of Power," *Texas National Security Review*, 1, no. 3 (May 2018), https://tnsr.org/2018/05/artificial-intelligence-international-competition-and-the-balance-of-power/.

90. Syndney Freedberg Jr., "Pentagon Studies Weapons that Can Read Users' Mind," *Breaking Defense*, July 14, 2017, https://breakingdefense.com/2017/07/pentagon-studies-weapons-that-can-read-users-mind/; and "Nomination Hearing: Selva," United States Senate Committee on Armed Services, July 18, 2017, www.armed-services.senate.gov/hearings/17-07-18-nomination_--selva.

91. Andrew Illachinski, "Artificial Intelligence and Autonomy: Opportunities and Challenges," CNA, October 2017, www.cna.org/CNA_files/PDF/DIS-2017-U-016388-Final.pdf.

92. Andrew Ilachinski, "AI, Robots, and Swarms: Issues, Questions, and Recommended Studies," CNA, January 2017, www.cna.org/cna_files/pdf/DRM-2017-U-014796-Final.pdf.

93. Nathan Leys, "Autonomous Weapon Systems and International Crises," *Strategic Studies Quarterly*, 12, no. 1 (Spring 2018).

94. Defense Innovation Board, "AI Principles: Recommendations on the Ethical Use of Artificial Intelligence by the Department of Defense," October 31, 2019, https://media.defense.gov/2019/Oct/31/2002204458/-1/-1/0/DIB_AI_PRINCIPLES_PRIMARY_DOCUMENT.PDF, p. 8. In February 2020, the Pentagon formally adopted these principles with small adjustments. See Nathan Strout, "The Pentagon Now Has 5 Principles for Artificial Intelligence," C4ISR-NET, February 24, 2020, www.c4isrnet.com/artificial-intelligence/2020/02/24/the-pentagon-now-has-5-principles-for-artificial-intelligence.

95. Adapted from Mara Karlin, "The Implications of Artificial Intelligence for National Security Strategy," Brookings, November 1, 2018, www.brookings.edu/research/the-implications-of-artificial-intelligence-for-national-security-strategy.

96. James Gerstenzang and Greg Miller, "Bush Warns of Long War," *Los Angeles Times*, September 16, 2001, www.latimes.com/archives/la-xpm-2001-sep-16-mn-46416-story.html.

97. Joel Rayburn, Frank Sobchak, and others, *The U.S. Army in the Iraq War, Volume 2: Surge and Withdrawal, 2007–2011* (U.S. Government Printing Office, 2019), p. 622.

98. Robert M. Gates, *Duty* (New York: Alfred A. Knopf, 2014), p. 119.

99. David Barno and Nora Bensahel, *Adaptation under Fire: How Militaries Change in Wartime* (Oxford University Press, 2020), chapter 6.

100. Eric Schmitt, "Iraq-Bound Troops Confront Rumsfeld over Lack of Armor," *New York Times*, December 8, 2004, www.nytimes.com/2004/12/08/international/middleeast/iraqbound-troops-confront-rumsfeld-over-lack-of.html; and George Edmonson, "Humvee Makers Dispute Rumsfeld Remarks," *Seattle Pi*, December 9, 2004, www.seattlepi.com/national/article/Humvee-makers-dispute-Rumsfeld-remarks-1161662.php.

101. Schmitt, "Iraq-Bound Troops Confront Rumsfeld."

102. Barno and Bensahel, *Adaptation Under Fire,* chapter 6.

103. Gates, *Duty*, pp. 119–22.

104. Ibid., 122–23.

105. Rayburn, Sobchak, and others, *The U.S Army in the Iraq War,* pp. 313–15.

106. Robert Gates, *A Passion for Leadership* (New York: Vintage Books, 2017), pp. 73, 100; Gates, *Duty*, p. 124; and Andrew Feickert, "Mine-Resistant, Ambush-Protected (MRAP) Vehicles: Background and Issues for Congress," Congressional Research Service, January 18, 2011.

107. Gates, *Duty*, p. 309.

108. Sharon K. Weiner, "Organizational Interests versus Battlefield Needs: The U.S. Military and Mine-Resistant Ambush Protected Vehicles in Iraq," *Polity*, 42, no. 4 (October 2010), p. 463.

109. Robert Komer, *Bureaucracy Does Its Thing: Institutional Constraints on U.S.-GVN Performance in Vietnam* (RAND, 1972).

110. Quoted in Michael J. McNerney, "Stabilization and Reconstruction in Afghanistan: Are PRTs a Model or a Muddle," *Parameters* (Winter 2005-2006), p. 36.

111. McNerney, "Stabilization and Reconstruction in Afghanistan," p. 44.

112. Rumsfeld, *Known and Unknown*, p. 687.

113. Ibid., pp. 690–91.

114. McNerney, "Stabilization and Reconstruction in Afghanistan," p. 40; and Henry Nuzum, "Shades of CORDS in the Kush: The False Hope of 'Unity of Effort' in American Counterinsurgency," U.S. Army War College Strategic Studies Institute, April 2010, p. 37.

115. Lieutenant Colonel Robin L. Fontes, as quoted in *Enduring Voices: Oral Histories of the U.S. Army Experience in Afghanistan 2003–2005*, edited by Christopher N. Koontz (Washington: Center of Military History, 2008), pp. 458, 465.

116. Rayburn, Sobchak, and others, *The U.S Army in the Iraq War,* pp. 309–10.

117. Ibid., p. 310.

118. Nuzum, "Shades of CORDS in the Kush," p. 51.

119. Interview with Marin Strmecki, "The Afghanistan Papers," *Washington Post,* Conducted November 19, 2015, Released December, 2019, www.washingtonpost.com/graphics/2019/investigations/afghanistan-papers/documents-database/?document=background_ll_01_xx_xx_10192015.

120. Nuzum, "Shades of CORDS in the Kush," pp. 51, 56.

121. Interview with Brian Copes, "The Afghanistan Papers," *Washington Post,* Conducted February, 25, 2016, Released December, 2019, www.washingtonpost.com/graphics/2019/investigations/afghanistan-papers/documents-database/?document=copes_brian_ll_05_c15_02252016.

Chapter 6

1. James Jones, *The Thin Red Line: Every Man Fights His Own War* (New York: Delta Books, 1998).

2. As noted earlier, the term "iron triangle" related to defense was initially conceptualized by Gordon Adams and refers to the relationship among the Defense Department, Congress, and defense contractors. Gordon Adams, *The Iron Triangle: The Politics of Defense Contracting* (New York: Council on Economic Priorities, 1981).

3. Kathleen Hicks, "Defense Strategy and the Iron Triangle of Painful Trade-Offs," *Defense 360,* June 21, 2017, https://defense360.csis.org/defense-strategy-and-the-iron-triangle-of-painful-tradeoffs/.

4. "Summary of the 2018 National Defense Strategy of the United States of America: Sharpening the American Military's Competitive Edge," https://dod.defense.gov/Portals/1/Documents/pubs/2018-National-Defense-Strategy-Summary.pdf.

5. For a suggested U.S. policy approach toward the Middle East, see Mara Karlin and Tamara Cofman Wittes, "America's Middle East Purgatory: The Case for Doing Less," *Foreign Affairs,* January 2019, www.foreignaffairs.com/articles/middle-east/2018-12-11/americas-middle-east-purgatory.

6. Portions from this section are excerpted from Mara Karlin, "How to Read the 2018 National Defense Strategy," Brookings, January 21, 2018, www.brookings.edu/blog/order-from-chaos/2018/01/21/how-to-read-the-2018-national-defense-strategy/.

7. Readers seeking to understand the history of each military service would be well served by reading the following books: Paula Thornhill, *Demystifying the American Military* (Naval Institute Press, 2019); Jeffrey W. Donnithorne, *Four Guardians: A Principled Agent View of American Civil Military Relations* (Johns

Hopkins University Press, 2018); and Carl Builder, *Masks of War* (Johns Hopkins University Press, 1989).

8. Elizabeth Samet, *No Man's Land: Preparing for War and Peace in Post-9/11 America* (New York: Farrar, Straus, and Giroux, 2014), p. 100.

9. Jennie Wenger, Caolionn O'Connell, and Linda Cottrell, *Examination of Recent Deployment Experience across the Services and Components* (RAND, 2018).

10. David Baiocchi, "Measuring Army Deployments to Iraq and Afghanistan," RAND, 2012, www.rand.org/content/dam/rand/pubs/research_reports/RR100/RR145/RAND_RR145.pdf, p. 2.

11. Kyle Rempfer, "Iraq Killed More US Troops in Iraq than Previously Known, Pentagon Says," *Military Times*, April 4, 2019, www.militarytimes.com/news/your-military/2019/04/04/iran-killed-more-us-troops-in-iraq-than-previously-known-pentagon-says/.

12. Stanley McChrystal, *My Share of the Task: A Memoir* (New York: Portfolio, 2013), p. 15.

13. Readers seeking more detail on failed Army procurement programs should read Russell Rumbaugh, "What We Bought: Defense Procurement from FY01 to FY2010," Henry Stimson Center, 2011, www.stimson.org/wp-content/files/file-attachments/Contentv2_1.pdf, pp. 7–10.

14. To be sure, this historical record is generally not enthusiastically welcomed by the Army, whose leaders proclaim that it is shortsighted because it takes decades to grow an experienced and capable soldier.

15. Kyle Rempfer, "It'll be Tight, but the Army Expects to Meet Recruiting Goals this Year," *Army Times*, June 25, 2019, www.armytimes.com/news/your-army/2019/06/25/itll-be-tight-but-the-army-expects-to-meet-recruiting-goals-this-year/.

16. T. R. Fehrenbach, *This Kind of War* (New York: Potomac Books, 1961), p. 290. To be sure, Fehrenbach's book suffers from a number of problems, particularly in its racist portrayal of Koreans. See, also, Eric Scigliano, "The Book Mattis Reads to be Prepared for War with North Korea," *Politico*, October 15, 2017, www.politico.com/magazine/story/2017/10/15/the-book-mattis-reads-to-be-prepared-for-war-with-north-korea-215712; and Barry Strauss, "This Kind of War: The Classic Korean War History by TR Fehrenbach," Hoover Institution, June 7, 2016, www.hoover.org/research/kind-war-classic-korean-war-history-t-r-fehrenbach.

17. Scigliano, "The Book Mattis Reads to be Prepared for War with North Korea."

18. As quoted in Drew Brooks, "The Big Guns are Back," National Guard Association of the United States, July 31, 2019, www.ngaus.org/about-ngaus/newsroom/big-guns-are-back.

19. Lizette Alvarez, "Recruitment of Felons Up in U.S. Army and Marine Corps," *New York Times*, April 22, 2008, www.nytimes.com/2008/04/22/world/americas/22iht-army.4.12232382.html. Worryingly, those numbers are increasing again. See Lolita Baldor, "Army Using Drug Waivers, Bonuses to Fill Ranks," AP, August 1, 2018, https://apnews.com/5414d68d6fdb4dc99fc70ac9ad2e7468.

20. This point was further underscored by a manager of Army professional military education programs. Email exchange with author, Chris Rizzo, Army War College and Senior Service School program manager, July 27, 2017.

21. Quoted in Leon Panetta with Jim Newton, *Worthy Fights* (New York: Penguin Press, 2014), p. 347.

22. Elizabeth Samet, *Soldier's Heart—Reading Literature through Peace and War at West Point* (New York: Farrar, Straus, and Giroux, 2007), p. 19.

23. Michael Gordon, "Army Buried Study Faulting Iraq Planning," *New York Times*, February 11, 2008, www.nytimes.com/2008/02/11/washington/11army.html. The study has since been published and can be found at www.rand.org/pubs/monographs/MG642.html. The author was an adjunct scholar at the RAND Corporation focusing on Middle East security affairs from 2009 to 2012.

24. Michael Gordon, "The Army Stymied Its Own Study of the Iraq War," *Wall Street Journal*, October 22, 2018, www.wsj.com/articles/the-army-ordered-an-unvarnished-iraq-war-historythen-let-it-languish-1540220153.

25. Jon Finer, "The Last War—and the Next? Learning the Wrong Lessons from Iraq," *Foreign Affairs*, July 2019, www.foreignaffairs.com/reviews/review-essay/2019-05-28/last-war-and-next, and Gordon, "The Army Stymied Its Own Study of the Iraq War."

26. For more detail on the study's flaws, see Finer, "The Last War—and the Next?"

27. Tony, "Army Determined to Eliminate All Operational Memory of War on Terror," *Duffel Blog*, May, 2013, www.duffelblog.com/2013/05/army-determined-to-eliminate-all-operational-memory-of-war-on-terror/.

28. Michael E. O'Hanlon, *The Future of Land Warfare* (Brookings Institution Press, 2015), chapter 5.

29. Samet, *No Man's Land*, p. 18.

30. Ibid., pp. 39, 95–96.

31. Paula Thornhill, *Demystifying the American Military: Institutions, Evolution, and Challenges Since 1789* (U.S. Naval Institute Press, 2019), p. 7; and Thomas Mahnken, *Technology and the American Way of War Since 1945* (Columbia University Press, 2008), p. 8.

32. Leo Spaeder, "Sir, Who Am I? An Open Letter to the Incoming Commandant of the Marine Corps," *War on the Rocks*, March 28, 2019, https://

warontherocks.com/2019/03/sir-who-am-i-an-open-letter-to-the-incoming
-commandant-of-the-marine-corps/.

33. James Dao, "With Recruiting Goals Exceeded, Marines Toughen Their Ad Pitch," *New York Times*, September 17, 2009, www.nytimes.com/2009/09/18/us/18marines.html?referringSource=articleShare. While the Marines aimed to have 202,000 Marines by 2012, they fulfilled this goal by 2009. See Office of the Under Secretary of Defense, Personnel, and Readiness, *Population Representation in the Military Services: Fiscal Year 2006–2009 Summary Report.* Published in 2007, 2008, 2009, and 2010, respectively, www.cna.org/research/pop-rep.

34. Tara Copp, "Marine Corps Aviation Mishaps on the Rise, Up to 80 Percent," *Military Times*, April 8, 2018, www.militarytimes.com/news/your-military/2018/04/08/marine-corps-aviation-mishaps-on-the-rise-up-80-percent/.

35. "What We Do: Rapid Response," Marines.com, https://www.marines.com/what-we-do/rapid-response.html.

36. General Robert Neller, "White Letter 3-18: Sustaining the Corps," Department of the Navy, www.marines.mil/portals/1/Publications/3-18%20-%20SUSTAINING%20THE%20CORPS.pdf?ver=2019-03-22-113020-300.

37. General David Berger, "Commandant's Planning Guidance," United States Marine Corps Headquarters, 2019, www.hqmc.marines.mil/Portals/142/Docs/%2038th%20Commandant's%20Planning%20Guidance_2019.pdf?ver=2019-07-16-200152-700, p. 1.

38. Michael O'Hanlon, "The Questionable Future of Amphibious Assault," Brookings, June 23, 2020, www.brookings.edu/blog/order-from-chaos/2020/06/23/the-questionable-future-of-amphibious-assault/.

39. While Navy and Marine aircraft were also involved, their roles have not become a part of their respective service's narrative in the way that it has for the Air Force.

40. Nora Bensahel and David Barno, "The Catastrophic Success of the U.S. Air Force, *War on the Rocks*, May 3, 2018, https://warontherocks.com/2016/05/the-catastrophic-success-of-the-u-s-air-force/.

41. Quoted in Barno and Bensahel "The Catastrophic Success of the U.S. Air Force," May 3, 2016, https://warontherocks.com/2016/05/the-catastrophic-success-of-the-u-s-air-force/.

42. "USAF Posture Statement: Fiscal Year 2018," The Committee on Appropriations, Subcommittee on Defense, 2018, www.af.mil/Portals/1/documents/airpower/FY18%20AF%20Posture%20Statement%20Final.pdf?ver=2017-06-30-093831-353. See, also, Mark Cancian, "U.S. Military Forces in FY 2020: Air Force," Center for Strategic and International Studies, October 21, 2019, www.csis.org/analysis/us-military-forces-fy-2020-air-force.

43. Readiness Subcommittee of the Committee on Armed Services, "The Use of In Lieu Of, Ad Hoc, and Augmentee Forces in Operations Enduring Freedom and Iraqi Freedom," 110th Congress, 1st Session, 2007, www.govinfo.gov/content/pkg/CHRG-110hhrg38670/html/CHRG-110hhrg38670.htm.

44. Blodesoverbaghdad, "Air Force Decreases Deployments to Afghanistan to 3-Hour Tour," *Duffel Blog*, November, 2018, www.duffelblog.com/2018/11/air-force-3-hour-tour-deployment/.

45. Gates, *Duty*, pp. 130, 319

46. Schwartz, *Journey*, pp. 255–56

47. Andrew Gray, "Air Force Fires Commanders Over Nuclear Mix-up," Reuters, October 19, 2007, www.reuters.com/article/us-usa-military-nuclear/air-force-fires-commanders-over-nuclear-mix-up-idUSN1930047820071019; and Josh White, "Nuclear Parts Sent to Taiwan in Error," *Washington Post*, March 26, 2008, www.washingtonpost.com/wp-dyn/content/article/2008/03/25/AR2008032501309.html?tid=a_inl_manual.

48. Gates, *Duty*, pp. 239–43.

49. Schwartz, *Journey*, p. xvii.

50. Gates, *Duty*, pp. 318–19.

51. Tobias Naegele, "USAF Moving Ahead with Biggest Change to Promotion System in Decades," *Air Force Magazine*, October 21, 2019, www.airforcemag.com/usaf-moving-ahead-with-biggest-change-to-promotion-system-in-decades/.

52. Stephen Losey, "New in 2019: Growing the Force—The Road to 386 Squadrons," *Air Force Times*, January 2, 2019, www.airforcetimes.com/news/your-air-force/2019/01/02/new-in-2019-growing-the-force-the-road-to-386-squadrons/.

53. Mara Karlin and Jim Mitre, "Three Urgent Questions for the Air Force's New Chief of Staff," *Defense One*, July 28, 2020, www.defenseone.com/ideas/2020/07/three-urgent-questions-air-forces-new-chief-staff/167179.

54. Christopher Cavas, "Defense, Navy Secretaries Spar Over Budget," *Defense News*, December 8, 2016, www.defensenews.com/naval/2016/12/09/defense-navy-secretaries-spar-over-budget/.

55. Mabus was a controversial secretary of the Navy for many reasons, including his penchant for building ships rather than ensuring their warfighting capability and the many social changes he instituted. W. T. Door, "Grief-Stricken Navy Mourns the Departure of Beloved Secretary Ray Mabus," *Duffel Blog*, January, 2017, www.duffelblog.com/2017/01/entire-navy-overjoyed-to-be-led-by-army-officer-instead-of-ray-mabus/; Christopher Cavas, "Defense, Navy Secretaries Spar over Budget," *Defense News*, December 8, 2016, www.defensenews.com/naval/2016/12/09/defense-navy-secretaries-spar-over-budget/; and Ray Mabus, "Secretary of Navy: Why Our Fleet Is Growing after Years of Decline,"

Time, September 15, 2016, https://time.com/4033459/secretary-of-navy-why-our-fleet-is-growing-after-years-of-decline/.

56. Cavas, "Defense, Navy Secretaries Spar over Budget."

57. Sam LaGrone and Megan Eckstein, "Navy Wants to Grow Fleet to 355 Ships; 47 Hull Increase Adds Destroyers, Attack Subs," *USNI News*, December 16, 2016, https://news.usni.org/2016/12/16/navy-wants-grow-fleet-355-ships-47-hull-increase-previous-goal.

58. Notably, Davidson was promoted to commander, U.S. Indo-Pacific Command, despite serving as Fleet Forces commander during the 2017 mishaps. "Comprehensive Review of Recent Surface Force Incidents," U.S. Navy Fleet Forces Command, October 26, 2017, http://s3.amazonaws.com/CHINFO/Comprehensive+Review_Final.pdf.

59. Readiness Subcommittee of the Committee on Armed Services, "The Use of In Lieu Of, Ad Hoc and Augmentee Forces in Operations Enduring Freedom and Iraqi Freedom."

60. Craig Whitlock, "Trump Nominee Sunk by 'Fat Leonard' Corruption Scandal, *Washington Post*, November 26, 2018, www.washingtonpost.com/world/national-security/trump-nominee-sunk-by-fat-leonard-corruption-scandal/2018/11/26.

61. Quoted in David Ignatius, "What It Will Take to Fix the Navy—and Who Can Do It," *Washington Post*, July 31, 2020, www.washingtonpost.com/opinions/2020/07/31/michael-gilday-fix-navy/.

62. Matthew Cox, "Decades of Combat Led to SEAL Team Disciplinary Issues, Acting Navy Secretary Says," *Military.com*, December 6, 2019, www.military.com/daily-news/2019/12/06/decades-combat-led-seal-team-discipline-issues-acting-navy-secretary-says.html.

63. David Larter, "Analysis: Spencer's Firing is Latest in String of Disasters for US Navy Leadership," *Defense News*, December 2, 2019, www.defensenews.com/naval/2019/12/02/for-navy-leadership-spencers-firing-is-latest-in-a-string-of-disasters/.

64. Epitomizing the contradictory stories behind Spencer's firing by Secretary of Defense Esper is Spencer's official story and the Defense Department spokesman's official story found in Richard Spencer, "I Was Fired as Navy Secretary: Here's What I've Learned because of It," *Washington Post*, November 27, 2019, www.washingtonpost.com/opinions/richard-spencer-i-was-fired-as-navy-secretary-heres-what-ive-learned-because-of-it/2019/11/27/9c2e58bc-1092-11ea-bf62-eadd5d11f559_story.html; and "Jonathan Hoffman, "Statement on the Resignation of Secretary of the Navy," US Department of Defense, November 24, 2019, www.defense.gov/Newsroom/Releases/Release/Article/2025157/statement-by-dod-spokesman-jonathan-hoffman/.

65. Maxx Butthurt, "Navy Fires More Captains than Torpedoes," *Duffel Blog*, April, 2015, www.duffelblog.com/2015/04/navy-fires-more-captains-than -torpedoes/.

66. Frederick Taub, "Army-Navy Game Prepares West Pointers for Similar Battlefield Results," *Duffle Blog*, December, 2014, www.duffelblog.com/2014/12 /army-navy-prepares-west-pointers-for-battlefield-results/; and Blondsoverb- aghdad, "Navy Pranks Army with 17 Years of Sustain Land-Based Combat just before Army-Navy Game, *Duffel Blog*, December, 2018, www.duffelblog.com/ 2018/12/navy-pranks-army-game.

67. "Education for Seapower Strategy 2020," Department of Defense, www .navy.mil/strategic/Naval_Education_Strategy.pdf.

68. Thomas Gibbons-Neff, "The Lies the Generals Told about Afghanistan," *New York Times*, December 20, 2019.

69. Cynthia Watson, *Combatant Commands: Origins, Structure, and Engage- ments* (Santa Barbara, Calif.: Praeger Security International, 2011), p. 18.

70. Kathleen Hicks, "Invigorating Defense Governance," CSIS, March 2008, https://csis-prod.s3.amazonaws.com/s3fs-public/legacy_files/files/media/csis/ pubs/080311-hicks-invigoratingdef4web.pdf, p. 2.

71. Gates, *Duty*, p. 39.

72. Joel Rayburn, Frank Sobchak, and others, *The U.S. Army in the Iraq War, Volume I: Invasion and Civil War, 2003–2006* (U.S. Government Printing Office, 2019), p. 38.

73. DeLong, *A General Speaks Out*, p. 18.

74. Michael E. O'Hanlon and Adam Twardowski, "How the U.S. Military is Prioritizing Great Power Competition," *Order from Chaos* (blog), September 29, 2020, www.brookings.edu/blog/order-from-chaos/2020/09/29/how-the-us -military-is-prioritizing-great-power-competition/.

75. Readers interested in learning more about how to do so should read Mara E. Karlin and Melissa G. Dalton, "Toward A Smaller, Smarter Force Pos- ture in the Middle East," *Defense One*, August 26, 2018; Mara E. Karlin and Me- lissa G. Dalton, "How Should the Pentagon Reshape Its Mideast Posture? Four Indicators to Watch," *Defense One*, January 20, 2018; and Mara E. Karlin and Melissa G. Dalton, "It's Long Past Time to Rethink US Military Posture in the Gulf," *Defense One*, August 2, 2017.

76. RAND's Scorecards is the preeminent unclassified study of Chinese mil- itary modernization. See Eric Heginbotham and others, *The U.S.-China Mili- tary Scorecard: Forces, Geography, and the Evolving Balance of Power, 1996–2017* (RAND, 2015), www.rand.org/pubs/research_reports/RR392.html.

77. The Center for Strategic and International Studies (CSIS) has done the best work examining gray zone conflict, which it defines as "an effort or

series of efforts intended to advance one's security objectives at the expense of a rival using means beyond those associated with routine statecraft and below means associated with direct military conflict between rivals. In engaging in a gray zone approach, an actor seeks to avoid crossing a threshold that results in open war." Kathleen Hicks and others, "By Other Means: Campaigning in the Grey Zone," CSIS, July, 2019, https://csis-prod.s3.amazonaws.com/s3fs-public/publication/Hicks_GrayZone_interior_v4_FULL_WEB.pdf, p. 4.

Chapter 7

1. For further background on the AVF, see Bernard Rostker, *I Want You: The Evolution of the All-Volunteer Force* (RAND, 2006); and Amy Schafer, "Generations of War: The Rise of the Warrior Caste and the All-Volunteer Force," Center for a New American Security, May, 2017, https://s3.amazonaws.com/files.cnas.org/documents/CNASReport-WarriorCast-Final.pdf?mtime=20170427115046.

2. For an overview of concerns, see Thomas S. Gates Jr., "The Report of the President's Commission on an All-Volunteer Armed Force" (Government Printing Office: Washington, 1970), www.rand.org/content/dam/rand/pubs/monographs/MG265/imag- es/webS0243.pdf.

3. Hugh Liebert and James Golby, "Midlife Crisis? The All-Volunteer Force at 40," *Armed Forces & Society*, 43, no. 1 (January 2017), pp. 115–238. For greater detail on the force's diversity, see "2015 Demographics: Profile of the Military Community," Department of Defense, 2015, pp. 23, 74.

4. Andrea Asoni, Andrea Gilli, Mauro Gilli, and Tino Sanandaji, "A Mercenary Army of the Poor? Technological Change and the Demographic Composition of the Post-9/11 U.S. Military," *Journal of Strategic Studies* (January, 2020), pp. 4, 34.

5. Phillip Carter, Katherine Kidder, Amy Schafer, and Andrew Swick, "AVF 4.0: The Future of the All-Volunteer Force," Center for a New American Security, March 28, 2017, www.cnas.org/publications/reports/avf-4-0-the-future-of-the-all-volunteer-force, p. 3.

6. Quoted in Robert M. Gates, *Duty* (New York: Alfred A. Knopf, 2014), pp. 58–59.

7. "Post-9/11 Veterans More Likely to Have Been Deployed, Seen Combat, Experienced Emotional Trauma," Pew Research, November 7, 2019, www.pewresearch.org/fact-tank/2019/11/07/key-findings-about-americas-military-veterans/ft_19-11-07_veteransfacts_post-911-veterans-deployed/.

8. Liebert and Golby, "Midlife Crisis?"

9. See footnote 6 in Golby and Liebert for more detail. Liebert and Golby, "Midlife Crisis?"

10. Tim Kane, "Why Our Best Officers are Leaving," *The Atlantic*, January/

February 2011; James Fallows, "The Tragedy of the American Military," *The Atlantic*, January/February 2015; Carter, Kidder, Schafer, and Swick, "AVF 4.0."; Margaret Harrell and Nancy Berglass, "Losing the Battle: The Challenge of Military Suicide," Center for a New American Security, October 31, 2011, www.cnas .org/publications/reports/losing-the-battle-the-challenge-of-military-suicide; Amy Schafer, "The War on Apathy," Center for a New American Security, October 31, 2017, www.cnas.org/publications/commentary/the-war-on-apathy; and Rajiv Chandrasekaran, "A Legacy of Pain and Pride," *Washington Post*, March 29, 2014, www.washingtonpost.com/sf/national/2014/03/29/a-legacy-of-pride-and -pain/?utm_term=.fbc05501c783.

11. Dave Phillips and Tim Argango, "Who Signs Up to Fight? Makeup of US Recruits Shows Glaring Disparity," *New York Times*, January 10, 2020, www -nytimes-com.cdn.ampproject.org/c/s/www.nytimes.com/2020/01/10/us/ military-enlistment.amp.html.

12. Liebert and Golby, "Midlife Crisis?"; and "2015 Demographics: Profile of the Military Community," p. IV. More detail on regional recruitment rates from the South can be found at "Military Recruitment 2010," National Priorities Project, June 30, 2011, www.nationalpriorities.org/analysis/2011/military -recruitment-2010/.

13. Statistics by military service: Army (79 percent); Navy (82 percent); Marines (77 percent); and Air Force (86 percent) JAMRS New Recruit Survey, Wave 1 Findings, Department of Defense, October 2012–March 2013, https://jamrs .defense.gov/Market-Research-Studies/Reports/.

14. "Army Family Provided Backup at Chief of Staff Nominee McConville's Confirmation Hearing," *Stars and Stripes*, May 3, 2019, www.stripes.com/news /army/army-family-provided-backup-at-chief-of-staff-nominee-mcconville-s -confirmation-hearing-1.579540.

15. Yochi Dreazen, "A Class of Generals," *Wall Street Journal*, July 25, 2009, www.wsj.com/articles/SB10001424052970204886304574308221927291030.

16. Anne Gearan, Phillip Rucker, and John Wagner, "John Kelly, Trump's Chief of Staff Whose Son Died in Combat, Defends President's Call to Gold Star Widow," *Washington Post*, October 19, 2017, www.washingtonpost.com/ politics/trumps-chief-of-staff-whose-son-died-in-combat-defends-presidents -call-to-gold-star-widow/2017/10/19/2091ee0a-b502-11e7-be94-fabb0f1e9ffb_ story.html.

17. I'm grateful to Eliot Cohen for crystalizing this point. William Shakespeare, *Coriolanus* (New York: Penguin, 1999), p. 122.

18. Corey Dickstein, "Army Misses 2018 Recruiting Goal," *Stars and Stripes*, September 21, 2018, www.stripes.com/news/army/army-misses-2018-recruiting -goal-which-hasn-t-happened-since-2005-1.548580.

19. Some background on the current system's challenges and efforts to change them can be found at Brad Carson, "You Don't Get to the NDAA Personnel Reforms without Force of the Future," *War on the Rocks*, August 13, 2018, https://warontherocks.com/2018/08/you-dont-get-to-the-ndaa-personnel -reforms-without-force-of-the-future/; and Blaise Misztal, Jack Rametta, and Mary Farrell, "Personnel Reform Lives, but Don't Call it 'Force of the Future,'" *War on the Rocks*, August 9, 2018, https://warontherocks.com/2018/08/personnel -reform-lives-but-dont-call-it-force-of-the-future/.

20. Paula Thornhill, *The Crisis Within: America's Military and the Struggle between the Overseas and Guardian Paradigms* (Rand, 2016).

21. Carter, Kidder, Schafer, and Swick, "AVF 4.0.," p. 5.

22. A useful primer on this history can be found in Agnes Gereben Schaefer and others, *Implications of Integrating Women into the Marine Corps Infantry* (RAND, 2015).

23. Andrew Tilghman, "All Combat Jobs Open to Women in the Military," *Military Times*, December 3, 2015, www.militarytimes.com/2015/12/03/all -combat-jobs-open-to-women-in-the-military/.

24. Quoted in Gereben Schaefer and others, *Implications of Integrating Women into the Marine Corps Infantry*, p. 16.

25. "General Lori Robinson," U.S. Air Force Command Biographies, www .af.mil/About-Us/Biographies/Display/Article/108119/general-lori-j-robinson /; and Nora Bensahel, David Barno, Katherine Kidder, and Kelley Sayler, "Battlefields and Boardrooms: Women's Leadership in the Military and Private Sector," Center for a New American Security, January 2015, https://s3 .amazonaws.com/files.cnas.org/documents/CNAS_BattlefieldsVsBoardrooms _BensahelBarnoKidderSayler.pdf?mtime=20160906080519, p. 9.

26. "DoD is Expanding Combat Service Opportunities for Women, but Should Monitor Long-Term Integration Progress (Report 15-1589)," Government Accountability Office, July 2015, www.gao.gov/assets/680/671963.pdf, p. 1.

27. See Tilghman, "All Combat Jobs Open to Women in the Military" for more detail on the decisionmaking process to open combat positions to women. Also, see Ash Carter, *Inside the Five Sided Box: Lessons from a Lifetime of Leadership in the Pentagon* (New York: Dutton, 2019), pp. 394–407.

28. Ash Carter, "No Exceptions: The Decision to Open All Military Positions to Women," Belfer Center, December 2018, www.belfercenter.org/publication/ no-exceptions-decision-open-all-military-positions-women.

29. "DOD to Save Funds by Paying Women 73 Cents on the Dollar," *Duffel Blog*, February 2016, www.duffelblog.com/2016/02/dod-to-pay-women-73-cents/.

30. Kyle Rempfer, "Army 'Ahead of Schedule' in Integrating Women in Combat Arms, Outgoing SMA Says as He Departs," *Army Times*, August 16, 2019,

www.armytimes.com/news/your-army/2019/08/16/army-ahead-of-schedule-in
-integrating-women-in-combat-arms-outgoing-sma-says-as-he-departs.

31. Ibid.

32. "Inspired to Serve," National Commission on Military, National, and
Public Service, March 2020, https://inspire2serve.gov/sites/default/files/final
-report/Final%20Report.pdf, p. 8.

33. Rosa Brooks, "Civil-Military Paradoxes," in *Warriors and Citizens: American Views of our Military*, edited by Kori Schake and Jim Mattis (Stanford, 2016),
p. 57.

34. "Mattis Speech to Cadets at Virginia Military Institute," *USNI News*, September 26, 2018, https://news.usni.org/2018/09/26/secdef-mattis-speech-cadets
-virginia-military-institute; and Melanie Sisson, "Mattis is Poisoning the Well
on Women in Combat," *The Hill*, September 30, 2018, https://thehill.com/
opinion/national-security/408982-mattis-is-poisoning-the-well-on-women-in
-combat?amp.

35. Dianna Cahn, "Poll Asks Troops, Veterans Thoughts on Women in
Combat, Mixed-Gender Training and More," *Stars and Stripes*, January 2, 2019,
www.stripes.com/news/poll-asks-troops-veterans-thoughts-on-women-in
-combat-mixed-gender-training-and-more-1.562898.

36. For more detail, see Nancy Youssef, "The Military Offers Women Pay
Equity and Opportunity, but Few Still Make Top Ranks; Though the Armed Services Tout Themselves as a Meritocracy, for Women the Promise Remains Elusive," *Wall Street Journal*, October 13, 2019, www.wsj.com/articles/the-military
-is-more-open-to-women-than-in-the-past-but-obstacles-remain-11570959001.

37. For a thorough history, see Bernard Rostker and others, *Sexual Orientation and U.S. Military Personnel Policy* (RAND, 1993).

38. Ironically, Powell's handwritten notes illustrate that he may have helped
conceptualize Don't Ask, Don't Tell. "A starred section of the notes indicates
Powell's possible contribution to history: A "possible solution," he said, was
that "we stop asking." Russell Berman, "The Awkward Clinton-Era Debate over
'Don't Ask, Don't Tell,'" *The Atlantic*, October 10, 2014, www.theatlantic.com/
politics/archive/2014/10/the-awkward-clinton-era-debate-over-dont-ask-dont
-tell/381374/.

39. Robert Gates, *A Passion for Leadership* (New York: Vintage Books, 2017),
p. 77–79.

40. Rostker and others, *Sexual Orientation and U.S. Military Personnel Policy*,
p. xxiii.

41. See footnote 3 in Aaron Belkin, Morten G. Ender, and others, "Readiness
and DADT Repeal: Has the New Policy of Open Service Undermined the Military?" *Armed Forces & Society*, 39, no. 4 (October 2013), p. 587–601.

42. Elisabeth Bumiller, "Top Defense Officials Seek to End 'Don't Ask Don't Tell,'" *New York Times*, February 2, 2010, www.nytimes.com/2010/02/03/us/politics/03military.html.

43. "DoD Ends All Future LGBT Events, Declares Military 'Gay Enough Already,'" *Duffel Blog*, October, 2012, www.duffelblog.com/2012/10/dod-ends-all-future-lgbt-events-declares-military-gay-enough-already/.

44. Gates, *Duty*, p. 445.

45. Quoted in Andrew Bacevich, *Breach of Trust: How Americans Failed their Soldiers and their Country* (New York: Metropolitan Books, 2013), p. 77.

46. Belkin and others, "Readiness and DADT Repeal."

47. Ibid.

48. Agnes Gereben Schaefer and others, *Assessing the Implications of Allowing Transgender Personnel to Serve Openly* (RAND, 2016).

49. Ibid., xiii.

50. "Secretary of Defense Ash Carter Announces Policy for Transgender Service Members," Department of Defense, June 30, 2016, www.defense.gov/Newsroom/Releases/Release/Article/821675/secretary-of-defense-ash-carter-announces-policy-for-transgender-service-members/; and Jonah Engel Bromwich, "How U.S. Military Policy on Transgender Personnel Changed under Obama," *New York Times*, July 26, 2017, www.nytimes.com/2017/07/26/us/politics/trans-military-trump-timeline.html.

51. "Memorandum for the President: Military Service by Transgender Individuals," Office of the Secretary of Defense, February 22, 2019, https://media.defense.gov/2018/Mar/23/2001894037/-1/-1/0/MILITARY-SERVICE-BY-TRANSGENDER-INDIVIDUALS.PDF; Donald Arthur and others, "DOD's Rationale for Reinstating the Transgender Ban is Contradicted by Evidence," *Palm Center*, April 2018, www.palmcenter.org/wp-content/uploads/2018/04/Transgender-troops-are-medically-fit-1.pdf, p. 2.

52. Shannon L. Dunlap, Ian W. Holloway, Chad E. Pickering, and others, "Support for Transgender Military Service from Active Duty United States Military Personnel," *Sex Res Soc Policy* (2020).

53. Admiral Mike Mullen, "Testimony to the US Senate Armed Services Committee," C-SPAN, February 2, 2010, www.c-span.org/video/?291857-1/gays-lesbians-military.

54. Jacqueline E. Whitt and Elizabeth A. Perazzo, "The Military as Social Experiment: Challenging a Trope," *Parameters*, 48, no. 2 (Summer 2018), p. 5.

55. Ibid., p. 7.

56. Ibid., p. 5.

57. Leila Fadel, "After Falling Short, U.S. Army Gets Creative with New Recruiting Strategy," *National Public Radio*, January 6, 2019.

Chapter 8

1. According to NVivo word frequency analysis of interviews.

2. Army Doctrinal Publication 6-22: Army Leadership and the Profession, U.S. Department of the Army, July 2019, https://fas.org/irp/doddir/army/adp6_22.pdf.

3. See General Montgomery C. Meigs, "Generalship: Qualities, Instincts, and Character," in *Military Leadership in Pursuit of Excellence*, edited by Robert L Taylor, William E Rosenbach, and Eric Rosenbach (New York: Routledge, 2008).

4. Sarah Sewall, "Leading Warriors in the Long War," in *Military Leadership in Pursuit of Excellence*, edited by Robert L. Taylor, William E. Rosenbach, and Eric Rosenbach (New York: Routledge, 2008).

5. Leonard Wong, Paul Bliese, and Dennis McGurk, "Military Leadership: A Context Specific Review," *Leadership Quarterly*, 14, no. 6 (December 2003), p. 669.

6. Quoted in Risa Brooks, "Paradoxes of Professionalism: Rethinking Civil-Military Relations in the United States," *International Security*, 44, no. 4 (Spring 2020), p. 7.

7. Richard Myers, *Eyes on the Horizon: Serving on the Front Lines of National Security* (New York: Simon & Schuster, 2007), p. 60.

8. Myers, *Eyes on the Horizon*, p. 59.

9. Norton Schwartz, *Journey: Memoirs of a U.S. Air Force Chief of Staff* (New York: Skyhorse, 2018), p. 11.

10. Donald Rumsfeld, *Known and Unknown: A Memoir* (New York: Penguin, 2011), p. 671.

11. His dissertation found that in addition to blaming civilian leaders for debacles in Vietnam, "the younger generation [in the military] also blames the older generation for some of the problems the United States experienced in Vietnam." David H. Petraeus, *The American Military and the Lessons of Vietnam: A Study of Military Influence and the Use of Force in the Post-Vietnam Era* (Princeton University, 1987), p. 279.

12. Yochi Dreazen, "A Class of Generals," *Wall Street Journal*, July 25, 2009, www.wsj.com/articles/SB10001424052970204886304574308221927291030.

13. The top three leaders at CENTCOM are defined as the commander, the deputy commander, and the chief of staff. "Biographies: General Joseph Votel," Department of Defense, 2016, www.defense.gov/Our-Story/Biographies/Biography/Article/602777/general-joseph-l-votel/; "Biography: Deputy Commander LTG Thomas Bergeson," CENTCOM, www.centcom.mil/ABOUT-US/LEADERSHIP/Bio-Article-View/Article/1631857/deputy-commander-lieutenant-general-thomas-w-bergeson/; and "Biography: Chief of Staff Major General Michael "Erik" Kurilla," CENTCOM, www.centcom.mil/ABOUT-US

/LEADERSHIP/Bio-Article-View/Article/1627071/chief-of-staff-major-general
-michael-erik-kurilla/.

14. David Sanger, *The Perfect Weapon: War, Sabotage, and Fear in the Cyber Age* (New York: Penguin Random House, 2018), pp. 18, 31. However, the lack of support around the Pentagon for Cartwright's appointment to chairman can be attributed to his bumpy relations with Secretary of Defense Gates and Chairman of the Joint Chiefs Admiral Mullen plus his tendency to operate outside the system. See Robert M. Gates, *Duty* (New York: Alfred A. Knopf, 2014), pp. 102–03, 377–78, 379, 537.

15. David Cloud and Greg Jaffe, *The Fourth Star: Four Generals and their Epic Struggle for the Future of the United States Army* (New York: Broadway Books, 2010), pp. 114–15, 164.

16. Elizabeth Samet, *Soldier's Heart—Reading Literature through Peace and War at West Point* (New York: Farrar, Straus, and Giroux, 2007), p. 157.

17. Rumsfeld, *Known and Unknown*, pp. 299–300. Notably, Colin Powell recounts in his memoirs that, during the Carter administration, Special Assistant to the Deputy Secretary of Defense John Kester aided Secretary of Defense Brown in shaping general officer promotions. "No longer would lists for brigadier and major general be signed pro forma by Secretary Brown. Kester would carefully review them. John also changed the service chief's traditional prerogative of recommending generals and admirals for promotion to three and four stars. Past practice had been for the chiefs to submit a single name for each opening. No, Kester said, they must now submit two candidates and the Secretary of Defense would choose. The chiefs were not happy." See Colin Powell with Joseph E. Persico, *My American Journey* (New York: Ballantine Books, 1995), pp. 225–28.

18. Rumsfeld, *Known and Unknown*, pp. 500–02.

19. Ricardo Sanchez, "How Much Did Rumsfeld Know?" *Time Magazine*, May 1, 2008, http://content.time.com/time/nation/article/0,8599,1736831,00.html. Interestingly, Abizaid kept Sanchez in place despite multiple missteps and Abizaid, ultimately, ignored the advice of Acting Chief of Staff of the Army General Jack Keane to push Sanchez out. Cloud and Jaffe, *The Fourth Star*, pp. 129, 152–53.

20. Rumsfeld, *Known and Unknown*, pp. 299–300.

21. Andrew Hoehn, Albert Robbert, and Margaret Harrell, *Succession Management for Senior Military Positions: The Rumsfeld Model for Secretary of Defense Involvement* (RAND, 2011), p. xvii, www.rand.org/pubs/monographs/MG1081.html.

22. Hoehn, Robbert, and Harrell, *Succession Management for Senior Military Positions*, p. iii; and Rumsfeld, *Known and Unknown*, pp. 299–300.

23. Hoehn, Robbert, and Harrell, *Succession Management for Senior Military Positions*, pp. iv, xv; and Rumsfeld, *Known and Unknown*, pp. 299–300.

24. Hoehn, Robbert, and Harrell, *Succession Management for Senior Military Positions*, pp. xv–xx.

25. Ibid., pp. 20–28.

26. Ibid., p. 39.

27. Schwartz, *Journey*, pp. 179, 188.

28. Hoehn, Robbert, and Harrell, *Succession Management for Senior Military Positions*, pp. 35, 49.

29. Ibid., p. 45–47.

30. Gates, *Duty*, p. 86.

31. Marcus Weisgerber, "Trump's New Joint Chiefs Chair is a Savvy Political Operator," *Defense One*, September 29, 2019, www.defenseone.com/politics/2019/09/milley-trump-joint-chiefs-chair-savvy-political-operator/160232/; and Richard Sisk, "Carter Surprises by Picking Neller as Next Marine Commandant," Military.com, July 1, 2015, www.military.com/daily-news/2015/07/01/carter-surprises-by-picking-neller-as-next-marine-commandant.html.

32. Dr. Paula Thornhill discussion with author.

33. Rumsfeld, *Known and Unknown*, pp. 548–51.

34. Jaffe and Cloud, *The Four Star*, pp. 127–28.

35. Ibid., p. 135–37.

36. Adding eeriness to the comparison, Westmoreland himself had given Casey his father's medals after his father died in Vietnam. David Cloud and Greg Jaffe, "Age of Anarchy," *Washington Post*, December 20, 2009, www.washingtonpost.com/wp-srv/style/longterm/books/chap1/thefourthstar.htm.

37. Stanley McCrystal, *My Share of the Task: A Memoir* (New York: Portfolio, 2013), p. 254.

38. Quoted in Tom Ricks, *The Generals* (New York: Penguin Books, 2013), p. 431.

39. Gates, *Duty*, p. 54.

40. Cloud and Jaffe, *The Fourth Star*, p. 248.

41. An initial illustrative list would include Secretary of Defense Rumsfeld, Deputy Secretary of Defense Paul Wolfowitz, and Under Secretary of Defense for Policy Doug Feith.

42. Steven Metz, "Don't Blame the Generals for the Strategic Shortcoming of America's Forever Wars," *World Politics Review*, May 17, 2019, www.worldpoliticsreview.com/articles/27865/don-t-blame-the-generals-for-the-strategic-shortcomings-of-america-s-forever-wars.

43. Peter Feaver, "The Right to be Right: Civil-Military Relations and the Iraq Surge Decision," *International Security*, 35, no. 4 (Spring 2011), p. 94.

44. Paul Yingling, "A Failure in Generalship," *Armed Forces Journal*, May 1, 2007, http://armedforcesjournal.com/a-failure-in-generalship/.

45. Cloud and Jaffe, *The Fourth Star*, p. 272.

46. Ibid., p. 271.

47. Ibid., pp. 271–72, 294.

48. Daniel P. Bolger, *Why We Lost* (New York: Mariner Books, 2014), Author's notes, pp. xv, xvi, 431.

49. Ibid., pp. 424, 430.

50. Thomas Ricks, "General Failure," *The Atlantic*, November 2012, www .theatlantic.com/magazine/archive/2012/11/general-failure/309148/.

51. Ricks put this well: "Generals did not fire other generals." Ricks, "General Failure."

52. Gates, *Duty*, p. 487.

53. Christopher N. Koontz, editor, *Enduring Voices: Oral Histories of the U.S. Army Experience in Afghanistan 2003–2005* (Washington: Center of Military History, 2008), p. 79.

54. Gates, *Duty*, p. 66.

55. Eric Schmitt, "'Career of General in Charge during Abu Ghraib May End," *New York Times*, January 5, 2006, www.nytimes.com/2006/01/05/world/middleeast /career-of-general-in-charge-during-abu-ghraib-may-end.html?auth=login-email.

56. Greg Jaffe, "The President's Difficult Relationship with War and His Warriors," *Washington Post*, June 3, 2016, www.washingtonpost.com/graphics/ national/obama-legacy/military-generals-commander-of-us-forces.html.

57. Gates, *Duty*, pp. 217, 346.

58. Ibid., p. 346.

59. Noah Shachtman, "Gates Sacks Stealth Jet Chief," *Wired*, February 1, 2010, www.wired.com/2010/02/gates-sacks-stealth-jet-chief-blasts-troubling -record-of-crucial-plane/.

60. Rajiv Chandrasekaran, "Two Marine Generals Fired for Security Lapses in Afghanistan," *Washington Post*, September 30, 2013, www.washingtonpost .com/world/national-security/two-marine-generals-fired-for-security-lapses -in-afghanistan/2013/09/30/b2ccb8a6-29fe-11e3-b139-029811dbb57f_story .html; and David Cloud, "General is Fired over Conditions at Walter Reed," *New York Times*, March 1, 2007, www.nytimes.com/2007/03/01/washington/01cnd -general.html.

61. Yingling, "A Failure in Generalship."

62. Cloud and Jaffe, *The Fourth Star*; Thomas Ricks, *The Gamble: General Petraeus and the American Military Adventure in Iraq* (New York: Penguin Books, 2010); and Linda Robinson, *Tell Me How This Ends: David Petraeus and the Search for a Way Out of Iraq* (New York: Public Affairs, 2009).

63. See Kris Alexander, "David Petraeus Can Run Your Ass Off," *Wired*, January, 2008, www.wired.com/2008/01/david-petraeus/; and Mark Bowden, "David Petraeus' Winning Streak," *Vanity Fair*, March 30, 2010.

64. To take one example, "in the first six months of 2007, Bush mentioned Petraeus's name 150 times in speeches." Greg Jaffe and Rajiv Chandrasekaran, "Petraeus Scandal Puts Four-Star General Lifestyle under Scrutiny," *Washington Post*, November 17, 2012, www.washingtonpost.com/world/national-security/petraeus-scandal-puts-four-star-general-lifestyle-under-scrutiny/2012/11/17/33a14f48-3043-11e2-a30e-5ca76eeec857_story.html.

65. Scott Wilson, "A Mix of 'President . . . and Pope,'" *Washington Post*, May 16, 2003, www.washingtonpost.com/archive/politics/2003/05/16/a-mix-of-president-and-pope/3882bb73-e20c-4bd5-8359-d6396179ecac/; Bowden, "David Petraeus's Winning Streak." As senior adviser to President Obama, Benjamin Rhodes recounts in his memoir that Petraeus "was so popular in some circles that he was mentioned as a potential Republican presidential candidate, though he volunteered to me more than once on the sidelines of Situation Room meetings that he had no interest in politics." Benjamin Rhodes, *The World as it is: A Memoir of the Obama White House* (New York: Random House, 2018), p. 64.

66. Justin Moyer, "Gen. Petraeus: From Hero to Zero," *Washington Post*, April 24, 2015, www.washingtonpost.com/news/morning-mix/wp/2015/04/24/gen-david-petraeus-from-hero-to-zero/.

67. Jessica Bennett, "Paula Broadwell, David Petraeus, and the Afterlife of a Scandal," *New York Times*, May 28, 2016, www.nytimes.com/2016/05/29/fashion/david-petraeus-paula-broadwell-scandal-affair.html.

68. James Dao, "No Food for Thought: The Way of the Warrior," *New York Times*, May 16, 2009, www.nytimes.com/2009/05/17/weekinreview/17dao.html.

69. George Packer, "The Lesson of Tal Afar," *New Yorker*, April 10, 2006, www.newyorker.com/magazine/2006/04/10/the-lesson-of-tal-afar.

70. Kori Schake, "Dereliction of Duty Reconsidered: The Book that Made the National Security Advisor," *War on the Rocks*, March 28, 2017, https://warontherocks.com/2017/03/dereliction-of-duty-reconsidered-the-book-the-made-the-national-security-advisor/.

71. These dynamics are nicely highlighted in: Patrick Radden Keefe, "McMaster and Commander," *New Yorker*, April 30, 2018, www.newyorker.com/magazine/2018/04/30/mcmaster-and-commander; Jonathan Stevenson, "The Failure of H. R. McMaster," *New York Times*, March 23, 2018, www.nytimes.com/2018/03/23/opinion/mcmaster-bolton-trump.html; and Carlos Lozada, "20 Years Ago, H. R. McMaster Wrote a Cautionary Tale. Now He Risks Becoming One," *Washington Post*, May 19, 2017, www.washingtonpost.com/news/book

-party/wp/2017/05/19/20-years-ago-h-r-mcmaster-wrote-a-cautionary-tale
-now-he-risks-becoming-one/?utm_term=.6b107e2324c3.

72. Tanisha M. Fazal, "Dead Wrong? Battle Deaths, Military Medicine, and Exaggerated Reports of War's Demise," *International Security*, 39, no. 1 (Summer 2014), p. 102.

73. Fazal, "Dead Wrong?" p. 95–125.

74. Ellen Ioanes, "More US Contractors Have Died in Afghanistan than US Troops—But the Pentagon Doesn't Keep Track," *Business Insider*, December 10, 2019, www.businessinsider.com/more-us-contractors-have-died-in-afghanistan-than-us-troops-2019-12.

75. Martin Dempsey and Ori Brafman, *Radical Inclusion* (New York: Mission Day, 2017), p. 91.

76. "President Barack Obama Remarks at the Farewell Ceremony for Gen. Martin Dempsey," *Stripes*, September 25, 2015, www.stripes.com/news/president-obama-s-remarks-at-gen-martin-dempsey-s-farewell-ceremony-sept-25-2015-1.370297.

77. Greg Jaffe, "Fighting to Get Out of the Way, U.S. Troops Battle to Hand Off a Valley Strongly Resistant to Afghan Governance, *Washington Post*, December 27, 2010, A7.

78. McChrystal, *My Share of the Task*, p. 361.

79. David Wood, *What Have We Done: The Moral Injury of Our Longest Wars* (New York: Little, Brown and Company, 2016), p. 10.

80. Katie Bo Williams, "Top US General Defends Afghanistan War," *Defense One*, December 20, 2019, www.defenseone.com/politics/2019/12/top-us-general-defends-afghanistan-war/162057/?oref=defense_one_breaking_nl). For a transcript of these remarks see "Department of Defense Press Briefing by Secretary Esper and General Milley," US Department of Defense, December 20, 2019, www.defense.gov/Newsroom/Transcripts/Transcript/Article/2045725/department-of-defense-press-briefing-by-secretary-esper-and-general-milley-in-t/.

81. Obama, *A Promised Land*, p. 325.

82. Ibid.

83. Gates, *Duty*, p. 109.

84. Quoted in Gates, *Duty*, p. 499.

85. Panetta, *Worthy Fights*, p. 459.

86. Robert McNamara, *In Retrospect: The Tragedy and Lessons of Vietnam* (New York: Vintage Books, 1996).

87. Quoted in Tom Wells, *The War Within: America's Battle Over Vietnam* (New York: Open Road, 2016), p. 198.

88. Gates, *Duty*, p. 209.

89. Leon Panetta and Jim Newton, *Worthy Fights: A Memoir of Leadership in War and Peace* (New York: Penguin Press, 2014), p. 359.

90. Leo Shane III, "Rumsfeld to Personally Sign All Condolence Letters," *Stars and Stripes*, December 17, 2004, www.stripes.com/news/rumsfeld-to-personally-sign-all-condolence-letters-1.27255.

Donald Rumsfeld to Larry Di Rita, "Condolences," January 10, 2002, released December, 2019 in "The Afghanistan Papers," *Washington Post*, www.washingtonpost.com/graphics/2019/investigations/afghanistan-papers/documents-database/?document=snowflake_casualties_derita_nsarchive_01102002. General George Marshall personally signed condolence letters in the first part of WWII, but as casualties mounted, he was no longer able to do so. As he explained to his biographer, "During the early part of the war, when we had so many losses and no victories or successes, I made it my business to write a personal letter to the parents or the wives of many of our casualties. . . . I continued this until the numbers grew beyond me. Unfortunately, the casualties had gone beyond my personal, individual attention." "George Marshall Interviews and Reminiscences for Forrest C. Pogue," The George C. Marshall Foundation, www.marshallfoundation.org/library/collection/george-c-marshall-interviews-reminiscences/#!/collection=341, Tape 18, p. 11.

91. Quoted in *The War of the Rebellion: Official Records of the Union and Confederate Armies*, Series 1, Volume XI, Part 1 (Government Printing Officer, 1899), p. 61, https://babel.hathitrust.org/cgi/pt?id=pst.000007608933&view=1up&seq=77.

92. See, for example, Kathleen Kowalski and Charles Vaught, "Judgement and Decision-Making Under Stress: An Overview for Emergency Managers," *International Journal of Emergency Management*, 1, no. 3 (2003), pp. 278–89, www.cdc.gov/niosh/mining/UserFiles/works/pdfs/jadmus.pdf.

93. General Stanley McChrystal, *My Share of the Task: A Memoir* (New York: Portfolio/Penguin, 2013), p. 135.

94. Ibid.

95. Jeffrey Record, "Failed States and Casualty Phobia: Implications for Force Structure and Technology Choices," Maxwell Airforce Base, Ala.: Center for Strategy and Technology, Air War College Air University (2000), p. 8.

96. Yagil Levy, "How Casualty Sensitivity affects Civilian Control: The Israeli Experience," *International Studies Perspectives*, 12 (2012), p. 68.

97. Gates, *A Passion for Leadership*, p. 217. Readers interested in learning more about the impact of sleep deprivation in combat environments would do well to review N. L. Miller, P. Matsangas, and L. G. Shattuck, "Fatigue and Its Effect on Performance in Military Environments," in *Performance Under Stress*, edited by Peter A. Hancock and James L. Szalma (Monterey: Ashgate Publications, 2007).

98. Italics in original. McChrystal, *My Share of the Task*, pp. 187, 288.

99. Quoted in Steven Gerras and Leonard Wong, *Lying to Ourselves: Dishonesty in the Army Profession* (Carlisle: SSI Publications, 2015), p. 15.

100. Army Doctrinal Publication 6-0: Mission Command. Command and Control of Army Forces, July 2019, https://armypubs.army.mil/epubs/DR_pubs /DR_a/pdf/web/ARN19189_ADP_6-0_FINAL_WEB_v2.pdf.

101. C. Todd Lopez, "Future Warfare Requires 'Disciplined Disobedience,' Army Chief Says," May 5, 2017, www.army.mil/article/187293/future_warfare_ requires_disciplined_disobedience_army_chief_says.

102. Stanley McCrystal, *Team of Teams: New Rules of Engagement for a Complex World* (New York: Portfolio, 2015).

103. For more, see John C. McManus, "The Man Who Would be President," *Military History Quarterly*, 31, no. 2 (Winter 2019).

104. Colin L. Powell, "Why Generals Get Nervous," *New York Times,* October 8, 1992.

105. The most cogent work on this topic is by Colonel Heidi Urben, "Like, Comment, Retweet: The State of the Military's Nonpartisan Ethic in the World of Social Media," National Defense University Center for Complex Operations Case Study, May 2017, https://cco.ndu.edu/Portals/96/Documents/case-studies /CCO%20Case%20Study%20Urben%20Final%20for%20Web.pdf?ver=2017-05 -18-155848-287.

106. Mara Karlin and James Golby, "The Case for Rethinking Politicization of the Military," *Task & Purpose,* June 12, 2020, https://taskandpurpose.com/ opinion/us-military-politics-politicization.

107. See, for example, Gallup Poll, June 8–July 24, 2020, https://news.gallup .com/poll/317135/amid-pandemic-confidence-key-institutions-surges.aspx.

108. Karlin and Golby, "The Case for Rethinking Politicization of the Military"; and Dan Lamonthe, "Senator Who Lost Her Legs Challenges Mattis to Explain Why He Stood by as Trump Signed Travel Ban," *Washington Post,* January 31, 2017, www.washingtonpost.com/news/checkpoint/wp/2017/01/31/ senator-who-lost-her-legs-in-iraq-challenges-mattis-to-explain-why-he-stood -by-as-trump-signed-travel-ban/. See, for example, Aric Jenkins, "Read President Trump's Speech Where He Claims the Media Doesn't Report Terrorist Attacks," *Time,* February 6, 2017, https://time.com/4661658/donald-trump-terror -attacks-speech-macdill-air-force-base/; Phillip Carter, "Trump is Ordering Service Members to Support the Republican Agenda," *Slate,* July, 2017, https:/ /slate.com/news-and-politics/2017/07/trump-is-ordering-service-members-to -support-the-republican-agenda.html; Leo Shane, Meghann Myers, and Carl Prine, "Trump Grants Clemency to Troops in Three Controversial War Crimes Cases," *Military Times,* November 16, 2019, www.militarytimes.com/news/ pentagon-congress/2019/11/16/trump-grants-clemency-to-troops-in-three

-controversial-war-crimes-cases/; and Maggie Haberman, "Trump Brings Two Officers Pardoned for War Crimes Onstage at Fundraiser," *New York Times*, December 8, 2019, www.nytimes.com/2019/12/08/us/politics/trump-war-crimes-pardons.html.

109. Rebecca Balhaus and Gordon Lubold, "White House Wanted USS *John McCain* Out of Sight during Trump's Japan Visit," *Wall Street Journal*, May 30, 2019, www.wsj.com/articles/white-house-wanted-uss-john-mccain-out-of-sight-during-trump-japan-visit-11559173470; and John Fritze, "Trump Defends Signing MAGA Hats during Trip," *USA Today*, December 27, 2018, www.usatoday.com/story/news/politics/2018/12/27/donald-trump-signs-maga-hats-military-iraq-visit/2427103002/.

110. General Mark Milley, "Class Graduation Address," *National Defense University*, June 10, 2020, https://livestream.com/ndulivestream/events/9129550.

111. National Defense Staff, "Exclusive: Q&A with Air Force Chief of Staff Gen. David Goldfein," *National Defense Magazine*, August 4, 2020, www.nationaldefensemagazine.org/articles/2020/8/4/qa-with-air-force-chief-of-staff-gen-david-goldfein.

112. Every military unit has a voting assistance officer whose mandate is to ensure that its members understand their voting rights and to facilitate their ability to exercise those rights. However, historically, some leaders, like General (and not yet president) Dwight D. Eisenhower, did not vote, even when it was their right to do so—perhaps missing the irony of planning his political transition while still in uniform. See Chester Pach Jr., "Dwight Eisenhower: Campaigns and Elections," Miller Center, June 20, 2020, https://millercenter.org/president/eisenhower/campaigns-and-elections.

113. "State of the Military Voter," Federal Voting Assistance Program, June 20, 2020, www.fvap.gov/info/reports-surveys/StateoftheMilitaryVoter.

114. Jim Garamone, "Active-Duty Personnel Must Remain Apolitical, Nonpartisan, Dunford Say," *DoD News*, August 1, 2019, www.defense.gov/Explore/News/Article/Article/881624/acti/.

115. Jason Dempsey, *Our Army: Soldiers, Politics, and American Civil-Military Relations* (Princeton University Press, 2010), p. 2.

116. Zachary Griffiths and Olivia Simon, "Not Putting Their Money Where Their Mouth Is: Retired Flag Officers and Presidential Endorsements," *Armed Forces & Society*, December 9, 2019.

117. James Golby, Heidi Urben, Kyle Dropp, and Peter D. Feaver, "Brass Politics: How Retired Military Officers are Shaping Elections," *Foreign Affairs*, November 5, 2012, www.foreignaffairs.com/articles/2012-11-05/brass-politics.

118. To take one example, fewer than one-third of Americans polled in mid-2019 correctly identified former Secretary of Defense James Mattis as a retired

general officer. Heidi Urben, "Generals Shouldn't be Welcome at these parties," *War on the Rocks*, www.warontherocks.com/2020/07/generals-shouldnt-be -welcome-at-these-parties-stopping-retired-flag-officer-endorsements.

119. Risa Brooks, "Paradoxes of Professionalism: Rethinking Civil-Military Relations in the United States," *International Security*, 44, no. 4 (Spring 2020), pp. 7–44.

120. Heidi Urben, "Party, Politics and Deciding What is Proper: Army Officers' Attitudes after Two Long Wars," *Orbis*, 57, Iss. 3 (Summer 2013), p. 360.

121. The most cogent work on social media, politicization, and the U.S. military is by Colonel Urben, "Like, Comment, Retweet: The State of the Military's Nonpartisan Ethic in the World of Social Media."

122. Leo Shane, "Another Former Joint Chiefs Chairman Blasts Generals Involvement in Politics," *Military Times*, August 16, 2016, www.militarytimes .com/news/2016/08/16/another-former-joint-chiefs-chairman-blasts-generals -involvement-in-politics/; General Martin Dempsey, "Keep Your Politics Private, My Fellow Generals and Admirals," *Defense One*, August 1, 2016, www .defenseone.com/ideas/2016/08/keep-your-politics-private-my-fellow-generals -and-admirals/130404/.

123. Jim Garamone, "Active-Duty Personnel Must Remain Apolitical."

124. Mara Karlin and Jim Golby, "The Case for Rethinking the Politicization of the Military," *Task and Purpose*, June 12, 2020, www.taskandpurpose.com/ opinion/us-military-politics-politicization; and David Barno and Nora Bensahel, "How to Get Generals Out of Politics," *War on the Rocks*, September 27, 2016, https://warontherocks.com/2016/09/how-to-get-generals-out-of-politics/.

125. Jim Garamone, "Chairman Promises Vigorous Military Ethics Campaign," *American Forces Press Service*, February 7, 2014, www.jcs.mil/Media/ News/News-Display/Article/571642/chairman-promises-vigorous-military -ethics-campaign/.

126. "As indicated in Figure 1, the number of senior official misconduct complaints dramatically increased from FY 2008 to FY 2012, rising from 395 in FY 2008 to 815 in FY 2012, but has remained relatively steady since then. The IG tally includes both general and flag officers and civilian senior executive service members," Glenn A. Fine, Senior Leader Misconduct: Prevention and Accountability," Statement before Subcommittee on Military Personnel, House Armed Services Committee, February 7, 2018, https://docs.house.gov/meetings/AS/ AS02/20180207/106815/HHRG-115-AS02-Wstate-FineG-20180207.PDF, pp. 7, 9.

127. Cheryl Pellerin, "Panetta Directs Review of Officers' Culture of Stewardship," *DOD News*, November 15, 2012, http://archive.defense.gov/news/ newsarticle.aspx?id=118551; and Jim Garamone, "Panetta Briefs President on

Dempsey Ethics Findings," *DOD News*, December 7, 2012, http://archive.defense
.gov/news/newsarticle.aspx?id=118741.

128. Thom Shanker, "Concern Grows over Top Military Officers' Ethics,"
New York Times, November 12, 2012, www.nytimes.com/2012/11/13/us/petraeuss
-resignation-highlights-concern-over-military-officers-ethics.html.

129. "Statement of Glenn A. Fine, Senior Leader Misconduct: Prevention
and Accountability," pp. 11, 13.

130. Ibid., p. 13–14.

131. Yossarian, "Colonel Who Gave Reenlistment Oath to Dinosaur Puppet
Forced to Retire at Same Rank as Jeffrey Sinclair," *Duffel Blog*, April, 2018, www
.duffelblog.com/2018/04/colonel-gave-reenlistment-oath-dinosaur-puppet
-forced-retire-rank-jeffrey-sinclair/.

132. Gerras and Wong, *Lying to Ourselves*, p. ix.

133. Ibid.

134. Ibid., pp. 20–23.

135. Ibid., p. 27–28.

136. Ibid., p. 3.

137. Mark Cancian, "Tell Me How This Ends: Military Advice, Strategic
Goals, and the 'Forever War' in Afghanistan," CSIS, July 10, 2019, pp. 30–31. For
more details, see Paul Szoldra, "Here's How Top Military Leaders Have Described US 'Progress' in Afghanistan over the Last Decade," *Task and Purpose*,
August 23, 2018, https://taskandpurpose.com/code-red-news/us-military-prog
ress-afghanistan.

138. Dan Lamothe, "Departing Top Admiral Acknowledges Navy's Struggle
with Character Issues," *Washington Post*, August 27, 2019, www.washingtonpost
.com/national-security/2019/08/27/departing-top-admiral-acknowledges
-navys-struggle-with-character-issues/?utm_campaign=EBB%2008.28.19&utm
_medium=email&utm_source=Sailthru.

139. Chief of Naval Operations Admiral Mike Gilday, "CNO's Guidance to
the Fleet," December 2, 2019," *USNI News*, https://news.usni.org/2019/12/02/
document-cno-gildays-fleet-guidance.

Chapter 9

1. Michael Vickers and Robert Martinage, "The Revolution in War," Center
for Strategic and Budgetary Assessments, December 1, 2004, https://csbaonline
.org/research/publications/the-revolution-in-war, p. 2.

2. The United States suffered 148 battle deaths during the conflict. "America's Wars," Department of Veterans Affairs, November, 2019, www.va.gov/opa/
publications/factsheets/fs_americas_wars.pdf.

3. Eliot Cohen and Thomas Keaney, *Gulf War Air Power Survey Summary Report* (U.S. Government Printing Office, 1993).

4. For an overview, see Eliot A. Cohen, "A Revolution in Warfare," *Foreign Affairs* (March 1996), pp. 37–54.

5. "Report of the Quadrennial Defense Review," Department of Defense, May 1997, https://history.defense.gov/Portals/70/Documents/quadrennial/QDR1997.pdf?ver=2014-06-25-110930-527.

6. "2001 Quadrennial Defense Review Report," Department of Defense, September 30, 2001, https://archive.defense.gov/pubs/qdr2001.pdf.

7. Donald H. Rumsfeld, "Transforming the Military," *Foreign Affairs* (May/Jun 2002), pp. 20–32.

8. Barry Watts, "The Maturing Revolution in Military Affairs," Center for Strategic and Budgetary Assessments, 2011, p. 6.

9. For additional background, see Watts, "The Maturing Revolution in Military Affairs."

10. These terms are explored more deeply in Eliot Cohen, "Technology and Warfare," in *Strategy in the Contemporary World*, edited by John Baylis, James Wirtz, and others (Oxford University Press, 2002), pp. 235–52.

11. Rather ironically, this phrase was introduced into U.S. defense lingo by Thomas A Callaghan more than forty years ago, who argued for more spending on high-technology assets, but it has now morphed into arguing for greater Army end-strength. Thomas A. Callaghan, "Quantity Has a Quality All Its Own," *Allied Interdependence Newsletter*, no. 13, Center for Strategic and International Studies, June 21, 1979.

12. Joel Rayburn, Frank Sobchak, and others, *The U.S. Army in the Iraq War, Volume 2: Surge and Withdrawal (2007–2011)* (U.S. Government Printing Office, 2019), p. 615.

13. The author worked on the development and implementation of the Third Offset while serving as the deputy assistant secretary of defense for strategy and force development. Cheryl Pellerin, "Deputy Secretary: Third Offset Strategy Bolsters America's Military Deterrence," Department of Defense, October 31, 2016, www.defense.gov/Explore/News/Article/Article/991434/deputy-secretary-third-offset-strategy-bolsters-americas-military-deterrence/.

14. "Remarks of Deputy Secretary Work on Third Offset Strategy," Department of Defense, April 28, 2016, www.defense.gov/Newsroom/Speeches/Speech/Article/753482/remarks-by-deputy-secretary-work-on-third-offset-strategy/; and Jesse Ellman, Lisa Samp, and Gabriel Coll, "Assessing the Third Offset Strategy," CSIS, https://csis-prod.s3.amazonaws.com/s3fs-public/publication/170302_Ellman_ThirdOffsetStrategySummary_Web.pdf, p. 3.

15. Paula Thornhill, *The Crisis Within* (RAND, 2016), p. 52.

16. Excerpted from Mara Karlin, "Military Superiority: More than Meets the Eye," *War on the Rocks*, June 28, 2018, https://warontherocks.com/2018/06/military-superiority-more-than-meets-the-eye/.

17. Christopher N. Koontz, editor, *Enduring Voices: Oral Histories of the U.S. Army Experience in Afghanistan 2003–2005* (Washington: Center of Military History, 2008), p. 25.

18. David Galula, *Pacification in Algeria: 1956–1958* (RAND, 2006); David Galula, *Counterinsurgency Wafare: Theory and Practice* (New York: Praeger, 1964); and T. E. Lawrence, *Seven Pillars of Wisdom: A Triumph* (New York: Anchor Books, 1926). To take one example, General (retired) Jack Keane recommended Galula's work to Secretary of Defense Rumsfeld after telling him the Iraq War was a disaster. Thomas Ricks, *The Gamble: General Petraeus and the American Military Adventure in Iraq* (New York: Penguin Books, 2010), p. 89.

19. John Nagl, *Learning to Eat Soup with a Knife*: *Counterinsurgency Lessons from Malaya and Vietnam* (University of Chicago Press, 2002); and David Kilcullen, *The Accidental Guerrilla: Fighting Small Wars in the Midst of a Big One* (Oxford University Press, 2009).

20. Michael Shurkin, "France's War in the Sahel and the Evolution of Counterinsurgency Doctrine," *Texas National Security Review* (Winter 2020), www.tnsr.org/2020/11/frances-war-in-the-sahel-and-the-evolution-of-counter-insurgency-doctrine/.

21. Douglas Porch, "David Galula and the Revival of COIN in the US Military," in *The New Counter-Insurgency Era in Critical Perspective*, edited by Celeste Ward Gventer, David Martin Jones, and M. L. R. Smith (London: Palgrave Macmillian, 2014).

22. Porch argues that the French attempt to wage counterinsurgency in Algeria contributed France's civil-military crisis in its aftermath. Porch, "David Galula and the Revival of COIN in the US Military."

23. Joshua Rovner, "Questions about COIN after Iraq and Afghanistan" in *The New Counter-Insurgency Era in Critical Perspective*, p. 34.

24. *The U.S. Army and Marine Corps Counterinsurgency Field Manual*, U.S. Army No. 3-24/MC No. 3-33.5, December 15, 2006.

25. For a history of the COIN manual from a not unbiased observer, see General David Petraeus, "The Surge of Ideas: COINdinistas and Change in the U.S. Army in 2006," Remarks at AEI upon receipt of Irving Kristol Award, May 6, 2010, www.aei.org/publication/the-surge-of-ideas-2/.

26. Mark Bowden, "David Petraeus' Winning Streak," *Vanity Fair*, March 30, 2010.

27. Colleen Bell, "Celebrity Power and Powers of War: The Rise of the COINdinistas in American Popular Media," *Critical Military Studies* (2018), p. 245.

28. Interview with Martin Schweitzer, "The Afghanistan Papers," *Washington Post*, Conducted September 19, 2017, Released December, 2019, www .washingtonpost.com/graphics/2019/investigations/afghanistan-papers/ documents-database.

29. Two good examples are Gian Gentile, *Wrong Turn: America's Deadly Embrace of Counterinsurgency* (New York & London: The New Press, 2013), p. 189; and Fred Kaplan, *The Insurgents: David Petraeus and the Plot to Change the American Way of War* (New York: Simon & Schuster Press, 2013). p. 418.

30. Kaplan, *The Insurgents*, p. 365.

31. Emphasis in original. Stephen D. Biddle, "Afghanistan's Legacy: Emerging Lessons of an Ongoing War," *Washington Quarterly*, 37, no. 2 (2014), pp. 75–76, 80.

32. Biddle, "Afghanistan's Legacy, p. 70.

33. Mara Karlin, "Why Military Assistance Programs Disappoint: Minor Tools Can't Solve Major Problems," *Foreign Affairs*, November 2017, www .foreignaffairs.com/articles/2017-10-16/why-military-assistance-programs-dis appoint; and Mara Karlin, *Building Militaries in Fragile States: Challenges for the United States* (University of Pennsylvania Press: 2018).

34. This follows Max Weber, who argues that the state must hold a monopoly on the legitimate use of violence. See Max Weber, "Politics as a Vocation," Lecture delivered at Munich University, 1918, in *From Max Weber: Essays in Sociology*, translated and edited by H. H. Gerth and C. Wright Mills (Oxford University Press: 1946), pp. 77–128.

35. Robert Gates, "Helping Others Defend Themselves: The Future of U.S. Security Assistance," *Foreign Affairs*, May 2010, www.foreignaffairs.com/articles /2010-05-01/helping-others-defend-themselves.

36. Mara Karlin and Frances Brown, "Friends with Benefits: What the Reliance on Local Partners Means for U.S. Strategy," *Foreign Affairs*, May 8, 2018, www.foreignaffairs.com/articles/united-states/2018-05-08/friends-benefits.

37. Andrew Krepinevich, *The Army and Vietnam* (Johns Hopkins University Press, 1988).

38. As quoted in Joel Rayburn and others, *The U.S. Army in the Iraq War Volume II*, p. 4.

39. Rachel Elizabeth Tecott, "The Cult of the Persuasive: Explaining U.S. Strategy Selection in Military Assistance," Draft dissertation as of May 1, 2020, chapter VI.

40. "SIGAR Quarterly Report," Special Inspector General for Afghanistan Reconstruction, October 30 2019, www.sigar.mil/pdf/quarterlyreports/2019-10 -30qr-section3-security.pdf, pp. 78–84; and SIGAR Quarterly Report," Special

Inspector General for Afghanistan Reconstruction, July 30, 2019, www.sigar .mil/pdf/quarterlyreports/2019-07-30qr.pdf, p. 89.

41. "Statement of General Joseph Votel, Commander of USCENTCOM before the Senate Armed Services Committee on the Posture of USCENT-COM," March 13, 2018, www.armed-services.senate.gov/imo/media/doc/Votel _03-13-18.pdf.; "Secretary Mattis Visits Allies, Partners during Indo-Pacific Trip," US INDOPACOM, January 23, 2018, www.pacom.mil/Media/News/News -Article-View/Article/1421853/mattis-visits-allies-partners-during-indo-pacific -trip/; "Statement of USSOCOM Commander General Tony Thomas before the Senate Armed Services Committee," May 4, 2017, www.armed-services.senate .gov/imo/media/doc/17-41_05-04-17.pdf; and "Statement of General Thomas D. Waldhauser, USMC, Commander USAFRICOM before the Senate Commit-tee on Armed Services," March 13, 2018, www.armed-services.senate.gov/imo/ media/doc/Waldhauser_03-13-18.pdf.

42. Adapted from Karlin, "Why Military Assistance Programs Disappoint: Minor Tools Can't Solve Major Problems," *Foreign Affairs* (November/December 2017).

43. Hajib Shah, Melissa Dalton, and Erol Yayboke, "Assessment, Monitor-ing, and Evaluation in Action for Security Sector Assistance," CSIS, June 27, 2019, www.csis.org/analysis/assessment-monitoring-and-evaluation-action -security-sector-assistance; Aaron Mehta, "A New Defense School Could Change American Weapon Sales Abroad," *Defense News*, September 27, 2019, www.defensenews.com/pentagon/2019/09/27/a-new-defense-school-could -change-american-weapon-sales-abroad/; and "Lieutenant General Charles Hooper, Director, Defense Security Cooperation Agency, Opening Statement to the Committee on Foreign Relations, United States Senate," September 26, 2017, www.foreign.senate.gov/imo/media/doc/092617_Hooper_Testimony.pdf.

44. Excerpted from Karlin and Brown, "Friends with Benefits."

45. "Syria Study Group Final Report and Recommendations," United States Institute of Peace, September 2019, www.usip.org/sites/default/files/Syria% 20Study%20Group%20Final%20Report.pdf, pp. 32, 44; and Mara Karlin, "On Syria, Washington Cannot Simply Throw Up Its Hands," September 24, 2019, www.brookings.edu/blog/order-from-chaos/2019/09/24/on-syria-washington -cannot-simply-throw-up-its-hands/.

46. Excerpted from Karlin and Brown, "Friends with Benefits."

47. Karlin and Brown, "Friends with Benefits."

48. "Quadrennial Defense Review Report," Department of Defense, Feb-ruary 6, 2006, https://archive.defense.gov/pubs/pdfs/QDR20060203.pdf, pp. 84–87.

49. Michèle Flournoy and others, "Beyond Goldwater-Nichols Project," CSIS, July 2005, https://csis-prod.s3.amazonaws.com/s3fs-public/legacy_files/files/media/csis/pubs/bgn_ph2_report.pdf.

50. Stewart Patrick and Kaysie Brown, *Greater than the Sum of Its Parts? Assessing "Whole of Government" Approaches toward Fragile States* (New York: International Peace Academy, 2007).

51. Ronan Farrow, *War on Peace: The End of Diplomacy and the Decline of American Influence* (New York: Norton and Company, 2018), p. xxiii.

52. Dana Priest, *The Mission: Waging War and Keeping Peace with America's Military* (New York: W. W. Norton and Company, 2004), p. 14.

53. William J. Burns, *The Back Channel: A Memoir of American Diplomacy and a Case for Its Renewal* (New York: Random House, 2019).

54. Priest, *The Mission*, p. 14.

55. To take just a few examples: "Defense Secretary Gates Discusses US Foreign Policy Budget Imbalance with Committee Members," U.S. House of Representatives Committee on Foreign Affairs, March 6, 2008, https://foreignaffairs.house.gov/2008/3/defense-secretary-gates-discusses-us-foreign-policy-budget-imbalance-committee; and "Letter from Secretary of Defense Dr. Robert Gates to Chairman of the Senate Budget Committee Kent Conrad," U.S. Department of State, April 21, 2010, https://2009-2017.state.gov/secretary/20092013clinton/rm/2010/04/140674.htm.

56. Dan Lamothe "Retired Generals Cite Past Comments from Mattis while Opposing Trump's Proposed Foreign Aid Cuts," *Washington Post*, February 27, 2017, www.washingtonpost.com/news/checkpoint/wp/2017/02/27/retired-generals-cite-past-comments-from-mattis-while-opposing-trumps-proposed-foreign-aid-cuts/.

57. This popular phrase took on a new life when the retail chain Staples placed the "easy button" concept at the heart of their advertising efforts. See Jane Levere, "Press a Button and Your Worries are Gone," *New York Times*, July 21, 2008.

58. Interview with Lieutenant General David Barno in *Enduring Voices: Oral Histories of the U.S. Army Experience in Afghanistan 2003–2005*, edited by Christopher N. Koontz (Washington: Center of Military History, 2008), p. 81

59. Senior civilian official. Full quote: "'Whole of government': when the military doesn't know what to do or doesn't want to do it, it becomes 'whole of government.' I'd hear four stars talk about the h-o-l-e of government."

60. Priest, *The Mission*, p. 187.

61. The joke became especially relevant in 2018 when former PACOM Commander Admiral Harry Harris was nominated and confirmed as the U.S. ambassador to South Korea. Twenty years earlier, another PACOM commander,

Admiral Joseph Prueher, was appointed U.S. ambassador to China right out of that position.

62. Kathleen McInnis, "Right-Sizing the National Security Staff?" CRS Insight (IN 10521), June 30, 2016, https://fas.org/sgp/crs/natsec/IN10521.pdf.

63. Donald Rumsfeld, *Known and Unknown: A Memoir* (New York: Penguin, 2011), p. 325.

64. Robert M. Gates, *Duty*, (New York: Alfred A. Knopf, 2014), pp. 482, 587.

65. Italics in original. Barack Obama, *A Promised Land* (New York: Crown, 2020), p. 317.

66. Obama, *A Promised Land*, pp. 434–35.

67. Gates, *Duty*, p. 383.

68. Gates, *Duty*, pp. 351, 377–78, 537; and Leon Panetta with Jim Newton, *Worthy Fights* (New York: Penguin Press, 2014), pp. 339–40.

69. Stanley McChrystal, *My Share of the Task: A Memoir* (New York: Portfolio, 2013), p. 287.

70. The Center for Strategic and International Studies has done the most thoughtful work on this topic: Kathleen Hicks and others, "By Other Means," CSIS, July 8, 2019, www.csis.org/analysis/other-means-part-i-campaigning-gray-zone.

71. Lewis Carroll, *Alice's Adventures in Wonderland* (New York: CreateSpace, 2014).

72. More information on the Army's study of the Russian invasion of Crimea can be found in: Brigadier General Peter Jones, Major General Ricky Waddell, Major Wilson C. Blythe Jr., and Mr. Thomas Pappas, "Unclassified Summary of the U.S. Training and Doctrine Command (TRADOC) Russian New Generation Warfare Study," *U.S. Army Training and Doctrine Command*, 2016, www.armyupress.army.mil/Portals/7/online-publications/documents/RNGW-Unclassified-Summary-Report.pdf. More detail on Army views of the 1973 war and its connection to the 1991 war can be found in: Robert Scales, *Certain Victory* (Office of the Chief of Staff of the U.S. Army, 1993), pp. 9–10.

73. Rayburn and others, *The U.S Army in the Iraq War, Volume II*, p. 622.

74. Author question to chairman of the joint chiefs of staff, at Halifax 2018, "2018 Halifax International Security Forum," November, 2018, https://halifaxtheforum.org/forum/2018-halifax-international-security-forum/.

75. Gates noted in front of the Corps of Cadets at West Point: "I must tell you, when it comes to predicting the nature and location of our next military engagements, since Vietnam, our record has been perfect. We have never once gotten it right, from the Mayaguez to Grenada, Panama, Somalia, the Balkans, Haiti, Kuwait, Iraq, and more—we had no idea a year before any of these missions that we would be so engaged," "Robert Gates Speech to the Corps of Cadets," United

States Department of Defense, May 2011, https://archive.defense.gov/Speeches
/Speech.aspx?SpeechID=1539. For an example of the latter, George Marshall
worried about World War II from the 1920s on. See David Roll and George Marshall, *Defender of the Republic* (New York: Dutton Caliber, 2019).

Chapter 10

1. Last line of Orson Welles's screenplay "The Big Brass Ring," in Joseph
McBride, *Writing in Pictures: Screenwriting Made (Mostly) Painless* (New York:
Random House, Inc., 2012).

2. See, for example, James S. Corum, *The Roots of Blitzkrieg: Hans von Seeckt
and German Military Reform* (University of Kansas Press, 1992), p. 1.

3. Corum, *The Roots of Blitzkrieg*, p. 2

4. Williamson Murray, "Armored Warfare: The British, French and German
Experiences," in *Military Innovation in the Interwar Period*, edited by Allan R.
Millett and Williamson Murray (Cambridge University Press, 1998), pp. 36–37.

5. Corum, *The Roots of Blitzkrieg*, p. 2.

6. Matt M. Matthews, "The Israeli Defense Forces Response to the 2006
War with Hezbollah," *Military Review* (July-August 2009), p. 42.

7. Matthews, "The Israeli Defense Forces Response to the 2006 War with
Hezbollah," p. 44.

8. Eliot Cohen and Thomas Keaney, *Gulf War Air Power Survey Summary
Report* (U.S. Government Printing Office, 1993); Richard Lock-Pullan, "An Inward-Looking Time: The United States Army, 1973–1976," *Journal of Military
History*, 67, no. 3 (2003), pp. 488, 500.

9. See, for example, some of the literature on military innovation: Stephen
Rosen, *Winning the Next War: Innovation and the Modern Military* (Cornell University Press, 1994); *Military Innovation in the Interwar Period*, edited by Williamson Murray and Alan Millet (Cambridge University Press, 1998); and Barry
Posen, *The Sources of Military Doctrine: France, Britain, and Germany between the
World Wars* (Cornell University Press, 1986).

10. Mitt Regan, "Citizens, Suspects, and Enemies: Examining Police Militarization," *Texas National Security Review* (Winter, 2020).

11. Thucydides, *The History of the Peloponnesian War*, edited by M. I. Finley
(New York, Penguin Classics, 1972), p. 142.

12. Mara Karlin, "Policy Roundtable: The Pursuit of Military Superiority,"
Texas National Security Review, June 26, 2018, https://tnsr.org/roundtable/policy
-roundtable-the-pursuit-of-military-superiority/.

13. Craig Whitlock, "At War with the Truth," *Washington Post*, December
9, 2019, www.washingtonpost.com/graphics/2019/investigations/afghanistan
-papers/afghanistan-war-confidential-documents/.

14. "State of the Wars" is a spinoff from a set of conferences that I helped convene titled "State of the Strategy" while serving as deputy assistant secretary of defense for strategy and force development. "State of the Strategy" involved multiple gatherings with a senior internal Department of Defense audience, external thinkers, and close U.S. allies to assess the defense strategy. They benefited from the heavy involvement and vision of Bob Scher, Chris Skaluba, Kaleb Redden, Stephanie Ahern, and Nina Wagner. See, also, Mara Karlin and Christopher Skaluba, "Strategic Guidance for Countering the Spread of Strategic Guidance," *War on the Rocks*, July 20, 2017, https://warontherocks.com/2017/07/strategic-guidance-for-countering-the-proliferation-of-strategic-guidance/.

15. As a Defense Department official, I encouraged congressional colleagues to enact this legislative requirement.

16. "National Defense Authorization Act for Fiscal Year 2017," 114th Congress, November 30, 2016, www.congress.gov/114/crpt/hrpt840/CRPT -114hrpt840.pdf.

17. Mara Karlin and Christopher Skaluba, "What has Become Clear to You? Reflections on Assessing the National Defense Strategy," October 16, 2018, https://warontherocks.com/2018/10/what-has-become-clear-to-you-reflections -on-assessing-the-national-defense-strategy/.

18. Brian VanDeMark, *Road to Disaster: A New History of America's Descent into Vietnam* (New York: Harper Luxe, 2018), p. xv.

19. David Wood, *What Have We Done: The Moral Injury of Our Longest Wars* (New York: Little Brown Spark, 2016), p. 248.

20. James Thomon, "How Could Vietnam Happen? An Autopsy," *The Atlantic*, April 1968, www.theatlantic.com/magazine/archive/1968/04/how-could -vietnam-happen-an-autopsy/306462/.

21. For example, Nick Burns, in his interview with SIGAR, noted that it was remarkable that no one asked "why" in the years after 2003. "Interview with Nick Burns," in Craig Whitlock, "At War with the Truth," *Washington Post*, December 9, 2019, www.washingtonpost.com/graphics/2019/investigations/afghanistan-papers/afghanistan-war-confidential-documents/.

22. Bryan Doerries interview with author, February 20, 2020.

23. Bryan Doerries, *The Theater of War—What Ancient Greek Tragedies Can Teach Us Today* (New York: Vintage, 2016), pp. 75, 83.

24. Bryan Doerries interview with author, February 20, 2020.

25. Quoted in Doerries, *The Theater of War*, p. 108.

26. Adapted from Mara Karlin, "Bridging America's Civil-Military Gap— At Sea," *Defense One*, November 11, 2017, www.defenseone.com/ideas/2017/11/bridging-americas-civil-military-gap-sea/142474/print/.

27. Phillip Bump, "Nearly a Quarter of Americans have Never Experi-

enced the U.S. in a Time of Peace," *Washington Post*, January 8, 2020, www
.washingtonpost.com/politics/2020/01/08/nearly-quarter-americans-have
-never-experienced-us-time-peace/.

28. Gregory Foster, "Civil-Military Relations on Trial: Through the Eyes of
Tomorrow's US Military Leaders," *RUSI Journal*, 161, no. 4 (2016), p. 36.

29. Max Brooks, "Privatizing the United States Army was a Mistake," *Washington Post*, February 3, 2020, www.nytimes.com/2020/02/03/opinion/future
-privatized-army-strike.html.

30. Italics in original. "Inspired to Serve: Final Report of the National
Commission on Military, National, and Public Service," March, 2020, https://
inspire2serve.gov/sites/default/files/final-report/Final%20Report.pdf, p. 9.

31. Richard Sisk, "Design Approved for Gulf War Memorial on National
Mall," *Military.com*, December 2, 2019, www.military.com/daily-news/2019/12
/02/design-approved-gulf-war-memorial-national-mall.html. Note that the
Vietnam War memorial is formally known as the Vietnam Veterans Memorial.

32. David Roza, "29 Years after Desert Storm, an Air Force General Says We've
Forgotten the Lessons that Made It So Successful," *Task and Purpose*, January
29, 2020, https://taskandpurpose.com/chuck-horner-desert-stormlessons?mc_
cid=b814167706&mc_eid=f263dbbf38.

33. Rachael Riley, "Bragg Boot Display Honors Fallen Service Members,"
Fayetteville Observer, May 25, 2019, www.fayobserver.com/news/20190525/bragg
-boot-display-honors-fallen-service-members.

34. Robert Poole, *Section 60: Where War Comes Home* (New York: Bloomsbury, 2015).

35. David Montgomery, "A Wave of War Memorials Is Coming to D.C. Are We
All at Peace with That?" *Washington Post*, July 31, 2020, www.washingtonpost
.com/lifestyle/magazine/a-wave-of-war-memorials-is-coming-to-dc-are-we-all
-at-peace-with-that/2018/07/30/87980d18-794d-11e8-93cc-6d3beccdd7a3_story
.html.

Index

Page numbers followed by f and t represent figures and tables, respectively.